CHURCHILL'S ENEMIES

1927–1940

PART 2 OF CHURCHILL'S CHALLENGES

CHURCHILL'S ENEMIES

1927–1940

PART 2 OF CHURCHILL'S CHALLENGES

JOHN HARTE

Pen & Sword
MILITARY
AN IMPRINT OF PEN & SWORD BOOKS LTD.
YORKSHIRE – PHILADELPHIA

First published in Great Britain in 2025 by
PEN AND SWORD MILITARY
An imprint of
Pen & Sword Books Limited
Yorkshire – Philadelphia

ISBN 978 1 03610 319 4

Typeset in Times New Roman 10/12 by
SJmagic DESIGN SERVICES, India.
Printed and bound in the UK by CPI Group (UK) Ltd.

The Publisher's authorised representative in the EU for product safety is Authorised Rep Compliance Ltd., Ground Floor, 71 Lower Baggot Street, Dublin D02 P593, Ireland.
www.arccompliance.com

For a complete list of Pen & Sword titles please contact
PEN & SWORD BOOKS LIMITED
George House, Units 12 & 13, Beevor Street, Off Pontefract Road,
Barnsley, South Yorkshire, S71 1HN, England
E-mail: enquiries@pen-and-sword.co.uk
Website: www.pen-and-sword.co.uk

or

PEN AND SWORD BOOKS
1950 Lawrence Rd, Havertown, PA 19083, USA
E-mail: uspen-and-sword@casematepublishers.com
Website: www.penandswordbooks.com

Contents

I: INSIDE GERMANY

II: THE GERMAN CRISIS

III: THE ROAD TO WAR

Dates beside chapter headings are intended only as guidelines, which cannot be completely accurate in a tapestry of moving events.

Author's Note

This account of Winston Churchill's life and times between two world wars, from 1918 to 1940, is described in two volumes. The first is entitled *Churchill's Challenges* (1918-1927). This second volume entitled *Churchill's Enemies* (1927-1940) completes the interwar period by describing what led to the Second World War and the Holocaust.

'Devoured by egoism, adoration of his mother Jennie, and enduring love for Clementine whom he married, young Winston Churchill's gifts and flaws are described against a background of a world crisis and their love of country. The Middle-East was in peril. The Communist Revolution was spreading over Europe. The Nazis were taking over Germany when he was out of office in a government reshuffle. And the women in Winston's life were united by a common purpose to make him prime minister.'

Preface to *Churchill's Challenges.*

I

INSIDE GERMANY

Preface

Preface

This book continues where the previous volume called *Churchill's Challenges* left off in 1927.

It described how Winston Churchill was confronted by the grim realities of the spread of communism over Soviet Russia's borders, and Islamic fanaticism across the Middle East. It barely touched upon the alarming news emerging from post-First World War Germany soon after the 1918-1919 Peace Conference at Versailles, with the terrorism of the Spartacus Revolution and assassinations and brutal murders of leading political figures. This volume is devoted very largely to informing a new generation of readers what ensued to cause the Second World War and the Holocaust.

The objective of scrutinising history is to learn the mistakes of the past in the hope of avoiding a repetition. The saga of the rise of Germany's Nazi Party demonstrates how easy it can be to stumble in the wrong direction and be confronted by previously hidden dangers. More people suffered a more miserable fate in the twentieth century than at any other time in history. It raised a question which has been asked repeatedly all over the world for thousands of years: 'Why do awful things happen to decent people?'

The young Winston Churchill had considered that question seriously and read as much history as he was able to find to answer it. He had been influenced by his father's close friendships with leading Jewish scholars and his own Jewish friends in a guiding principle of Jewish ethics, known as 'the repair of the world, righting the wrongs, facing and addressing injustice and poverty'.[1]

Most violence and terrorism was perpetrated by young men aged from fifteen to twenty-four who lacked sufficient knowledge or experience to understand how the world worked and what responsibilities were required to establish social cohesion. We have the advantage of hindsight to add to our own experiences of a belligerent and rebellious mindset which triggered two incidents in more recent times that demonstrate the irrationality of human nature and the extraordinary waste of valuable time by idle teenagers. The first was when an Islamic State (ISIS) terrorist eagerly confronted television cameramen at the prospect of beheading innocent hostages in front of TV audiences for the first time in 2016. While shouting, 'We love death as you love life,' he warned audiences, 'We are coming for you!'[2]

The simple but profound fact that Islamist fanatics diligently searched for ways to die because of delusions about an afterlife instilled into them from the age of five, seemed not to have occurred to genuine peace negotiators striving, year after year, towards conclusions to terrorist atrocities. Terrorists do not want peace when they can enjoy violence and be paid for their services as mercenary suicide squads.

The other incident which provided a similar thrill in threatening innocent people with death was the false student demonstrations that hoaxed western college campuses in 2023, when mean-spirited teenage students rioted in support of terrorist groups in the Middle East. Some peace negotiators at least, began to realise that terrorists, and political agitators inspired by them, were little different from German students during the rise of the Nazi Party in the 1920s and 1930s, which led to the Second World War and the Holocaust. That was the link between the world crisis then and the world crisis now. When Winston Churchill was appointed Colonial Secretary in 1920, he was confronted by three different cultures of death which shared those same aims. They were communist, fascist, and Islamist fanatics. What all three had in common was a determination to destroy liberalism and democracy and seize control of the future by imposing terror all over the world.

The Militant Muslim International

Terrorism has been defined as 'the deliberate and systematic murder, maiming, and menacing of the innocent to inspire fear for political ends'.[3] Author Christopher Harmon, who specialised in the nature and global spread of terrorism, pointed out how it can emerge from the hot rage and hatred that produces fascism or the cold contempt and indifference to life of communism. Both passions were demonstrated daily in one corner of the world or another by cynical political agitators and followers of the suicidal murder squads of Islamist fanatics, the Fedayeen, which have become the 'militant Muslim international'.*

Hitler's official interpreter, Paul Schmidt, who observed the rise of the Nazis at firsthand, emphasised in his post-war memoir that 'The real enemies of mankind are the fanatics, in whichever camp they may be.'

The fate of Germany's Weimar Republic soon after the end of the First World War was most likely the clearest example of a nation led by a fanatic and poisoned by hate. And with a passion for death. This volume explains how Hitler succeeded in destroying democracy and replacing it with a fascist code of force, violence, and death.

* Their training manual was 'recovered in an Al Qaeda safe house in Manchester, England'. The terrorist manual described ways to make and deploy poisons.[4]

If both world wars and the Holocaust seem irrational and hardly real to a new generation which might view them as products of a madman's imagination, they were inconceivable then. Despite all previous revolutions and invasions by conquering hordes, history had not reached anything like that level of barbarism until the twentieth century. Even so, violent terrorism has always been the refuge of failures who could not succeed by legitimate means and turned to criminality instead. The intention of all three terrorist doctrines of the extreme political right and the far left was to extinguish every spark of humanity in the world, because they hated liberal modernity and believed that neither their supporters nor their antagonists possessed any rights, other than as units of production in peacetime or useful idiots to be packed off to the battlefront in war.

The phenomenon of death cults existed since ancient times. There are plenty of examples. The Persian Prophet Zoroaster saw the world divided into two camps, which he called 'the sons of darkness' and 'the sons of light'. All three rigid adversarial doctrines that Churchill faced – beginning with Islamist slave traders at Khartoum in the Sudan in 1898; continuing with the Communists in Russia from 1917 onwards; and followed by the Nazi Party in Germany from 1924, belonged to the dark satanic forces which became known as 'the axis of evil.' It rejected moral principles in a belief that life had no meaning and there are no such things as human rights. All who venerated life would be suppressed or killed by death cults which felt uneasy with modern life and want to escape from it into an imaginary parallel one.

An impression conveyed from Germany's past history was that the nation was in a state of collapse after the First World War ended in 1918. While it was true that defeat was followed by outbreaks of civil war, and hundreds of assassinations by the political far-right, followed by sporadic revolutions to impose a Soviet-style Republic by the far-left, in fact its infrastructure and its society remained intact, at least for a while. The Weimar Republic was otherwise stable. And so was Austria. Although many imagine that bad times produced Hitler, there is ample evidence to show that it was Hitler who brought bad times to Germany and Austria and the rest of the world. Economist Karl Polanyi was a contemporary observer of the rise of the Nazis before fleeing to Britain:

> 1918 initiated an equally unexampled moral and intellectual rise in the condition of a highly developed working class which, protected by the Vienna system, withstood the degrading effects of grave economic dislocation and achieved a level never reached before by the masses of the people in any industrial city.[5]

Those who read *Churchill's Challenges* may understand how and why a new generation of young people in the West might have felt diminished soon after Winston Churchill retired as Britain's prime minister in 1955. They and following generations would certainly become confused and unhappy without moral guidance;

some even mentally ill. Discontent would become widespread in universities and other institutions that failed to educate and prepare each new generation for career and lifetime opportunities.

The Weimar Republic

The final chapter of *Churchill's Challenges* was devoted to the Weimar Republic as a bridge between that book and this one. Churchill's major ministerial portfolios were accomplished as a Liberal Member of Parliament up until 1925, when he rejoined the Conservative Party after Liberalism failed to attract enough support. Just as he had encountered grotesque incidents in the Middle East and Soviet Russia, now they were followed by equally grotesque situations that developed from the rise of Hitler in Nazi Germany. That is the main subject of this book.

The word 'grotesque' has special significance for clinical psychiatrists and professional institutions like The American Association of Psychiatrists in the United States, which studies mental disorders. The grotesque is characterised in literature too by bizarre distortions in which people's behaviour becomes caricatured. Human nature becomes grotesque when alienated from reality and disoriented between normal expectations and the challenges of confronting reality. In *The Psychology of Grotesque in Modern American Literature,* the word 'grotesque' is continually used to 'explore the anxieties of a given period'.[6]

The postwar period in the Weimar Republic was packed with an abundance of *Sturm und Drang,* meaning turmoil, high emotions, and apprehension for the future, like thunder and lightening heralding a storm

Grotesque attitudes inspired the crazed histrionics of Hitler and the savagery of ordinary Germans in the postwar Weimar Republic. Despite revealing information already harvested by historians and psychologists about that schizoid period in Germany, it would be rewarding to read the clinical details of delusions suffered by vagrants and political agitators who were patients in Vienna's polyclinic at the time. It was managed for Sigmund Freud by the 23-year-old Wilhelm Reich, who developed his theory when working there of what he called 'the impulsive character'. His patients were men with unbridled passions who could not restrain themselves.

'The real cause of the crisis, we submit,' wrote economist Polanyi with caution, while sharing his controversial opinion in his new book, 'was the threatening collapse of the international economic system.'

> It had only haltingly functioned since the turn of the century, and the Great War and the Treaties had wrecked it finally. This became apparent in the twenties when there was hardly an internal crisis in Europe that did not reach its climax on an issue of foreign economy. Students of

> politics now grouped the various countries, not according to continents, but according to the degree of their adherence to a sound currency... 'Flight of capital' was a new thing. Neither in 1848, nor in 1866, nor even in 1871 was such an event recorded... That and "the development of a fascist movement in Germany in 1930, was patent."[7]

'But,' he emphasised elsewhere, 'if the breakdown of our civilisation was timed by the failure of world economy, it was certainly not caused by it.'[8]

To understand the rise of the Nazi Party – and several historians admitted that they did not understand Hitler – the collapse of the Weimar Republic was not an either-or situation of politics versus economics. There were numerous influential factors that swept democracy aside in favour of fascism. Populism inspired mob hysteria and an intimidating theatre of the streets. There was an 'us and them' mentality that encouraged Prussia's and Austria's traditional antisemitism. There was faith in the Gold Standard, a tradition of cheap labour, and much more besides. According to Polanyi, 'A kind of sinister intellectual superiority accrued to those of her [Germany's] statesmen in the thirties who turned their minds to this task of disruption...'[9]

Expectations versus Reality

Readers who have been misled by cinema or TV versions of Winston Churchill's life and times, might well have expected a cozy or amusing account of the challenges that confronted him between the two World Wars. But he has been falsely characterised on cinema and TV screens. The cinema was first and foremost part of an entertainment industry that prized box office receipts above all other considerations, whereas historians are always conscious of a responsibility to do their best to remain true to historical facts. In the eyes of history, Churchill was a thoughtful, serious, and dedicated Member of Parliament, and an influential Minister of the Crown, who was well versed in political judgements and goals from an early age. Although he enjoyed entertaining guests in a mischievous spirit of mockery, his impishness was exploited by film-makers aiming to entertain audiences by glossing over the extraordinary mental scope and skills of the real man.

Young Winston's awareness of politics most likely emerged from his father's Progressive Conservatism and the political influence that his famous ancestor, the First Duke of Marlborough, impressed on the monarchy in the seventeenth and eighteenth centuries. Winston built on that foundation as a young soldier by studying Ancient Greek and Roman forms of government, from monarchies to republics, tyrannies and democracies, nationalists and oligarchs, which had been described by Plato, Aristotle and Plutarch. He had also been at the sabre-end of tribalism in his cavalry skirmishes on the Indian and Afghan borders with experienced Sikh troops in his early twenties.

Perhaps that was why he had not been surprised by the unchanging primitive tribalism in the Middle East when he became Colonial Secretary on 13 February in 1921, because he had expected little more. He was a modern man who believed in the results of reasoning with facts and logical arguments. He always hoped for the best, while seldom being surprised when he was met by the worst of human failings. He continually encountered primitive emotions in his adversaries. He was challenged repeatedly by superstitious, irrational, and hostile tribal passions that frequently prevented cool and responsible reasoning, whether with Palestine, India, or Ireland.

His study of Reade's *The Martyrdom of Man,* and his own military experiences, confronted him with a sense of fatalism at man's inability to influence world events by reason. He shared Sigmund Freud's scepticism of the flawed and misguided human condition. But his acquisition of experience and knowledge had since made him positive about the influence he could have on world affairs by using his determination to succeed in his career as a soldier, a war correspondent, a politician, and an international statesman.

Reade's experiences in Africa, and his studies of the rise and fall of previous civilisations had embedded in Winston's mind a keen awareness of the whims and fancies and strange notions and doctrines that vied with reason to overwhelm societies from time to time. Few of those weird notions lasted for long, but they caused chaos while they did.

Winston had attempted to stem the communist tide from its very beginning, and continued to struggle against it. But in the course of his appointments to different ministries he would also be confronted by a surge of nationalism that appealed to the innate tribal jostling to compete for limited resources in order to survive by domination.

Churchill was sceptical of all forms of nationalism preached by populist politicians driven by personal ambition. He knew that they rarely, if ever, represented the interests of the people, but were opportunistic adventurers with the skill to stir up the passions of impressionable audiences. Some were motivated by greed for wealth, others by power. Churchill's attitude to third-world countries was to guide and develop them towards self determination. It was the principal goal set for him as Colonial Secretary by Prime Minister Lloyd George and the League of Nations.

Europe, Asia, Africa, and the Middle East had been left in a state of chaos by the end of the First World War, without effective leadership after the collapse of four huge empires. Now Churchill no longer headed the Colonial Office; he had become Chancellor of the Exchequer. Even so, his instincts stirred him to continue to seek justice for all.

Enemies of an Open Society

This book continues describing what was the first half of Winston Churchill's military, political and literary career, during the rise of dictatorships in the 1920s, and 1930s, and brings readers to the Second World War in 1940. One of the most influential books about totalitarian police states ruled by tyrants would not be published until 1945. It would be written by modern philosopher Karl Popper, who called it *The Open Society and its Enemies*. Those enemies were Winston Churchill's enemies, too. Churchill maintained that justice was only possible in an open society, not the closed societies of secret police and concentration camps that kept their populations imprisoned in an iron cage.[10]

That description of the Prussian military influence over German society came from sociologist Max Weber, because it was a traditional society where people gave and took orders instantly and without question, on pain of death. The bureaucracy and secret police enforced orders from above, also without question: *Folgen sie den Anführer* (follow the leader).

Reminders of the capricious nature of fate can still be found around us. We live in a constantly changing world that evolves much faster than before. Those continual changes presented Winston Churchill with endless challenges that confronted him throughout his life. All were reactions to economic and social change. Most resulted from nations being unprepared, and from poor judgements made in the past without consideration for the consequences. Karl Popper remarked that in Ancient Athens, 'Plato reacted to this situation by attempting to arrest all change.' An alternative was to accept, and even welcome, change. Another was 'to bring it under rational control by attempting to tame it'.[11]

All three tyrannical societies that caused continual global problems during Churchill's lifetime attempted to resist change rather than accommodate it. Restrictions imposed on the lives of their subjects hindered progress. Having established communism in Soviet Russia, none of its leaders could permit change, because the regime would disintegrate if it fell out of their control. As for the iron cage of Prussian society, it was based on officers and families alike obeying orders instantly. Men bowed, clicked their heels, and did what they were told. Women submitted to male authority. Germany's social contract was as locked in and changeless as the authority of Islam in the Middle East, under the Caliphate, where it meant total submission and obedience to despots.

The following narrative describes all three types of tyranny in the closed police states that Churchill faced throughout his life when outside the 'English Democracy' favoured by parliamentary democracy in the British Isles. He was forced to recognise in dealing with fanatics that not every problem had a solution. Some required compromises or trade-offs. But he found that none of those three closed societies allowed change or compromise.

When young Winston had absorbed the main message of Reade's *The Martyrdom of Man*, about the rise and fall of civilisations which had seemed almost destined to disappear into the fog of lost causes by their errors of judgement, he had studied the many reasons that Reade gave for their demise. He had read of open societies that welcomed new ideas and opportunities, and closed ones that failed to assimilate them. A terminal problem of closed societies was that, in their isolation from reality, they turned to fantasies that became delusions. Nevertheless, he was not discouraged, because he believed that he was destined for greatness if he could remain firmly in the saddle.[12]

The aim of English Democracy was to provide justice for all by means of an open society with new ideas constantly vying for attention in the marketplace. The most effective would be bound to rise to prominence. Unfortunately, the open society was always assailed by enemies.[13] The Enemy on the Right was Fascism. The Enemy on the Left was Communism. Islamist fanaticism was based on the Extreme Right doctrine of Wahabism, which resulted in submission and stagnation.

When Winston had been Home Secretary in 1910, he had discovered another destructive force which had left previous civilisations as puzzled as he was as to why so many different types of political subversives made a nuisance of themselves to others in their determination to destroy the foundations of their own society which sheltered and protected them. He had decided that troublemakers from within caused more harm to the country than threats from outside.

Heraclitus in Ancient Greece had been sceptical of human nature. He was aware from his observations that most people did not understand what was happening around them, either before it was explained to them, or even afterwards. Their lack of experience prevented them from understanding even simple truths. They were 'unaware of what they do when they are awake just as they are forgetful of what they do when they are asleep'.[14]

Whereas *Churchill's Challenges* described the rise of Arab nationalism in the Middle East, and the 'Enemy on the Left' in Europe, the narrative that follows describes the 'Enemy on the Right'. Readers might find it helpful to connect and visualise the following fragments of history holistically as a chain of cause and effect. As contemporary philosopher and mathematician David Berlinski pointed out, 'There is an obvious connection between the catastrophe of the First World War, the Russian Revolution, the Russian civil war, the development and rise of the Nazis in Germany, [and] the Holocaust…'[15]

The Kaiser's name might mean little or nothing to most people today, but Wilhelm the Second of the Hohenzollern dynasty had ruled the German Empire until the end of the First World War. He had been the key to each link in a chain, from the First World War and the Bolshevik Revolution in Russia in 1917 to the Second World War and the Holocaust. He had been treated almost as a god by his German subjects, and believed he was ordained by God to lead the Teutonic races as a warrior king. As the heir to the Hohenzollern dynasty, he had become more of a myth than a man. Churchill's description of him as a leader who had twice invited him to observe Prussian military manoeuvres, in 1906 and 1908, was clear. Photos of both occasions show Winston's mischievous grin of incredulity as he gazed at the conceited Kaiser, whom he could not take seriously. He would have known how much the Kaiser's English royal cousins despised him as an incompetent and irresponsible troublemaker. The manoeuvres of his Prussian cavalry were intended to warn England to take him seriously – that Germany's sword was sharply pointed and might be aimed at the British Isles.

'Kaiser Bill' – as Allied troops liked to call him with derision – would receive his come-uppance for his arrogance twelve years later, when he was a broken man fleeing from Germany to find refuge in a neutral country, with calls from the British to 'Hang the Kaiser!' How had he met his reverses?

'It is, indeed, impossible to exaggerate the fecklessness which across a whole generation led the German Empire in successive lurches to catastrophe.' The young Kaiser had dismissed Bismark on coming to adulthood – one of the greatest chancellors in history – and reversed all that Bismarck had achieved in national alliances. He had disdained friendship with his cousin Nicky, the Tsar of Russia, causing Nicholas to make an alliance with France instead of Germany. He had estranged himself from England, even though Queen Victoria was his grandmother, because he had continually ridiculed her successor, his cousin King Edward Vll. The Kaiser was jealous of him. All the connections he had inherited from Bismarck evaporated. "Born with everything to make a sovereign envied by all, the Kaiser proceeded to throw it all away through arrogance and condescension. He had proved to be too incompetent to rule."[16]

It was no surprise to Churchill that the Kaiser, having mistakenly ordered his troops to mobilise for war, had almost immediately had second thoughts about the consequences and changed his mind. He was stunned to be told by his Chief of Staff that it was too late to prevent the First World War; that once mobilised, the German troops could not be stopped from attacking neutral Belgium to invade France. He had blundered. So would his Chiefs of Staff blunder, after encouraging him. The instability of losing by your own incompetence what you value most was not limited to Germany, but also to Russia, Austria, Turkey, and among the Arab tribes in the Middle East, which were all 'ruled by terror, fanaticism, and the Secret Police'.

Churchill pointed out in 1937 that human beings 'are prepared to kill or be killed for the sake of an idea'. Ideas can be explosive, even though they don't have to make sense: they appeal to the emotions. They are 'independent of reasoning'. Ideas are dangerous when they turn into an article of faith. Although he referred particularly to Germany, Italy and Russia, the Middle East crisis was never far from his mind.[17]

1

Nazi Ideology

As Britain's empire continued to struggle for human rights, a contrarian view of society and a wave of oppression surged more powerfully across the Continent of Europe. Post-First World War Germany had sunk into social and economic instability. One typical leadership crisis was resolved temporarily when former Chancellor Dr Marx resumed office. But unemployment rose to 2 million when the economy worsened, and joblessness continued to increase. The rise in numbers of those without work channelled flows of new recruits into the ranks of the Nazi Party. There had been only 17,000 members at the beginning of 1926, whereas now, a year later, their numbers stood at 40,000, and continued to rise. The most feared members were those of the 'Protection Squad', known as *Schutzstaffeln*, or SS, who wore sinister black uniforms to intimidate any opponents who dared to protest.

The name of the squad of troops used expressly to put down civilian resistance by violent means, typified the use of propaganda in which anything threatening was described in innocent looking-glass language that suggested the public would benefit rather than be oppressed by brute force. Although, supposedly, it was intended to protect the nation from troublemakers, it did not protect members of the public. Most impressionable followers of the Nazi Party remained unaware of its real intentions, for now at least. They too were gulled by its innocent name. Nevertheless, the reason for their receptiveness to violence and cruelty lay in their mindset, already formed by their inherited Prussian belief that 'the destiny of the weak is to be devoured by the strong'. It was considered wise to be on the side of the strong by joining the Nazi Party.[1]

On 6 July, Hitler founded the Hitler Youth Movement. It attracted schoolboys and girls to sports activities and outdoor camps, where they soon bonded and were brainwashed with Nazi propaganda as they sang comradely songs together. One of its aims was to instil race hatred into receptive and impressionable young minds. By marching behind swastika-emblazoned banners and repeating simple slogans that conditioned them to be proud young Nazis ready to fight for the Fatherland, Hitler trained the next generation of German recruits for hatred, bloodshed and war.

'We love our race,' they chanted together, 'our people, our blood, and our fair upright youth ... but never the intellectual who is at home everywhere, who knows neither friendship nor fatherland.'[2]

Nazi ideology was clear. It was all about the alleged superiority of the German race, the German people, and German blood. They were 'supermen'. A woman's place was in the home, producing and rearing children and supporting her husband. Hitler sneered that the slogan 'Emancipation of women' was invented by Jewish intellectuals. According to him, a woman possessed exactly what nature had necessarily given her. The woman's world was a smaller one, comprising husband, family, children and home. "We do not consider it correct for the woman to interfere in the world of the man, in his main sphere."[3]

The main sphere of man was war, according to Nazi ideology, and Hitler carefully prepared adults, children, and even babies and their mothers, to collaborate in waging it, while brainwashed and conditioned with a will to fight persistently like robots for generations to come; to sacrifice their lives like a colony of ants defending their anthill:

> What the man gives in courage on the battlefield, the woman gives in eternal self-sacrifice, in eternal pain and suffering. Every child that a woman brings into the world is a battle; a battle waged for the existence of her people.[4]

Even less extremist institutions in Germany, like the Bavarian government, passed a law criminalising 'Gypsies, travellers and the Work-shy'. It sent them to forced labour in industries and mines, and categorised all Jewish people in a similar way; so that, in due course, they would be sent to their deaths together in concentration camps designed to murder them on reverse assembly line principles. Demonising other nationalities, religions, or so-called 'races', stemmed from desperation. It had nothing to do with the worthiness of Czechs, Poles, Slavs, Gypsies or Jews. Hitler had learnt when a teenager in Vienna that condemning immigrants of other nationalities was a sure way to achieve political popularity. No politician had been more popular than the antisemitic mayor, Karl Lueger. Antisemitism in Germany resulted from a defeatist attitude by incompetent Nazis, who found it easier to blame others for their problems than provide realistic solutions.

Hitler published his second volume of *Mein Kampf* on 10 December 1926. According to one book reviewer, 'These were the writings of an extremist with no prospect of political influence, let alone power. Hitler's readership was small. Every effort was being made to normalise life in Germany, to attract tourists to the many beautiful regions with which the country was endowed, and to enhance trade.'[5]

As a master of oratory, Hitler linked his political targets together in one catchy phrase as 'Jewish Bolshevism;' despite the fact that – according to economist Karl Polanyi who lived in Vienna at the time – 'Actually, there was never any serious danger of a Communist regime since the workers were organised in parties and unions actively hostile to the Communists.'

'The Peril,' according to Polanyi, 'was not Bolshevism, but disregard... of interruptions of public order and trading habits [which] might constitute a lethal threat.' He meant the breakdown of the economy through a sudden flight of capital from investors that could result in business losses and large-scale unemployment.

Hitler was still viewed as a traitor by Germans who wanted to move forward, while grievances and resentment persuaded others to join the Nazi ranks and obtain revenge on society for their misfortunes. Only the newly formed Viennese psychologists appeared to understand that the obsessive-compulsive push-and-pull towards a culture of death must be due to some type of mental condition. In Arabic countries it had been brushed aside as typical mob hysteria due to the climate and the influence of the Quran. 'Hysteria' was the erroneous word originally used by psychoanalysts for neuroses that frequently involved hallucinations and wild histrionic behaviour.*

Paradoxically, starting in 1922, and reaching a high point in 1926, communist Russia was unobtrusively building up German power. Nine facilities were developed at secret locations in Soviet Russia to train the German military, while Russian armament factories made weapons and ammunition in four locations to manufacture tanks, and poison gas for chemical warfare. A flying school was set up for German pilots at Lipetsk.

Aircraft production was undertaken in secrecy. Hugo Junkers was already running an aircraft factory in Dessau by 1926. Ernst Heinkel set up another one in Sweden. Claude Dornier organised others in Italy and Switzerland. Junkers, Heinkel and Dornier bombers would soon emerge from assembly lines in those factories to contribute to the destruction of cities and their civilian populations in another world war.[6]

What can posterity make of the mindsets of societies that inherit a well-established culture and infrastructure that they fail to build on, but spend all their time, energy, and resources on destroying it and its people, instead? Churchill had pondered on that question even as early as in 1910 when he had been Home Secretary and was confronted by a variety of contrarian subversive rebels aiming to bring down the establishment on their own heads. Now he was confronted by three types of rebellious regimes: communist Russia, Nazi Germany, and Islamic fundamentalist terrorists in the Middle East. Each was led by a warlord dictator who hated not only other people, but his own. Few orderly and peaceful Arab

* Hysteria symptoms included a wide range of physical and mental issues, including blindness, hearing loss, seizures, amnesia, uncontrolled bodily movements or complete loss of movement, heart palpitations, emotional outbursts, paralysis, fainting, chronic pain, loss of sensation, hallucinations, and histrionic behaviour. Functional neuroimaging has revealed selective decreases in the activity of frontal and subcortical circuits involved in motor control during hysterical paralysis, decreases in somatosensory cortices during hysterical anaesthesia, or decreases in visual cortex during hysterical blindness.

kingdoms remained for long without assassination of the king or murders of the entire royal family by Wahabi fanatics, Ikhwan warriors, or hate-filled and power-hungry Mullahs.

What those autocratic regimes also possessed in common was a psychological quirk that would become known as a death drive – as if they were in love with death and wanted to hasten their own end, as well as everyone else's. Not surprisingly, despite their inflated egos, each lasted for almost no time at all. A mystery that still remained to be solved was whether that drive to their doom was due to a cultural, or a psychotic, or a biological or chemical flaw – or mere stupidity. As Britain's empire continued its steady progress towards its goal of human rights for all after the end of the First World War, a wave of oppression from a contrarian view of society crept over much of the Continent of Europe – largely as a result of the collapse of four huge empires by 1918. The chaos caused by the return of large numbers of mind-numbed troops from the atrocities of war, coupled with the surge of millions of widows and orphans through the cities, searching for food and shelter, could not be managed by weak and incompetent governments. Germany and Austria had sunk into social and economic instability.

As the Nazi Party continued to grow, its most feared members comprised the 'Protection Squad,' known as the SS. They were used expressly to put down civilian resistance to authority by violent means. Although allegedly intended to protect the nation from troublemakers, they represented the brute force of authoritarianism.

Many of Hitler's impressionable followers remained unaware of his real intentions, for a while at least, because he withheld them. The Nazis had seen from the postwar experience in Italy how Mussolini and his black shirted army had abolished parliamentary democracy for fascism when he became sole dictator a year previously. He had claimed in his speech to Parliament on January 3, 1925 that Liberalism was dead because it could not protect the nation from chaos. What he had not mentioned was that much of the chaos had been deliberately caused by his Blackshirts in order to demonstrate how effectively they could restore law and order. Like all popular nationalist dictatorships, it was a hoax from the start.

Nevertheless, the reason for their receptiveness to violence and cruelty had already been formed by their Prussian heritage and its belief that 'the destiny of the weak is to be devoured by the strong.' They wanted to be on the side of the strong by joining the Nazi Party. Hitler founded the Hitler Youth Movement on July 6. It drew schoolboys and girls to organised sports events and outdoor camping. They soon bonded and were brainwashed with Nazi propaganda as they sang comradely songs together before campfires. One of its aims was to instill race hatred into receptive and impressionable young minds. They marched behind swastika emblazoned banners and repeated simple hate-filled slogans to demonstrate they were proud young Nazis, ready to fight for the Fatherland against the hateful Czechs and Slavs, and the 'subhuman' Poles and Jews, whom Hitler claimed, unscientifically, were inferior races.

Blockheaded Barbarism

Despite the industrialisation of Germany in what was considered to be the beginning of a modern age, a medieval culture still lingered beneath the surface of society from tribal and feudal times. It had been ritualised by the duelling fraternities of universities in Vienna in the early 1920s. They wore medieval ceremonial uniforms, and practised a tradition in German universities as 'a relic of medieval days', when the German student was known to be 'a proverbially wild and lawless swashbuckler whose only preoccupations, according to legend and folk-songs were gambling, drinking, transpiercing rivals with his sword, and seducing rustic *Gretchens* ...' Hungarian author Arthur Koestler, who studied in Vienna at that time, dismissed them as blockheads.

There were three main categories of fraternities which were split along quasi-racial lines – the Pan-Germanists, the Liberals, and the Zionists. The Pan-Germanist fraternities had 'adopted a racist doctrine long before the name of Hitler was known, and only admitted pure-bred Aryans to their ranks'.[7] It indicated that the false notion of the existence of such people as 'Aryans' had preceded Hitler, who had borrowed the fiction from a novel or some pseudo-scientific source.

Since two thousand years of victimisation had shown young Jewish men that they must stand up to bullies and beat them at their own game, there were twelve Zionist duelling fraternities in the University of Vienna. They were determined to show that they could duel, shout, drink, carouse and sing together like everyone else. Students of the first Zionist duelling fraternity practised duelling for eight hours a day for six months with cavalry sabres, before competing with the Pan-Germanist fraternities and beating them.

German duelling fraternities were not pleased at being humiliated and viewed as second best. A convention of Pan-Germanist duelling fraternities had responded with a formal resolution in 1920 that "Any son of a Jewish mother is to be regarded as devoid of honour; satisfaction by arms is therefore to be refused to him."

Prevented from answering insults with sabres, Zionists were now obliged to use fists and clubs instead. They would formally stare down the Austrians, then stride up to them and click their heels as a ritual, declaring; "*Herr Kollege*, you have provoked me. I invite you to follow me to the ramp."

The ramp was outside the jurisdiction of the university, where the duellists would again click heels and bawl out their names according to the customary formality. Seconds would be chosen, as if for a traditional duel with sabres. Now the ritual was for the Austrian offender to ask solemnly, "*Herr Kollege*, are you an Aryan?"

Rules for students required that the offended Zionist should slap the other student in the face or hit him over the head with his stick. Then a free-for-all would develop until blood ran.

When Arthur Koestler was enrolled in a Zionist duelling fraternity, he called the rituals 'blockheaded barbarism', where the very success of Jewish duelling fraternities condemned them in the bitter eyes of the losers. It established a ruthless attitude of intimidation towards Jews that would be learned by young Austrians and Germans who became officers in the Nazi forces.

The Vienna that Koestler wrote about was the same city to which a young Austrian student from the provinces arrived some three years later, and was so overawed by its grandeur, and the immense poverty concealed behind the Rococo architecture, that he fled to Munich and changed his name to Adolf Hitler. It was there that he made his notorious bid for power in a failed rebellion against the Weimar government in November 1923. His trial would be a farce that released him from Landsberg prison after only eight months and banned him from making public speeches. He wrote *Mein Kampf* while he was locked up.

Craving for Excitement in Germany

In order to renew his public speaking early in 1927, Hitler gave an assurance to the authorities that he would not pursue any unlawful aims or use unlawful means. As a result, the governments of Bavaria and Saxony ended their ban. His first public speech after more than three years took place at the *Krone* Circus in Munich on 9 March. Police observers made an official report:

> The only decoration is a red swastika flag hanging from the stage. A band on the stage plays rousing marches as crowds pour in to the hall. There is the excitement of anticipation from the waiting audience, who talk about Hitler and his former triumph.
>
> Most come from lower income groups – workers, small tradesmen and artisans, youths in windbreakers and knee-socks. But some are well-dressed, a few even in evening dress. A great many women appear still to be enthusiastic about him. There is a craving for excitement in the hot and humid building from so many eager bodies.[8]

'We have to make it like the old days,' some people murmur as the arena fills up.

Vendors walk about selling the *Völkischer Beobachter*. Each entrant is given a slip with their programme, warning them to maintain order and not react to provocation. Tiny swastika flags are bought for 10 pfennig each, particularly by the women.

It is half past eight. About seven thousand people pack the venue and watch as roars of '*Heil*' emerge when Brownshirts enter. The band lurches into martial music, and the crowd cheers loudly as Hitler enters in a brown raincoat, accompanied by his entourage. He marches swiftly across the length of the circus and up onto the stage, with roars of excitement to welcome him. Led by two rows of drummers, columns of Brownshirts follow him in. The men give fascist salutes as they '*Heil!*' They are cheered continuously by the audience. Hitler returns the salutes of his followers with his own arm raised in the fascist salute. The music swells. Swastika flags move past like Roman military standards as about two hundred men file across the front of the stage.

Then Hitler steps swiftly to the forefront and speaks without notes. He begins slowly but emphatically, until his emotions tumble forth almost incoherently. Gesticulating with his arms and hands, he jumps around in agitation, while his audience is mesmerised by his antics and listens with keen attention. The pageantry might be described as the Hitler Circus.

Hitler spoke fifty-six times that year. But the question still remained as to if and how his Nazi Party could seize power. His most eager follower, Joseph Goebbels, published a pamphlet on what the Nazi Party should do if it could not win enough votes by the normal process of the ballot box: 'What then?'

His answer was, 'Then we'll clench our teeth and get ready. Then we'll march against this government; then we'll dare the last great coup for Germany; then revolutionaries of the word will become revolutionaries of the deed. Then we'll make a revolution!'[9]

What Germany's fascists found so appealing about Stalin's total power over the Soviet Union and his determination to accelerate history by using deliberate and decisive violence, was that they instantly wanted to do it themselves. 'It confirmed for them that a party can make a revolution, seize a state and govern by force if necessary.'[10]

Mother India

In the summer of 1927, a book was published titled *Mother India.* It challenged the aim of the Indian National Congress to obtain self-government for India. Its author was the American journalist Kathleen Mayo, who gave details of the abuse of child brides, often from the age of ten, and other cruel traditions that disregarded the human rights of many Indians. It created a surge of anti-Hindu and anti-Muslim sentiments in the West. British Viceroy Lord Irwin – better known later as Lord Halifax – remarked with understatement, "I think the general effect may be useful if it gives a shock to the unsatisfactory conditions of Hindu thought on many of these subjects."

Other human rights abuses that were abhorrent to the West included *suttee*, the tradition of Hindu widows to burn themselves alive on their husband's funeral pyre. Then there was female circumcision; and the callous treatment of the so-called 'Untouchables' that the British Government had been fighting against from the very beginning of the Raj. Almost as repugnant to the West were the 'Drugs and intoxicants, nautch dancers and courtesans, polygamy and polyandry, female infanticide, and abortion.'[11]

A question continually on Winston Churchill's lips and in his debates and reports was, in effect, 'How Indians could be left to rule themselves when they continued to accept such ghastly abuses of human beings as traditions?' He was convinced it was too soon for Home Rule. And now the American journalist's exposure of those awful customs to larger public audiences gave sound reasons to continue with British governance in India.

Even more alarming were the continually repeated riots between Hindus and Muslims. The main organisation initiating unrest was the Indian National Congress, composed of Hindus and Muslims working together. They had been confronted by the All-India Muslim League in 1906. Some 250 to 300 people had been killed in Hindu–Muslim clashes since 29 August, and more than 2,500 injured. Riots broke out in the predominantly Muslim city of Lahore as a result of an Indian article that belittled the Prophet Mohammed who had founded Islam.[12]

A Statutory Commission that the British Government was committed to under the India Act of 1919 was announced in November 1927: it would review the nature of British rule for the future. One of the members of the Commission was the moral idealist and socialist Clement Attlee, who had fought alongside Indian troops as a young man, just as young second lieutenant Winston Churchill had done. Since Churchill was now Chancellor of the Exchequer, India's problems with protests from right-wing nationalists seeking political power were no longer his.

A large minority group welcomed the Commission and wished to cooperate with it. It was composed of millions of 'Untouchables', who were excluded from society and cut off from the important and influential Hindu caste system. Muslims were divided, some deciding to support the Commission, others to boycott it.

Slavery over the border in the remote area of Kachin was also a cause for serious concern by the British Government. But Burma was beyond their jurisdiction. Even so, more than a hundred local chiefs were invited to an assembly, where they were told that slavery must stop. A British military expedition freed 4,000 slaves. Six hundred more remained to be freed, but the expedition was ambushed and its most senior officer was killed. Another expedition was organised the following year and succeeded in liberating the remaining slaves.

2

A Real Man of Genius

1928

Britain's Liberal Party had continued to decline in favour under the leadership of Prime Minister David Lloyd George by 1922, when it became splintered into 'fighting factions'. It seemed that a centrist party now lacked appeal in comparison with the passionate demands of more extreme Members of Parliament. Churchill and Lloyd George had been highly successful partners, each complementing the other, as well as rivals for greatness. Lloyd George had taken most of the credit as Prime Minister. But now it was Churchill who was greatly admired by the Conservatives and their leader Stanley Baldwin. Lloyd George was no longer trusted by the electorate.[1]

They were Lloyd George's wilderness years, while Churchill was now more at home as a Member of Parliament in a less malicious and mellower Conservative Party than before, so that his comfortably witty oratory in Parliament sounded more like friendly after-dinner speeches than his biting criticisms of the past.

Colleagues and critics thought they noticed a new sense of maturity in Churchill while he was Chancellor of the Exchequer. He developed the patience, not only to balance the nation's books, but also to banter with people, whereas he had previously focused his interest on being businesslike in his affairs and avoiding frivolous leisure pursuits. He had shown many of the symptoms of an introvert: he did not enjoy small talk, which he considered a waste of time; nor was he gregarious. He knew he was a hopeless dancer, and avoided balls. Instead, he had tended to talk only about his work, his department, or the challenging situations in which the Government was presently involved. He had been absorbed in the affairs of the House of Commons, and his political aspirations aimed at the supreme goal of presiding over the nation from 10 Downing Street.

Now, his accessibility and his genial and helpful manner drew people to him and made him more popular. His colleague and chief competitor in the Cabinet, Neville Chamberlain, even wrote to a friend that he thought Winston was a 'real man of genius', although their natures were completely different. While Churchill was broad-minded, worldly and imaginative, Chamberlain was provincial, small-minded, rigid and dull.

It was often remarked that Winston's obsessive-compulsive behaviour tired people who were unaccustomed to such single-minded devotion to high standards of professionalism, of politics, of management, and leadership. For Winston Churchill was an overachiever.

It was not a typical characteristic of the civil service or of government, which tended more towards a modest spirit of amateurism; as if to demonstrate that they were giving their services to the nation out of loyalty, chivalry, and dedication, and certainly not for their inadequate remunerations.

Winston Churchill Timeline

1874: Winston Spencer Churchill born at Blenheim Palace.
1895: Commissioned as second lieutenant in the cavalry by Queen Victoria.
1895: His father Lord Randolph Churchill dies.
1898: Publishes first book of his experiences in India and Afghanistan, *The Story of the Malakand Field Force: An Episode of Frontier War*.
1898: His cavalry charge at Battle of Omdurman in the Sudan River War.
1899: Taken prisoner by the Boers in South Africa and escapes.
1900: Elected Conservative Member of Parliament for Oldham.
1901: Visits North America when Queen Victoria dies.
1904: Gives his Maiden Speech in the House of Commons.
1904: Winston switches to Liberal Party.
1905: Colonial Under-Secretary of State with Liberal Campbell-Bannerman as PM.
1908: President, Board of Trade.
1908: Winston marries Clementine Hozier.
1910: Home Secretary.
1911: First Lord of the Admiralty in Asquith's Government.
1915: Gallipoli Campaign fails.
1916: Military Service on Western Front as lieutenant colonel in Royal Scots Fusiliers.
1917: Minister of Munitions in Lloyd George's Coalition Government.
1919: Secretary of State for War and Air.
1921: Secretary of State for Colonies.
1922: Loses seat in Parliament when Coalition Government voted out.
1924: Chancellor of the Exchequer.
1925: Rejoins the Conservative Party.
1932: Visits Munich and warns of a rearmed Germany.
1939: First Lord of the Admiralty in Chamberlain's Government.
1940: Prime Minister of Britain and Minister of Defence at age 66.

It was clearly apparent that most civil servants, and even some members of the government, possessed far less knowledge than he did of literature, history, philosophy, science or geography, or even none at all. If he had been unaware of his reputation for single-mindedness in earlier years, now he worked actively to overcome it and appear as leisurely as his colleagues.

The fourth budget of his term in office in 1928 was planned to improve industrial production and create more jobs. It was considered a great achievement, even 'a great moment in the history of British finance'. Lord Balfour wrote him a letter of congratulations.[2]

Now that he had settled down in his new country manor, which he had bought six years previously, he appeared to be more content as a family man. He entertained streams of visitors on weekends, including his close friend, the scientist, Professor Lindemann, whom they all called 'The Prof'. The Churchill children had all grown up and were at boarding schools, except for Mary, the youngest, who still lived at home at the age of five. Chartwell provided beautiful outlooks across the terraces and lawns and a narrow country lane, towards broad views of the Kent countryside. It was always filled with laughter, often initiated by Winston's own good-humoured impishness and his engaging wit.

'Churchill's capacity for work amazed those who saw it at first hand. The four or more hours after dinner, from ten or eleven in the evening until two or even three in the morning, were particularly busy ones, with long official memoranda, or chapters of the new book, being tested on Treasury officials or research assistants, and then dictated to one of the secretaries who worked special night shifts.'[3]

Foreign Secretary Sir Edward Grey considered Winston to be 'a genius'. His only fault, he felt, was that he became carried away on waves of his own rhetoric that persuaded him his proposals were right. But Grey predicted that 'his faults and mistakes will be forgotten in his achievements'. Another prescient remark from Grey, later on, was that 'his high-metalled spirit was exhilarated by the air of crisis and high events'. He thrived on such challenges.[4]

But Churchill's contentment at home and in Parliament would continue only for another year before the Conservatives were ousted at the General Election, when the Labour Party took over the reins of Government, led by the unworldly Prime Minister Ramsay MacDonald.

Grey was not the only political leader who would be shocked at Winston's exuberant reaction to ominous and threatening news. Winston saw it as a prime opportunity to demonstrate his mettle by outwitting sombre news. It was that thrill-imbued characteristic that made him a self-confident gambler at the gaming tables; a pastime that annoyed Clementine with her frugal nature. He was elated when things were at their blackest and he was at his brightest. Self-doubt was not one of his shortcomings.

The Flip Side of Genius

Churchill was bound to possess some human failings like everyone else, but most of his shortcomings and mistakes can be passed over as merely shadows cast by his brilliance, or the flip side of his engaging personality and genius. It was hardly worth mentioning them, particularly as many bickering remarks, such as those about his alleged drinking, were frivolous and irrelevant. But criticism and bickering were bound to come from those with opposing political views, or different sets of values and priorities, since different people tended to consider that their own personal interests should be prioritised. Winston was generally astute at focusing on matters of the greatest importance, providing his emotions did not sidetrack him. They were easily aroused whenever he became aware of social injustices.

If conclusions by some of Churchill's biographers about his character or judgements may appear contradictory or ambiguous, it could have been partly because of differing worldviews or different political loyalties. But above all, every journalist or biographer encounters gaps in information that lead to different interpretations of facts. And Churchill's character was complex. What created so many different opinions about him was that he appears to have been at the centre of every major historical event in his lifetime.[5]

He was certainly 'pushy, assertive, abrasive', and 'tiresome' to some, but he was not insensitive. He was a perfectionist, while some others were not, and he was not about to change his attitudes or lower his standards to please them. His vivid experiences at the centre of events informed him of different situations than his critics at the periphery – so that he frequently formed opinions that differed from theirs. He was certainly driven by ambition. And if that made some other politicians or civil servants with whom he worked feel insecure, there would have been very good reason for their apprehension, because, in general, it was an insular age, while his experiences and attitudes were unusually broad in comparison with those of, for example, the Foreign Office in his time.

How people dealt with those conflicts of ideas or memories, or opinions, depended on their own seriousness and devotion to the truth when choosing to investigate the past. Everyone had their own prejudices. Churchill did too. That is why his views on the British Empire – like Rudyard Kipling's –were misunderstood by so many of its critics who never knew it.

To say that he was not affectionate or even 'incapable of love' – as one author did – and then list no fewer than eleven terms of endearment he coined for his wife and their children, and even stated that his marriage to Clementine was a 'love match', misses the point that Englishmen of the times were naturally reserved. Emotions were suspect. Public shows of affection or love were considered unnecessary and embarrassing, even vulgar. Ladies and gentlemen intentionally restrained themselves from embarrassing each other and others by displaying their emotions. Other classes followed the same code of behaviour. It did not mean they did not feel emotions.[6]

What was acceptable behaviour then may not be considered acceptable now, and vice-versa. Whenever we reflect on the past, we always find ourselves in that then-and-now situation. Those who know what life was like then from first-hand experience are always likely to see the picture of those years differently from those who were not yet born. If we are serious about searching for the truth, we cannot accept other people's personal opinions at face value. There is plenty of trustworthy information available for serious research.

There is no doubt that Churchill possessed considerable self-love from the very beginning, most likely because his parents showed so little towards him that he had to provide it for himself. Parental neglect turned out to be to his advantage, since it forced him to prove his worth to himself and others. Had he not possessed the self-assurance to do so, he might otherwise have allowed their apparent indifference to erode his confidence. Fortunately for history, he was irrepressible.

'Churchill's experience with women was limited,' remarked another critic. It was typical of most boys and men at the time, isolated as they were in all-male institutions and societies, like prep school, boarding school, university, a male-only dining club, and the Army or Navy, where they bonded. Not only that, men were taught to be independent and manly. Womanising was regarded as irresponsible. It was thought to reveal weakness or dependency.

Those who worked closely with Churchill in the civil service or in government, like his Private Secretary Edward Marsh, or Attlee, Bevan, and Herbert Morrison, described his continual kindnesses, and how he would often weep sentimentally at the misfortunes of others when he thought no one else was around to see him. It was not considered unmanly to feel compassion for the less fortunate. It showed that – like Churchill – they understood their pain.

Foreign Affairs

Nevertheless, a sweeping generalisation often expressed of the English, particularly during the time of the British Empire, was that they were standoffish, judgemental, arrogant, and indifferent to others. There was always a section of society everywhere like that, but it hardly matched the compassionate attitude taken by better educated and more influential ones. Britain was known to be far more welcoming to refugees fleeing from oppression in other countries, so they could hardly be indifferent, as some people liked to claim.

Educated and upper classes who knew Europe's history and their families' influence on it, were still conscious of the losses they had suffered from the enormous number of deaths of their officer husbands or young sons, who had volunteered for combat at the battlefront straight out of school and led their men into artillery shell fire and machine gun fire from the front. The statistics were stark in their revelations of extraordinary bravery of men embattled in trench warfare. Part of the responsibility of older commissioned and non-commissioned officers was to uplift the spirits of the teenage infantrymen who fought under their command.

Despite their welcoming nature towards immigrants, the English were instinctively suspicious of foreigners who had dragged their country into one war after another, and always seemed to be up to mischief. The English of Churchill's time were viewed by others as insular. And they were. They were islanders, protected in their secluded domain from barbarians by a huge moat called the English Channel, while examples of previous wars were still lodged in their ancestral memories. They had been obliged to defend themselves from the armies and navies of Catholic France and Spain, and the meddlesome Papal States in Italy, as well as Napoleonic France and the Kaiser's Germany.

Churchill would have been influenced in his attitudes towards the leaders of other nations by his research to write the life of his ancestor the First Duke of Marlborough, who had countered the ambitions of King Louis XIV of France to conquer Europe, by defeating his troops in one battle after another. There had been the bloody aftermath of Napoleon Bonaparte, who had whipped up the French masses to a frenzy and turned them into extraordinarily effective soldiers who plundered their way across Europe, in order to fulfil his ambition to become Emperor. And yet, Churchill never allowed himself to become prejudiced against a whole nation or a race because of the actions of one emperor or one dictator, or a politician or a military force. His worldview remained detached from personal prejudices.

It was Britain to whom Europe's leaders begged to come to their rescue. And it was Britain, with its navy led by Admiral Nelson, and its army led by the Duke of Wellington, which had been obliged to intervene and defeat Napoleon's *Grand Armée.*

Repeated encounters with troublesome foreigners made the seafaring British islanders glad of the dangerous Channel that separated them from Europe. They wanted to have as little as possible to do with foreigners, other than trade with them. That attitude had been reinforced after Britain was dragged in to the first German war, which, once again, had been won by a narrow margin only ten years previously. Now the British wished to be left alone to depend on themselves rather than on other nations.

Churchill's prose might often seem flowery or poetic today, but the romantic description of the Britain he pictured affectionately in 1911 was little different from what most Britons still thought of their home in and up to 1939. According to Churchill it was, 'peace-loving, unthinking, little prepared', but powerful and virtuous, with 'her mission of good sense and fair-play'.[7]

Foreigners were generally thought to be unreliable, and could not be trusted not to invade Britain's shores. The island had often been invaded before, leaving doubts in the mind about the French and Germans in particular. Now that the French had become subdued after their heavy losses in the war, German-watchers continued to keep a suspicious eye on what further mischief was being plotted by the Huns.

3

German Blood

1928–29

A decade after the end of the First World War and the flight of the Kaiser to escape being blamed for it, the largest party placed in office in the 1928 German election was the Social Democrats with almost 30 per cent of the poll. They easily took 153 seats and formed the government. The German National People's Party won seventy-eighty seats, the Centre Party sixty-one. The Communist Party took only fifty-four seats. The new Chancellor Herman Müller was well-known.

Germany had been stripped of its armaments only ten years earlier, and forbidden to build up a navy, an air force or an army, in accordance with the terms of the Versailles Treaty. Its clauses were clear and binding. The old German fleet was still submerged beneath the waters of Scapa Flow, off the coast of Scotland, where it had been scuttled at the end of the First World War, and continued to rust out of sight.[1]

Industrial problems had escalated in Germany as a result of the Treaty, and foreign loans had become heavy burdens to repay. Many factories could no longer remain competitive, and the numbers of liquidations increased. Workers were laid off when profit margins shrank. Strikes erupted when trade unions fought for their members. Germany's shipbuilding industry was brought to a halt by 50,000 striking dock workers. Nearly a quarter of a million iron workers had demanded higher wages and shorter working hours. They were locked out by their employers in the Ruhr for a month for protesting.[2]

French troops still occupied the Rhineland zone of Germany's heavy industry, as stipulated in the Treaty, while Germany remained, technically, disarmed. It rankled with an ex-serviceman who supported the German National People's Party, which had just replaced its moderate leader with a more bellicose newspaper proprietor named Hugenberg.

Hitler was not discouraged that his party had only managed to obtain twelve seats in the Reichstag. He withdrew to the Bavarian mountains after the 1928 election, and began to write his new book. In it, he set out his anti-democratic political beliefs, and convictions similar to those of Mussolini. It featured two principles. One was the self-preservation of what he called the German 'Aryan' race. The other was the necessity of acquiring more 'Living Space' in Eastern Europe. For him, the struggle for space required an eternal battle between nations. He claimed it was an almost continuous legendary battle that necessitated a dedication to racial purity, meaning avoiding Germans of mixed blood who might be unreliable, even disloyal.

His romantic theory presupposed that there was such a thing as 'German blood', and that it was superior to any other type of blood. The fact that no such blood type existed did not worry him – it was a useful story to attract followers by flattering them. Evidently he thought that false science was good enough to unite a large section of German voters behind him who had thronged to hear his speeches. They were not interested in whether his claims were true or false, and would never know the difference, since the main mass of his supporters were semi-literate at best.

Hitler had recently swapped his Austrian passport for a German one. He was still a provincial Austrian with a limited world view but a passionate dream. His aim was to inspire others with the same passion for the same dream. He was aware that a fascist organisation in Vienna had already organised an armed force called the *Heimwehr*, to attack members of the Social Democrats or anyone else they chose to defeat in order to unite Austria with Germany. It became his priority, too.

The *Anschluss*, as it was called, was favoured not only by extremist Austrian fascists, but also by many moderates, ever since the Austro-Hungarian Empire had collapsed at the end of the war and they had been left as a tiny fragment of a country on their own. The justification for the merger of two nations was that their common language with Germany provided what they imagined was 'racial unity'. Austria's fascist leader, Dr Steidle, was President of the Upper House in Austria's parliament. He had warned that he intended to follow Mussolini's example in Italy, and march on Vienna.[3] When socialists organised their own march to challenge him, the government called out 12,000 Austrian troops to intervene with machine guns. A sudden and heavy downpour of rain cooled the passions of both sides.

Normal Life in the Balkans

The trend of imposing authoritarian regimes to halt the spread of chaos was not confined only to Italy, Austria and Germany. Once successfully established by Mussolini, fascism became a model for all types of populist leaders to follow in order to obtain autocratic power.

Balkan countries had joined together at Versailles for their own protection in a larger kingdom called Yugoslavia. Those countries had never got along together before. Even when they had been part of the former Austro-Hungarian Empire, their languages, religions, ethnicity, and ambitions had always clashed. They were as envious and jealous and suspicious of each other now as they had always been when part of the Habsburg Empire. The Croats felt overlooked and under-represented in the Administration and in Parliament. The abrasiveness between Roman Catholic countries and Orthodox Christian ones, Calvinists, and Islamic regions persisted. They lacked a strong enough leader to unite them against the aggressiveness of the Serbs, or the growing number of Muslims in Bosnia. Mussolini's machismo appeared to be the answer for the Balkans. It did not seem to matter much whether such a leader pursued fascism to appeal to the lower middle classes, or communism to appeal to the working classes: it was a game that could be won by overwhelming society with numbers.

The Communist Party organised demonstrations in the main square of Zagreb, Croatia`s capital city, on 1 May 1929. Among the many rebel contenders arrested was Josip Broz, the Secretary of the Zagreb Communist Party. He claimed it was fighting for Croatian independence, and supported the right of Germans, Hungarians, Albanians and other minorities, to break away from Yugoslavia. He was sentenced to prison for two weeks.*

That summer, four Croat deputies were dragged out of Belgrade's parliament by police for disrupting the proceedings for four days of protest against under-representation and Serbian dominance in the legislature. A Montenegrin deputy in the Serb Radical Party, Punisa Racic, shot and killed a Croat deputy named Paul Radic and wounded his victim's uncle, Stephen Radic, who was a Croat Peasant Party leader. Anti-Serbian riots erupted in Belgrade on 20 June, and riot police opened fire, killing five rioters.

The Balkan countries were no more stable that the Middle East, where everyone disagreed with each other. So it continued, with Croats claiming that the whole concept of Yugoslavian unity did not work, and demanding autonomy. King Alexander of Yugoslavia watched his multinational kingdom falling apart. In an attempt to save it, he went so far as to visit the wounded Stephen Radic in hospital in Belgrade, to kiss him as a fellow Christian and beg him to form a new government.

Radic declined and returned to Zagreb to die of his wounds. Power passed to the Serbs and Slovenes. Josip Broz's Communist Party led a riot in Zagreb – after which he disguised himself and went into hiding. When caught on 4 August, he was tried, and sentenced to five years in prison after confessing that the Communist Party was 'Moscow`s organisation'.*

Paranoia ran thick among the different tribes and religions in the Balkan States, as it had always done when part of the Habsburg Empire. When the Croats became anxious at the possibility of a Serb dictatorship, someone murdered a Serbian secret police agent in a Zagreb café in retaliation. Belgrade called for the Croat leaders to be arrested. It was all considered to be 'normal' in the Balkan states where everyone hated everyone else with a different religion.

Men Have Tired of Liberty

Having obtained total power in Italy through threats five years previously, Benito Mussolini incorporated the Fascist Grand Council into the Italian constitution,

* Churchill would have to deal with him when he became Prime Minister of a communist Yugoslavia two decades later under the pseudonym of Tito.

making Italy, in effect, subordinate to his Fascist Party. It would officially advise the government on political, social and economic issues. No constitutional changes could be made without its approval. Moreover, its members would be protected from arrest. It would be like a private nation within a nation, with its own private army of black shirts. Mussolini would set the agenda for all its meetings, which would be undertaken in secret. He informed the Italian parliament that a new generation had the right to make new laws that suited its needs and attitudes.

The fascist leader had repudiated liberal democracy and its belief in the rule of law in 1923, two years after his black-shirted forces had prepared to march threateningly on Rome, when he had declared that: 'Liberalism is not the last word, nor does it represent the definitive formula on the subject of the art of government.'[4]

He claimed that it did not follow that what had been good for the nineteenth century, which had been dominated by the growth of capitalism and nationalist sentiments, should be adapted to the twentieth century:

> I challenge Liberal gentlemen to tell if ever in history there has been a government that was based solely on popular consent and that renounced all use of force whatsoever … Consent is an ever-changing thing like the shifting sand on the sea coast. It can never be permanent. It can never be complete … If it be accepted as an axiom that any system of government whatever creates malcontents, how are you going to prevent this discontent from overflowing and constituting a menace to the stability of the State? You will prevent it by force. By the assembling of the greatest force possible. By the inexorable use of this force whenever it is necessary. Take away from any government whatsoever force – and by force is meant physical, armed force – and leave it only its immortal principles, and that government will be at the mercy of the first organised group that decides to overthrow it. Fascism now throws these lifeless theories out to rot … men have tired of liberty. They have made an orgy of it … For the gallant, restless and bitter youth who face the dawn of a new history there are other words that exercise a far greater fascination, and those words are, order, hierarchy, discipline …[5]

Normal Life in China

The Kuomintang nationalist leader Chiang Kai-shek accepted the post of Generalissimo in order to restore order by securing alliances with the two main warlords, General Feng, who ruled Hunan and had just put down a Muslim revolt by killing 200,000 of them, and General Li, who ruled Canton. China had become one country again after more than ten years of fierce struggles. Now all foreigners were subject to Chinese laws.

That did not deter communist leader Mao Zedong, who led numerous uprisings of the peasants, cajoling them to massacre their landlords. His persecution and execution of the more prosperous peasants was similar to what Stalin had done with the Kulaks in communist Russia. Mao's intention was to lead an uprising throughout China. But he was not too optimistic about the dumb and sullen peasant resistance: 'Only after our propaganda did they slowly move into action.'

The severe winter of 1928–29 added to the hardships of the small and isolated Chinese communist army, against which the Kuomintang – made confident by its many victories elsewhere – launched yet another offensive in China.[6]

This was the turbulent age in which Winston Churchill matured and established a successful, if precarious, career at the forefront of British politics. Every sign of friction in every corner of the world would affect his outlook and the actions he took to respond. He appeared to possess more knowledge and understanding of global events than most politicians. It was no accident that he called his book on the causes and effects of the First World War *The World Crisis.* He understood how even the faintest ripples of rebellion by massive and uninformed forces can spread swiftly around the globe in copycat fashion as a result of the madness of crowds that transform themselves suddenly into monsters.

4

Hard Times

1929

While the United States was urging disarmament in Europe, Britain's Government was concerned with defining a long-term defence policy. Churchill believed firmly that France required a powerful enough army to resist a German invasion, since Germany was dissatisfied at the poor response to its grievances with the terms of the Versailles Treaty. He was impatient with America and 'these stupid disarmament manoeuvres'. He knew that a disarmed nation invited attack. And yet, Britain's government possessed a naive idea that it would be seen as posing no threat to anyone if it began disarming; and that it would encourage other nations to disarm.

He had no desire to have to intervene again and again in Europe to prevent a war, or end one. It was not what he considered productive. He was convinced to the end of his life of the need to distract belligerent nations from attacking the British Isles by ensuring that their energies and resources would be used on the other side of the Channel, where a strong French Army in Europe could protect Britain as well as France. He opposed all efforts to persuade France to disarm.

In order to ensure that the British Isles would be protected, he pressed the Cabinet to make a detailed study of current foreign manufacturing techniques of armaments, particularly in Germany. Major General Desmond Morton and he had been friends ever since they had met in the war on the Western Front. Morton had undertaken intelligence work after the war, while Churchill had masterminded Britain's espionage as Secretary of State for War. Since Morton's cottage was within walking distance of Chartwell, it was convenient for them to meet often and privately to discuss matters of State.

Morton possessed invaluable expertise after being involved in military and economic preparations by Soviet Russia and Germany. He was appointed Head of the Industrial Intelligence Centre of the Committee of Imperial Defence at the beginning of the year. His responsibility now was to investigate and report on any plans in foreign countries for the manufacture of armaments and war stores.[1]

Churchill and the general studied as much information as they could obtain together. Their most frequent discussions involved the balance of power in Europe, and German rearmament. Churchill's friend, Lindemann, the former Oxford professor, was also a frequent visitor and adviser on scientific matters.

At the same time, Churchill continued writing his war memoirs, which he wanted to finish before an imminent general election. Publication of the fifth volume, which was about *The Aftermath* to *The World Crisis,* gave him time to reconsider how it related to the present situation in foreign affairs. Economist John Maynard Keynes would review it:

> With what feelings does one lay down Mr Churchill's two-thousandth page? Gratitude to one who can write with so much eloquence and feeling with things which are part of the lives of all of us of the war generation, but which he saw and knew much closer and clearer. Admiration for his energies of mind and his intense absorption of intellectual interest and elemental emotion in what is for the moment the matter in hand – which is his best quality. A little envy, perhaps, for his undoubting conviction that frontiers, races, patriotisms, even wars if need be are ultimately verities for mankind, which lends for him a kind of dignity and even nobility to events, which for others are only a nightmare interlude, something to be permanently avoided.[2]

Winston spoke in London and elsewhere in preparation for the general election campaign. He warned that the election of a socialist government would introduce subversion into the factories and the armed forces. It would probably lead to another General Strike. He was anxious about the misleading face of respectability behind which Labour Cabinet ministers pursued destructive socialist principles, whereas Churchill knew that 'ideas alone are not flesh and blood'. It was an allusion to doctrinaire politics based on theories and wishful thinking instead of on real people in real situations.[3]

The fundamental problem was – as in all cases when rebels ruthlessly followed the dogma of an ideology – that they 'manipulated the facts in the interests of the system', instead of protecting the interests of the electorate.[4] He reminded the electorate of his own achievements in the past five years. His entitlement legislation in 1925 had enabled over a million people to draw welfare benefits. They included 236,800 widows, 344,800 children, 450,000 seniors over sixty-five, and 227,000 over seventy.

After presenting his fifth budget as Chancellor of the Exchequer, he summarised the achievements of the Conservatives in a BBC broadcast on 30 April by announcing that there was peace abroad, steady stable government at home, clean, honest, impartial administration; goodwill in industry between masters and men; public and private thrift. But he warned that it would all be lost if there was a change in government. He cautioned voters to: 'Avoid chops and changes of policy; avoid thimble-riggers and three-card trick men; avoid all needless borrowings; and above all avoid, as you would the smallpox, class warfare and violent political strife.'[5]

Powerless

Despite all his warnings, the Conservative Party he had rejoined four years earlier was defeated at the polls by the opposition party on 30 May 1929. It was called the 'flapper election' because women were able to vote for the first time.

Churchill was now out of a job. The thought of inactivity made him disappointed and angry with himself. He had lost an opportunity by his unpopular performance as an austerity Chancellor. At least he had held on to his Epping seat, but with a much-reduced majority. But, more importantly, he had lost his position in the Cabinet.[6]

Nevertheless, unlike most other politicians, he had several other skills and opportunities, and immediately set about working on the biography of his famous ancestor, the First Duke of Marlborough. As usual when writing history, he benefited from the assistance of at least one experienced researcher. In this case it was a historian from Oxford, Maurice Ashley, who investigated all the relevant archives in Europe for him.

Since he was still a Member of Parliament, he was free to use his oratory in the House of Commons to support any Labour Party efforts to inject money into the economy in order to create more jobs through infrastructure spending, particularly in the coal mining areas of the country where there was unemployment.

In between times he analysed why the Conservatives had lost the election to the Labour Party, and considered how they could return to power. He was intrigued by the statistics: 8 million Conservatives, 8 million Labour, and 5 million Liberals. The Liberals held the balance of power. Better to have them in the Conservative camp than allied to the socialists. Otherwise the Conservatives would be isolated and powerless for years. He persuaded party leader Stanley Baldwin of the necessity for an alliance with the Liberal Party. With Baldwin's approval, he would approach his old colleague David Lloyd George, who still led the Liberal Party. They had been staunch friends during the war, but they were both strong minded and had often quarrelled since then.

As it turned out, there was a conflict of interests with Leon Amery, who was now First Lord of the Admiralty. He was a former Harrow schoolboy with Winston, but he was still dedicated to returning the country to protectionism, whereas Churchill supported free trade and considered it vital for the national economy and for providing more jobs.

Churchill left on a trip to North America at the beginning of August with several family members, and some relief at escaping from England and the weight of all the problems in the world. Clementine was not well enough to travel.

'My darling,' he wrote to her, while on board the Atlantic liner, 'I have been rather sad at times thinking of you in low spirits at home. Do send me some messages. I love you so much & it grieves me to feel you are lonely.'

Disillusion, Chaos and Fear

It was a relief to hear that the American President Herbert C. Hoover now favoured a return to United States' involvement with Europe, and even assuming possible international responsibilities. Such interest by America's leaders had been absent during the recent decade of the League of Nations, after the ailing President Woodrow Wilson had returned home from the Versailles Peace Conference in Paris and died.

British Prime Minister Ramsay MacDonald now decided to participate in the League's activities on disarmament, with the intention of preventing a possible future war.

The problem that the League of Nations had immediately encountered was a typically human situation, in which heavily armed nations were naturally against reducing their military power, whereas those that had been forced to disarm a decade earlier at Versailles were anxious to rearm again. The more the subject of disarming was pursued, the more obstacles were found. It depended on such insoluble questions as how large a nation's military forces should be, and the amount of military training that should be allowed; how much international supervision would be enough to prevent aggressive nations from having their way; and how to control military budgets of independent and sovereign nations, to prevent them from excessive spending on arms, which might create an arms race. Increased productivity of weaponry could easily build up heavy arsenals of war material that would inevitably be used to threaten others.

Everything depended on trust, which was in short supply between nations more concerned with power and self-preservation. And fear of war reigned in the Balkans, Soviet Russia, Germany and Italy. Every nation in Europe feared its neighbour becoming more powerful and aggressive, and formed alliances with old enemies. Just as Britain's history had taught it to be sceptical of foreign nations, so foreign leaders eyed each other anxiously.

The New York Stock Exchange crash in October, with the loss of Winston's investments and capital, made him even more conscious of the need to keep writing books and articles now that he had lost his Chancellorship salary. He had also lost the equivalent of £500,000 on the stock exchange.

He discovered that lecture tours of the United States paid even better than writing, and was able to obtain a lecturing engagement.

Devastation was taking place in America's depleted economy in which, as one example, the demand for US Steel would fall for three years following the Wall Street Crash, during which the firm had to lay off 225,000 workers. That was the effect of economic decline on only one company alone. The same situation rippled through thousands of others.

In less than a year after the Depression began, an extended drought dried up the farmlands. Powerful winds swept the Southern Plains and ripped off farms in an instant. Dust storms would continue to sweep through Texas and Nebraska from 1930 to 1936, where the land would become worthless. More than 35 million acres of cultivated farmland became useless, and another 125 million acres lost its topsoil. Some penniless farmers abandoned what had once been cultivated farms and somehow managed to travel west to reach California and search for work that provided only food and shelter but no pay, known as indentured labour. Others fled the country for work in Soviet Russia, which was industrialising and needed skilled workers, compared with their own peasant population.

Strikes and protests took place by bewildered and confused crowds that had lost their jobs and savings. They knew something was wrong but had no idea where to turn for help, or who to blame for the catastrophe. There were no safety nets. According to many, the country was on the edge of revolution.

The chaos in Germany was even worse, as soldiers mounted machine guns on street corners to subdue the crowds who searched vainly for order, jobs, and leadership. It was Hitler's opportunity to seize power.

By the end of that year in England, Churchill was almost bankrupt.[7]

5

The Unchanging Middle East

1928–29

Religions of Lamentation

A string of bad luck followed the Churchills' earlier series of misfortunes. Winston had barely started his speaking tour to help pay off his losses and meet his bills, when he was knocked down by a vehicle, after stepping out of a taxi on Fifth Avenue and rushed to hospital. His head, chest and thigh were badly injured. Now he had further costs from the Lennox Hill Hospital, as well as Clementine's hotel bill from the Waldorf Astoria. Unable to continue his series of lectures after completing only one booking, he forced himself to recover quickly and return to writing back home to pay his bills.

As a consequence of telegraphing news of his accident to the *Daily Mail*, which was syndicated all over the world, he was inundated with thousands of letters and telegrams wishing him well. Churchill was at the centre of the news once again, but in miserable shape. Now in desperate need of money, he sold the story of his accident to *Collier's* for about $3,000.

No sooner were they back at Chartwell than Clementine began a long period of ill-health. It started with a throat infection which led to blood poisoning. That was followed by a bout of mastoid fever – one of several life-threatening epidemics of the times. Although Winston was feverishly writing whatever he could to pay off part of his debt, he sat beside her hospital bed and read to her. They held hands and she told him it had brought them closer together again: 'You are always deep in my heart and now your tenderness has unlocked it.'

Nervous exhaustion and depression followed. Despite continual rumours of Churchill's famous 'black dog', in fact he was rarely depressed for long and had little patience with people's personal complaints; as if they were the price to be paid for the gift of life. He failed to understand what Clementine was going through during the deep depressions that overtook her from that time on. There had been a history of her frequently withdrawing to bed in the past, when it was thought that she was a hypochondriac.

Winston took such situations in his stride, without paying too much attention to them. His reaction to most people was to accept them for what they were, without questioning any quirks of character, or being judgemental, or wanting them to be someone else. As one member of the Churchill family noted, the Churchills 'expect their women to understand them totally. And they don't spend much time trying to understand their women.'

Each of the troublesome post-war territories which had been handed to the victorious Allies to administer as mandates by the League of Nations, after the collapse of several great empires, brought its own particular problems with it that the League was now obliged to reconsider. In the case of Britain's mandated territories, there had been continuous friction between Muslims and Jews in Jerusalem. Judaism, Christianity, and Islam are all religions of lamentation: so that administration included responsibility for keeping the peace at the traditional Jewish 'Wailing Wall'. It was a relic of the old Herodian Temple which had been destroyed by invading Roman legions a few thousand years previously.

The wall was the main Holy Place for religious and even secular Jews. It stood on the Temple Mount, which was administered by Muslim authorities, because it was situated in an area known to Islam as the Haram al-Sharif, or Holy Sanctuary, from which the Prophet Mohammad was claimed to have ascended to heaven on his death in the seventh century.

Some Muslims had deliberately harassed Jewish worshippers at the Holy Wall by opening up a passageway between it and the Holy Sanctuary. Jewish Orthodox worshippers had protested to the British Mandatory authorities, who had suspended work on the offending passageway. But then it was allowed to continue by the Law Officers of the Crown in London.

Population statistics showed that by now there were 150,000 Jews to more than 700,000 Arabs, because the Arab population now included an additional 100,000 economic immigrants who had fled from Egypt, Syria, Saudi Arabia and other Arab territories.[1]

An incident at the Wailing Wall resulted in 133 Jewish people being murdered in riots by Arab mobs, incited by their leader, Haj Amin al-Husseini; better known as the Mufti of Jerusalem, who harboured political ambitions for pan-Arabism, or global power. Other Jewish holy sites were attacked, like the Tombs of the Patriarchs in Hebron. As the British authorities did not allow any Jews to train or arm their own units to protect themselves and their settlements, British troops intervened to prevent more Arab attacks, and killed 113 rioting Arabs.

In accordance with the Balfour Declaration of 1917 and the 1922 Mandate legislation, the League of Nations was committed to allowing Jewish people to immigrate to Palestine as their right, and not on sufferance. So the League's Permanent Mandates Commission was requested to hold a special session to hear and consider a report of the causes of violence in Palestine, and recommend how to secure law and order in the territory. Some Arab rioters were tried and imprisoned.

The problem through western eyes appeared to be sullen envy by a peasant population at the arrival of educated Europeans who were more successful than them. However, there was more to it than envy or jealousy: there was the traditional Arab hatred of strangers who did not share their beliefs, even daring to step on the land that they imagined was holy to them, despite its sterility for thousands of years. It was even more infuriating to see those strangers succeeding by growing crops in the desert, whereas they had failed. Frustration created an attitude of anger and hostility at their own failings, which they took out on successful Jewish farmers.

It was not the only type of problem that Churchill had had to address when he had been responsible as Colonial Secretary. There were also continual clashes between Catholics and Protestants in Ireland, and Muslims and Hindus in India. Those problems shared many similarities. The Irish people and the Jews had suffered from bad luck for generations. Half the population of Ireland had left their homeland as a consequence of poverty, famine, or terrorism by IRA gunmen. Far more were now dispersed and living overseas than remained in Ireland.

A similar situation applied to Jews who had been forced to leave Judea and Israel – then called Palestine – when their homeland had been conquered by General Pompey's Roman legions and annexed by Rome in 63 BC. It was conquered again nearly eight centuries later by Islamic forces in the seventh century AD, when Muslims had built the Haram al-Sharif to emphasise their presence. It had more recently been ruled by the corrupt Ottoman Turks. Britain had defeated them in 1918. But, despite having been freed from oppression by the Turks, the Arab population showed no gratitude towards the English and were stubbornly uncooperative.

Arab peasants had turned out to be as stubborn and backward-looking as the Irish rebels, with their continual refusal to cooperate to improve their economic situation and the lives of their people. Revenge was at the forefront of their minds, rather than progress. Trauma imprisoned them in their history, and caused young idealists to become murderers for the sake of a cause.

The Middle East manifested that same quality of self-pity and frustration that prevented progress. It was enshrined in the word *inshallah:* It was 'God's will'. Muslims were commanded by their Mullahs to submit.

Other territories than Palestine had been mandated to British administration, like Syria, Transjordan, and Iraq. Ruled by King Abdullah, Transjordan's Bedouin troops would be trained and led by the British General Sir John Glubb to create stability in the region. He would officially take over leadership of the Arab Legion in 1930. Glubb Pasha, as he was known, would turn out to be an excellent choice for a general who identified personally with the Bedouin tribes and possessed a high regard for their bravery. He most probably understood the complexities of the Middle East better than most people, since he preferred to live with the Bedouin tribes.*

Glubb was a hero of the First World War, during which part of his jaw had been shot away. Unlike most British army officers, he was an Arabist who spoke the language fluently, dressed as an Arab, and lived and ate with his men. A somewhat shy and reserved man, he was more comfortable with the Arab Legion than in an English officers' club. And his rich knowledge of the region and its peoples would be invaluable, since what he would write about the people of Arabia on his

* Sir John Glubb had organised, trained, and would lead the Bedouin of Transjordan until 1956. After retiring from the military, he would write no fewer than eight informative books on Arabia and the Arabs.

retirement is still useful in attempting to sort out Arab differences and their hatred of each other and the West.

Iraq and Syria would become, and remain, trouble spots like Egypt. So that what had appeared to be a solution to governing the shapeless remains of the former Ottoman Empire when its power and leadership failed would become a continual burden, a heavy cost, and a thankless task for Britain. No doubt Churchill was happy at being no longer responsible for their destiny. He had fought against Islamist slave traders in the Sudan with General Gordon when he had been only twenty-three in 1897, and had seen the same chaos in the Middle East twenty-three years later when he was Colonial Secretary. Nothing seemed to have changed.

English Arabists

The British Empire had been served during the Victorian, Edwardian and Post-Edwardian periods by a number of dedicated secret agents who were fascinated with areas of the Middle East that they mapped and continued to study and observe on behalf of British Intelligence. The nomadic culture of the Bedouin appealed to them in much the same way that Orientalism had fascinated some of the more intelligent and well-read English army officers in India.

Harry St John Philby, the British Colonial Intelligence Officer and adviser to Ibn Saud, was an English eccentric who enjoyed dressing up as an Arab while exploring the Arabian Peninsula and Oman. He changed his name to Haji Abdullah after visiting the Kaba in Mecca. Explorer Wilfred Thesiger lived with the marsh Arabs in Iraq and worked in London with the Middle East Anti-Locust Unit. The archaeologist and Intelligence Officer Gertrude Bell, who worked in the Arab Bureau of British Intelligence in Cairo with T.E. Lawrence, was credited with the creation of Iraq. Freya Stark was another British Arabist. So was the Victorian adventurer Sir Richard Burton, who became a Muslim and a Haji in order to investigate Arabia and probe the origins of Islam. He became doubtful of what he heard and remained an atheist.

All identified themselves closely with the inhabitants of the region in which they enjoyed working. The reward in each case was a sense of purpose, as Gertrude described to her parents in February 1920: 'I'm acutely conscious of how much life has after all given me. I've gone back now, after many years, to the old feeling of joy in existence, and I'm happy in feeling that I've got the love and confidence of a whole nation … You must forgive me if it seems to preoccupy me too much …'[2]

The contrast between their sense of purpose in improving conditions in the Middle East compared with the defeatism of most Arab leaders and *fellahin* was disheartening for British administrators. The British attitude to misfortunes would rather have been to remark, 'Oh, what bad luck!' and move on. Self-pity was not an option for Anglo-Saxon temperaments. The cynical French in Syria, on the other hand, had no such patience with the Arabs in Syria and took the opportunity to exploit the territory.

Far more complicated Arabists, like St John Philby, enjoyed the deception that gave him two identities. There was something quintessentially English about dressing up splendidly for a particular official purpose. Austrians and Hungarians had loved dressing up in colourful uniforms in order to preen themselves in society, but Victorian Englishmen donned fancy dress to demonstrate their authority to undertake serious work, like ruling an empire, or serving their country as a secret agent in order to protect it in the 'great game' against Russian infiltration into India. The British loved entertaining friends and family at home with fancy dress parties, games of charades, and dressing up appropriately for *tableaux vivants*. They loved amateur theatricals.

A contemporary British philosopher described the custom as 'the familiar and constantly changing uniforms of the Edwardian gentry as they migrate from drawing room to dining room and back again, dropping one mask and picking up another in the hope that no one will accuse them of being who they are'.[3] In short, the British code of manners at the time was to be self-effacing. But it was rarely the case with Britain's more eccentric explorers and Arabists.

Apart from the Victorian explorer Richard Burton, the best known internationally of the Arabists was T.E. Lawrence. He had been present as an adviser at the Versailles Peace Conference a decade previously, and was still unhappy, suffering from what he considered to be a betrayal of his Arab comrades after he had led them in a revolt against the Ottoman Turks.

He was exhausted after writing his very long book describing his exploits as a guerrilla fighter in the desert, which he had called *The Seven Pillars of Wisdom*. Despite his heroic exploits in the First World War and his international fame, he was pleased to be able to earn £10 for an article on guerrilla warfare in the fourteenth edition of the *Encyclopaedia Britannica* in 1929. The eminent military historian of the First World War, Sir Basil Liddell Hart, edited it for him while Lawrence was serving in Karachi. He needed the fee because service life in India was more expensive than in Britain, and he was always short of cash.*

Lawrence was escaping from himself and unsure of his real identity by that time. Was it the withdrawn private intellectual or the vain and posturing 'Lawrence of Arabia' who loved dressing up in Arab robes for news photographers to take pictures of him?

His book described his experiences in the Arab Revolt against the Ottoman Turks in 1916–18, when poorly armed and untrained tribesmen had unsuccessfully attacked the Turkish garrisons in Medina and near Mecca. They had needed a leader to arm and train them.

While the undisciplined Arabs were still undergoing training, Turkish troops had suddenly advanced on Mecca and penetrated the hills in only twenty-four hours. Lawrence had realised that irregular Arab forces were undisciplined and unable

* Probably worth about £200 or more today.

to defend a position or attack one successfully. After some thought, it occurred to him how it could be done. Subsequently, he and Prince Faisal's tribesmen had succeeded in defeating the Turks in 1917, taking 35,000 prisoners of war, killing and wounding approximately the same number, and occupying about 100,000 square miles of enemy territory. The Wadi Rum would become part of Jordan.[4]

Man and Myth

Like some other intellectuals who became celebrities, Lawrence found the invasion of his privacy was irksome. In a desperate attempt to escape from the public glare, he re-enlisted anonymously in the lowest rank in the RAF as Aircraftsman Ross, and even preferred the anonymity of Aircraftsman 352087. When found out, he admitted that he must have suffered from a nervous breakdown.

He vanished again from the sight of the media as soon as he was recognised, and joined the Royal Tank Corps, this time under the name of 'Private Shaw', where he became fascinated with the idea of troop mobility by mechanised transport in time of war. Even then, he found himself caught between the desire for a private life and a wish to have his story known by more readers. It was suspected by some that although he cringed from publicity, he also suffered from delusions of grandeur when dressing up and posturing in Arab robes.

British Orientalism

The Victorian age had only recently passed away, and most of the British Arabists, explorers and naturalists with it, since most of the world had now been mapped and was 'known'. But contemporary Britons, including Churchill, were still keen to categorise people in order to understand them better.

Explorations of little-known Africa had taken place only about seventy years previously, and made the British more curious than ever. Burton had translated *The Arabian Nights* only thirty-four years previously. It created a fascination with the Middle East, and other lands that were foreign to them, and confronted them with even more different characteristics, like differently coloured skins and tribes, different religions and cultures, and bone and skull formations that identified the origins of different people.

Burton had been an army officer in Sind, like Churchill, but with the British East India Company in the 1840s. His travelling nature had been somewhat like Lawrence's; so that different cultures played a prominent role in his writings, which were part geographic, part anthropology and part philosophy. It was claimed that Burton was fluent in at least twenty-five different languages.[5]

That impulse by educated Englishmen appeared to contradict a belief that English people were narrow-minded. But the number of Britain's explorers amounted to little more than a handful who were motivated by curiosity and an adventurous spirit. What struck most of them was the enormous variety of different forms of life; humans, animals, insects, and plant life, as Darwin had found in South America. Most explorations had convinced Europeans that their civilisation was superior, but that 'no single system of religion enjoyed a monopoly on truth'.[6]

Churchill grew up to be keenly interested in each new exploration and its discoveries. Although those men who were motivated by curiosity about the world were very unusual types of people, they had in common 'a vast repertoire of ideas, practices, and values. Few if any scholars possess the breadth of knowledge needed to identify all the influences that informed this polymorphous polymath.' So wrote one analyst of their nature, which he attributed to each of them being what he called 'The Highly Civilised Man'.[7]

Young Winston had recorded his working trip to Africa with his private secretary in *My African Journey* in 1908. It differed from trips by other explorers in that it was to assess the value of one of Britain's colonies and how the territory and its economy could be improved.

The differences between highly intelligent adventurers and all the rest of the island nation was 'One of the peculiarities of the scholarship on nineteenth century Britain'. It had long been divided into two distinct histories: a national one concerned with 'the island story' of industrialisation, class conflict, and political reform, and an imperial historiography concerned with overseas trade, migration, and conquest.[8]

Despite the vast difference between rulers and the ruled, the English thought of themselves as individualists who differed from their European neighbours. As an example, their experience in ruling India produced qualities in them that made them exceptional. It was called 'Orientalism'.

> Orientalism as Burton understood it was the intellectual project associated with William Jones, Warren Hastings, and other late eighteenth-century and early nineteenth-century British officials in India whose systematic study of the languages, literature, laws, and religious beliefs of the subcontinent's inhabitants opened up an unfamiliar body of learning to the West. British Orientalism was in turn part of a wider European inquiry into the cultural traditions of people from the near to the Far East, an inquiry that came to assume over time a reputation as an impartial enterprise undertaken by a venerable scholarly fraternity.[9]

The main reason for the British military occupation of Sindh only a few months after Burton arrived in India, was that it was 'the gateway to India', which was considered, with its mountainous topography, to be 'a buffer against Russian expansion'. The threat of an invasion of India by Russian troops was a dominant theme in Britain during the Victorian era.

This was the British Empire that Churchill knew and loved – as opposed to the later theoretical view of colonialism by public intellectuals and political activists who refused to acknowledge its merits. Their mind was somewhere else: often in the heavy theories of Marx and Engels on capitalism and the communist experiment in Soviet Russia.

The close ties that were formed between the English and Indians were brought even closer by the fact that, according to Burton, 'there was hardly an officer in Baroda who was not more or less morganatically married' to an Indian woman. And 'an inspector general confirmed that nearly every officer in Burton's regiment in 1845 had a concubine'.[10]

Indian concubines were known as 'walking dictionaries', which, according to Isabel Burton, 'connected the white strangers to the country and its people'.[11] That custom provided a valuable source of information for British Intelligence. It also helped to explain Britain's fascination with Asia and the Middle East, as opposed to today's accusations that they 'interfered' in the affairs of other countries.

The Middle East was only part of a rich cultural tapestry that Britain's Colonial Office had been required to maintain and protect. If Churchill had mixed feelings when he had been forced to relinquish his ministerial responsibilities as a consequence of the General Election results that lost him his seat in 1922, his driving ambition to succeed in politics would have won out over any regrets. He was not sorry to have left the Colonial Office when all the emotional problems of the Middle East were unlikely to be resolved. They had existed for centuries and looked no better later on, after stewing for seven more years in the pitiless deserts of Syria, Iraq, Transjordan and Saudi Arabia.

The contrast between Churchill's more purposeful approach to life – that he seemed to have inherited from his ancestor John Churchill, the First Duke of Marlborough, and which no doubt was reinforced by the Victorian values of his youth – as against the apathy of the peasant multitudes in the Middle East, must have been disappointing. He abhorred apathy that resulted in defeatism, because he knew it was like a worm that penetrated the brain cells and portended failure. He was always positive, whereas they were negative with their stubborn resistance to progress and their preference for prayers and lamentations over a lost Caliphate.

6

Reason or Hysteria

1930

When Winston, his brother Jack and young Randolph, arrived in Québec on 9 August 1929, they were enchanted by their first motor car trip into the unspoiled Canadian countryside. Charles Schwab had provided a private railway car for them. He had built submarines for Churchill when Winston had been Minister of Munitions during the war, and reduced the construction time to less than six months, instead of the typical fourteen in the steel industry at that time.

They travelled from east to west across Canada by railway, past the Rockies to Vancouver in British Columbia, where he wrote to Clementine that he and Jack slept in large cabins with double beds and en suite bathrooms, with a large dining room that he used as an office.

He made two speeches in Montreal and one each in Ottawa and Toronto, remarking in his letter to Clementine that he had never been welcomed with such genuine interest and admiration: 'The workmen in the streets, the girls who work the lifts, the ex-servicemen, the farmers, up to the highest functionaries have shown such unaffected pleasure to see me & shake hands that I am profoundly touched; & and I intend to devote my strength to interpreting Canada to our own people & vice versa …'[1]

He was delighted to meet former servicemen in the middle west, whom he had last seen in several different wars more than three decades previously. They came to him 'in twos and threes' to welcome him and shake his hand. Among them was a former sergeant of engineers who had helped him to make his plans for the Battle of Omdurman in 1898. Churchill was deeply touched.[2]

Randolph enjoyed travelling with his father, and wrote in his diary, 'Papa came out looking magnificent, Jodhpur riding suit of khaki, his ten gallon hat, a Malacca walking stick with gold knob, and riding a pure white horse.'[3]

They visited the oilfields at Calgary. And, with all the adulation, Churchill's restless mind had evidently turned back from writing to politics again. His thoughts had flashed to how he could obtain the position of Britain's Prime Minister. He was only fifty-five. Writing from Banff, he remarked to Clementine that if Neville Chamberlain 'or anyone else of that kind', was made leader of the Conservative Party, 'I clear out of politics, & see if I cannot make you & the kittens a little more comfortable before I die.'

It was an insight into his personal opinion of Chamberlain, who was destined to become infamous later on in his career as the Prime Minister who led Britain into the open arms of Hitler during the Munich Crisis. It is likely that, even then, Winston saw him as a narrow-minded though well-meaning politician, who had become larger in public esteem than was warranted by his limited capabilities.

He began painting landscapes at Lake Louise; then headed south into the United States, and thence to San Francisco. He visited William Randolph Hearst's castle at San Simeon, and was not the only one to remark on the newspaper mogul's vast income, which was always overspent, and Hearst's not very discriminating works of art that he had collected and hoarded like an addict to possess things.

What was more interesting, he informed Clementine, was the circulation of Hearst's newspapers of 15 million a day. Hearst asked him to write for them. They would provide Winston with yet another source of income. From his writing in that month alone he had already earned the equivalent of two and a half years' earnings of a British Prime Minister.[4] It included the advance for his *Marlborough* biography, a fee for three articles in Nash's *Pall Mall* magazine, and royalties from the last volume of his war memoirs.

Churchill's welcome by New Yorkers astonished his bodyguard: 'Several hundred police in a whirling parade [we] rocked up Broadway with enough sirens to waken the dead.' Then they were on a train to his first engagement in Worcester, Massachusetts. Soon they were back at the Waldorf, where he dictated his next lecture to stenographers.[5]

He dined with the famous film star and producer Charlie Chaplin in Hollywood on 20 September. As Winston informed Clementine, Chaplin was, 'Bolshy in politics & delightful in conversation.'

He also talked to groups of American businessmen about England and the United States working together, and changed the minds of some who had been antagonistic towards Britain until then. Churchill always kept in the forefront of his mind the idea of a 'supreme reconciliation' of Britain and the United States. America's War of Independence was, to him, only a recent aberration.

'We must keep in step with them,' he told his constituents back in England during a wave of anti-Americanism. 'They are our kinsmen from across the ocean. They are our sons returned from a long estrangement.'[6]

Arab Atrocities

One of the questions the media asked him when in San Francisco was – as a recent member of the British Government and a former Colonial Secretary – how would the Arab killing of Jews and their destruction of Jewish property in Palestine affect Britain's promise to allow continued Jewish immigration?[7]

'The Arabs had no reason to be against the Jews,' he said at a luncheon on 11 September. 'The Jews have developed the country, grown orchards and grain fields out of the desert, built schools and great buildings, constructed irrigation projects and water power houses and have made Palestine a much better place in which to live than it was before they came a few years ago. The Arabs are much better off now than before the Jews came, and it will be a short time only before they realise it.'[8]

It was certainly true that Arab villagers who lived near Jewish settlements benefited considerably from the new water and electricity supplies, in addition to buying Arab produce. But Arab leaders could not resist playing political games for their own benefit, with little regard for the Arab population. They did not want western democracy in the Middle East, because it would take away their power. Arab *fellahin* were unimportant to them, because they were not constituents who could vote them in or out of office in a parliamentary democracy. What was not appreciated by the West's political leaders at the time was that the *fellahin* had always been tyrannised by powerful families headed by the most dominant local warlord. The West mistakenly believed that democracy would be viewed as a blessing in the Middle East. The result was that, although Churchill's original views on improvements were well-intentioned, they would turn out to be unrealistically hopeful in an atmosphere of ancient tribal defeatism.

The *New York Times* quoted him as adding that Arabs owe nearly everything they have in Palestine to Jewish enterprise, 'Fanaticism and a sort of envy have driven the Arab to violence, and for the present the problem is one of proper policing until harmony has been restored.'[9]

He wrote an article along the same lines for the *New York American* magazine. As an enthusiastic Zionist himself, he praised the results of Jewish work in Palestine. 'As for the Arabs of Palestine,' he wrote, 'they had been brought, as a result of the Jewish presence there, nothing but good gifts, more wealth, more trade, more civilisation, new sources of revenue, more employment, a higher rate of wages, larger cultivated areas, a better water supply – in a word, the fruits of reason and modern science.'

An Ullstein Press journalist who interviewed King Faisal of Iraq in 1929 described the king in the *Vossische Zeitung* as 'ruler of this wretched country of beggars, bandits and nomads …'[10]

He might have added that Faisal was a ruler who knew it was far too soon to expect the fruits of reason and modern science for his country, because they were not yet ready for it. Churchill still bore in mind the violence and tragedies of Bolshevism, which was the terrifying alternative to democratic law and order. He knew that democracy possessed many flaws, but was convinced that it was still the best alternative to tyranny from dictators of the extreme political right and the extreme left.[11]

They drove through the Yosemite Valley and then returned to their private carriage on the train to the Mojave Desert and the Grand Canyon. Reaching Chicago for another speech, Churchill pointed out the advantages if the British and American Fleets could work together to maintain peace. Then he switched from his private carriage to Bernard Baruch's railway car for the trip from Chicago to New

York. He toured the American Civil War battlefields. Back in Schwab's train again, he visited Bethlehem Steel on 29 October, where he toured their main plant.

He returned to New York on the same date as 'Black Tuesday', the day the stock market crashed. An American stockbroker in California had persuaded him to buy some American stocks with 'the greatest prospects'. It had been a delusion, and he became one of many victims of the market collapse on 28 and 29 October – down by nearly 25 per cent in only two days. His own losses exceeded £10,000 – more than £500,000 in today's currency.

When he attended a dinner in his honour that night, one of the forty businessmen present toasted their guest, beginning with the words, 'Friends and *former* millionaires'. It was the following day when Churchill saw from his bedroom window, 'a gentleman cast himself down fifteen stories and was dashed to pieces'.

He was invited on to the floor of the Stock Exchange and was surprised to find no one panicking, although blocks of securities were being offered around at a third of their old prices.

Despite the calm of the Stock Exchange, he was in a devastated mood over his losses when he left New York by ocean liner on 30 October. His finances were in poor shape and all of a sudden he was heavily in debt.

7

No Time for Self-Pity

1932

Churchill's article in the *Daily Mail*, after being knocked down by a taxi in New York, expressed his philosophy about life and death, which was very largely not to worry about it. There was no time for self-pity. Naturally, he had felt some shock at the incident, but it was endurable, just as a wound from a shell was endurable at the battlefront. And if a grey veil had descended at that moment and darkened into black, he would not have felt or been afraid of anything more. It was typical of the philosophy he always lived by, which was to challenge whatever he thought worth winning and brush aside what was not. He took what came and never stopped being defiant.

Behind his show of defiance, however, the truth was that he suffered from severe pains in his arms and shoulders. And he was impatient to recover, as usual.

'He is terribly depressed at the slowness of his recovery,' Clementine wrote to Randolph on 12 January 1932. Churchill had been in hospital for eight days and was now laid up in the Bahamas. On top of his questionable physical well-being was the anxiety at the loss of so much of his money on the stock markets that he had worked so hard to accumulate, and the loss of his position in the Conservative Government. He received no income as a Member of Parliament. He remarked privately that he didn't think he would ever recover from those three misfortunes. He was already preparing to return to the lecture circuit to earn back his losses.

He travelled across the United States on a tight schedule. On 28 January, he told his audience in Brooklyn that the great opposing forces of the future would be the English-speaking peoples against communism. And he felt it wrong for the English and Americans to go on gaping helplessly at the world when all that was needed was Anglo-American cooperation. It was a year before his visit to Germany on a fact-finding mission that would dash his optimism.

He travelled most days between then and 21 February to lecture in nineteen American cities. His earnings for the three-week lecture tour amounted to more than £7,500, at a time when a British Prime Minister was paid only £5,000 a year. Clearly, Churchill did not need to be Prime Minister for the modest financial rewards. But his ambition to achieve the highest office one day never left him. What was paramount was a need to show the world that he was worthy to lead Great Britain, as his famous ancestor had done. And, although his father was no longer alive, he was also motivated by a need for his approval.

Meanwhile, he urged bankers and industrialists in New York not to despair or panic because of the awful economy. But that was the public Churchill. As soon as he returned home to Chartwell, he wrote to one of his publishers 'You have no idea what I have been through.'

His bodyguard had expected trouble in both Detroit and Chicago, but there were only demonstrations in the former. At the end of his lecture in Chicago, when Churchill was talking to a group of people in the auditorium, near the glass door of the entrance hall, 'a very correctly dressed Indian hurried in and made straight for Winston in a determined way,' wrote Churchill's bodyguard. 'I pulled my gun and advanced on him, whereupon he spun like a top and crashed into the glass door behind, striking it with such force that he passed clear through the shattered frame and right into the arms of two detectives standing between the supporting columns of the forecourt.' The Indian's friends fled down the street.[1]

When he received a message from America's Secret Service that several subversives they had rounded up had declared that 'Winston will not get out of the USA alive,' Winston and Clementine decided it was time to leave the hotel and board the *Majestic.*

He perked up again when he broadcast from England to 30 million American listeners, and appealed for a joint Anglo-American policy to fight the economic depression.

Privately, he believed that the danger from Germany attempting to regain its lost territories would be far worse than the economic recession. At the same time, the World Disarmament Conference in Geneva was pressing for reductions in all armies, navies and air forces, while Hitler's share of the vote at the most recent German election was 40 per cent. When Churchill and his bodyguard parted company temporarily in January 1932, Churchill warned him to expect war within six months.

Despite that, British Foreign Secretary Sir John Simon demanded more speedy disarmament in Britain. He claimed that arms reductions by the wartime Allies could halt an arms race between the more powerful nations. But Churchill was convinced that any arms reductions in Britain would simply provide an opportunity for the enemy to attack when Britain was left denuded of weapons, unprepared for war, and militarily defenceless.

Britons still felt such a horror of war, so soon after the last huge and almost endless slaughter of young men on the Western Front, that Churchill was accused of warmongering when he pointed out how unprepared Britain was to protect itself. It almost seemed that the public and its leaders were in a hurry to throw away their weapons with revulsion, rather than use them to defend themselves when attacked. Their defeatism appalled him. To his mind, the situation was totally irrational, since France with a population of fewer than 40 million was faced by Germany with 60 million and double the number of young men now reaching military age every year. The French were highly unlikely to deprive themselves of all the necessary arms and armour required to prevent a fourth invasion by the Germans in little more than a hundred years.[2]

Political Turmoil in India

Churchill's mood was not helped by the Viceroy of India's decision to grant Dominion status to India, whereas Churchill was sure that – with the murderous hatred that existed between Muslims and Hindus – it was too soon for Indians to govern their own country. He was convinced it would take at least another twenty years before they could take charge of their own affairs.

He sat unhappily through Prime Minister Baldwin's pledge that the Conservative Party would grant Dominion status for India on 7 November. He wrote an article for the *Daily Mail* in which he emphasised that British rule had brought peace and prosperity to India. He pointed out that 60 million members of the so-called 'Untouchables' were still being branded on the face with hot iron, to identify them, so that they could be excluded from society and left unprotected by human rights.

Six weeks later, Nehru – who had been educated at Harrow, like Churchill – refused the offer of Dominion status, and demanded full independence for India, instead. He called for a campaign of disobedience and lack of cooperation with the British. When his Congress campaign was supported by Mahatma Gandhi, the viceroy arrested and imprisoned both of them for stirring up trouble.

Churchill celebrated his fifty-fifth birthday on 30 November. On 30 October the following year, his memoir was published under the title of *My Early Life.* It was a charming, entertaining and amusing account of his schooldays and his early army career. Stanley Baldwin openly admired it, wishing enviously that he could write something of the kind about himself.

T.E. Lawrence remarked with awe that, 'Not many people could have lived 25 years so without malice.'

It was an apt comment, since it was not in Churchill's nature to bear malice towards anyone. He accepted people as they were and incidents as they arose, without offence or rancour. Nor was it in his nature to waste time over negative thoughts or behaviour. He confronted each challenge that faced him, as it arrived – a new one at practically every hour of every day.

Churchill differed significantly from most other politicians and soldiers who tended to focus almost exclusively on reacting to immediate events, whereas he planned well ahead to prevent whatever he considered undesirable, and was generally well prepared to tackle it. He also considered how his actions would impact the more or less immediate future, and simultaneously bore in mind the effects of his actions on the long term. His mind was constantly active as he attempted to consider every possible challenge that might arrive from any direction. His panoramic and in-depth view of history also enabled him to consider the possibilities of unintended consequences, and where each might lead. It was the mind of a soldier considering how to act in every possible eventuality.

Ramsay MacDonald thanked him for his copy of the memoir and remarked ruefully 'what an interesting cuss' he was. And what a dull dog he was himself.

Churchill's attempts at sweet reasonableness did not always work. He became upset when the Conservative Party rejected free trade. Now an alliance between them and the Liberals would be impossible. But he did not plan to leave the party again, as he had done twenty-six years previously over the same issue.

Politics was a family affair. Just before Winston's fifty-sixth birthday, Clementine wrote to Randolph, who was still an undergraduate at Oxford, 'Politics as you say have taken an orientation not favourable to Papa. Sometimes he is gloomy about this, but fortunately not increasingly so. The success and praise that have greeted his new book counteract his sad moments.'

Churchill was the main speaker at a meeting of the Indian Empire Society on 12 December, which was the first organised to fight against Dominion Status for India. It revealed considerable Conservative opposition on the grounds that it was far too soon, and pointed out the rising civil disobedience in India, where tribalism still dominated political affairs. Neville Chamberlain admitted privately that he doubted if the Indians would be ready to govern themselves for at least another fifty years. Nevertheless, Baldwin's support for Dominion status had now become a political issue, and Viceroy Lord Irwin was committed to it.

Churchill warned of the dangers of a 'Gandhi Raj' and the necessity of avoiding political turmoil in India. He preferred to improve the living conditions of the Indian masses, to protect the Untouchables, and to treat extremism and all breaches of the law with 'swift severity'. He suggested a two-tier solution in which India's provincial governments should be better represented, while overall power would remain in British hands. He was totally convinced that India was not yet ready to govern itself, but he could do nothing about it without a ministerial portfolio. His only claim to relevance was that he was still a Member of Parliament.

But the Viceroy wavered, now feeling he should open negotiations with Gandhi and the Congress Party leaders who were still behind bars. So he released Gandhi – even though now he was worried that Winston might cause more mischief by interfering with his plans.[3]

Even without an official portfolio, politicians who knew Winston, like the Viceroy, were afraid of his influence. Their temperaments were diametrically opposed, and yet Winston managed to maintain a long-lasting condition of mutual respect, since he knew that the Viceroy represented the King-Emperor officially and was also the king's personal friend. The position lent Lord Irwin an aura of inviolability, almost like that of a Pope.

On 26 January 1933, Churchill spoke for the first time in a debate against the Conservative Party. His rebellion created a breach with the party leadership, which he accused of being weak in promising self-government before 'the gleaming eyes of excitable millions', while actually exerting formidable British powers. He was sure that India would not accept it, and pointed out that there were already 60,000 Indians behind bars for political offences.

Churchill warned that the All-India Parliament that Irwin proposed to set up would soon be dominated 'by forces intent on driving us out of the country as quickly as possible'.

He believed firmly that one of Britain's greatest achievements had been rescuing India from centuries of barbarism, tyrannical governments and civil wars. He took a similar view of the justification for Britain's control of Egypt. It was not a matter to him of conquest or exploitation, but knowledge that British administration had improved the lot of those confused and otherwise helpless populations who were unready for self-government and continued to be exploited by their own ambitious nationalist leaders whom, he was convinced, did not represent them.

His speech impacted on Conservative back-benchers, who felt that Churchill had said exactly what they were thinking. They began cheering him. However, since Baldwin opposed him, Churchill felt he had to resign from the Shadow Cabinet the next day. Then he began to rally support from members who felt that Baldwin had strayed from party beliefs.

His struggle to keep India British seemed unsound to most people. They failed to understand that he felt he had to protect Indians from internal exploitation by political activists he called 'criminally mischievous', who would propel India into a civil war that could become a bloodbath. He was sure that British rule provided a unifying culture that restrained Muslims and Hindus from extremism. He was genuinely concerned for the well-being of 300 million Indians.

Even so, Conservatives viewed him as politically self-serving. Now the Conservative Central Office decided to destroy Churchill's credibility rather than risk a revolt against them by their own back-benchers.

Civil Disobedience

Passionate and hysterical riots would often be aroused in the East by something that in the West would be considered trifling – like the Language War. As Churchill wrote, 'I had been made aware earlier that linguistic conflicts could assume violent and bloody forms in this country: demonstrations, street clashes, murders, even acts of self-immolation.'

Only 2 per cent of the Indian population spoke English at the time. They were the elite. There were dozens of other languages used by half a billion Indians, including Hindi, Bengali, Gujarati, Teluga, Urdu, Tamil, Punjabi, and so forth. It seemed obvious that a common language might help to unite them in a common purpose rather than with different tribal aims:

> They were prepared to give up their lives in the defence of their language, to burn on a pyre. This fervour and resolve stemmed from the fact that identity here is determined by the language one speaks ... Language is one's identity card, one's face and soul, even.[4]

The reason for this had been attributed, not so much to regionalism, but to the language of the great Hindu classics of literature that have been told and retold by word of mouth for thousands of years, like the *Mahabharata* and *Ramayana*, the *Upanishads*, the *Sangam* literature of the Tamils, and *Periya Puranam*. They contain the *Bhagavad Gita* and the *Vedas*. Although not necessarily factual records of history, those cultural memoirs described military invasions and wars, and other socially devastating incidents that contributed to that continent's many different identities, intermingled with philosophical insights and warnings, often told around a campfire, as if through the voices of ancestors or gods.

Myths or legends as they may be, when passed on from generation to generation, 'in the instant when they are first being related and heard, the tellers and the listeners believe in them as the holiest of truths, absolute reality'.[5]

Whatever was considered holy they thought was worth fighting and dying for.

Winston Churchill felt support growing for his opposition to Stanley Baldwin, and wrote to Randolph, 'At a stroke I have become quite popular in the Party and in great demand upon the platform.'

His hunch was confirmed by Brendon Bracken, who wrote to Randolph about Winston, 'He has … re-established himself as a potential leader & put heart into a great multitude here & in India.'

On 23 February, Churchill remarked to the West Essex Conservatives, 'It is alarming and also nauseating to see Mr Gandhi, a seditious Middle Temple lawyer, now posing as a fakir of a type well known in the East, striding half-naked up the steps of the vice-regal palace, while he is still organising and conducting a campaign of civil disobedience, to parley on equal terms with the representative of the King-Emperor.'

Only a few days later, the Principal Agent of the Conservative Party wrote to Neville Chamberlain that many Conservative supporters were worried about the India situation and 'lean more towards the views of Mr Churchill'.

Gandhi continued to talk with the Viceroy, and agreed on 4 March to abandon civil disobedience and permit Congress Party representatives to join another Round Table Conference on India's future, in London. A so-called Gandhi–Irwin Pact was announced the next day.

Churchill warned Parliament that the Indians were being encouraged to expect more concessions than could be given, and that appetites were mounting in India. He reminded them of recent anti-British riots in Bombay, and cautioned them that they would bring more bloodshed to the masses of Hindus by tantalising the Indians with Dominion status when they were unwilling to give them full independence.

He spoke at the Albert Hall a fortnight later, calling the policy of negotiating with Gandhi and Nehru 'a crazy dream with a terrible awakening'. Without British control and management, the medical, legal and administrative services, the railway services, irrigation, public works and famine prevention that Britain had created would vanish; the Hindus would drive out or destroy the Muslims; and profiteering and corruption would dominate trade and industry. Indian millionaires would grow rich on sweated labour and become even more powerful. And with the typical state of absent human rights, the Untouchables – men, women and children – would be victimised by the Hindus and deprived of hope. Their fate was worse than slaves because they were already demoralised at being deprived of any hope of equality under the laws.

Even so, a call for Conservative loyalty was made by the Whips, and the big battalions lined up behind Lord Irwin, and against Churchill.

Violence between Hindus and Muslims led to more than a thousand deaths in Cawnpore at the end of March, as Churchill had previously warned Parliament and the public to expect. He predicted that, if left to themselves, Muslims were in danger of being exploited and bled by the Hindus. In the meantime, Indian extremists continued to murder British officials.

8

A Flight of Capital

1931

Churchill gave his final approval for corrections to *The World Crisis: The Eastern Front* in Biarritz on 7 August, writing to his long-time friend and former private secretary Eddie Marsh, 'Thank God it is finished. I am longing to get on to *Marlborough*.'

His famous ancestor John Churchill was 'the greatest soldier in the history of the race', who won the Battle of Blenheim. It would be a worthy challenge to glorify the First Duke of Marlborough, who had been a controversial figure according to previous writers. Winston was determined to straighten out the records.

He ended his letter on a bleaker note. 'Everybody I meet seems vaguely alarmed that something terrible is going to happen financially.'

He returned home to England from North America on 30 October, where Ramsay MacDonald's Labour Government took a different stance towards Palestine that Churchill deplored for not being in the spirit of the Balfour Declaration. Fabian Socialist Sidney Webb – now Lord Passfield – had been appointed Colonial Secretary. He presented a new White Paper on Palestine that was aimed at appeasing the stubborn Arab hostility to a Jewish National Home.

Churchill wrote an article the following month that was headed, 'Fair Play to the Jews'. He pointed out in it that the Colonial Secretary had either overlooked or ignored the fact that the obligations in the Agreement 'are totally different in character' from Webb's new White Paper. In fact it 'diverged fundamentally from the 1922 White Paper which recognised an obligation not only to the inhabitants of Palestine – Arab or Jew – but to the Zionist Movement all over the world, to whom the original promise was made'.[1]

Although Churchill was still excluded from government office, he joined an informal committee from both Houses which favoured Zionist enterprise in Palestine, and 'made Zionism one of their parliamentary duties'.[2]

Feeling an unusual new sense of freedom from his former departmental limitations and pressures, Winston and Clementine drove through France for their summer holiday with Randolph. Churchill brought along his new secretary, Violet Pearman, to help him with his work. There was a great deal of writing to be done in the hope of paying his outstanding bills. She was soon known respectfully as 'Mrs P'.

The economy was so severe that, when Prime Minister Ramsay MacDonald required a much-needed American loan, he was ordered by the lenders to make a 10 per cent cut in unemployment benefits before they would approve it. Then, while Churchill was painting intently at Juan-les-Pins on 23 August, he heard that the trade unions refused to accept the proposed unemployment cuts. The Cabinet was forced to resign as a result of not being able to negotiate a loan; it was the end of a second Labour Government. The King asked Ramsey MacDonald to remain as Prime Minister and lead a National Government composed of a coalition of all political parties.

Churchill and Lloyd George were both away overseas. Neither was invited to join the new coalition government.

Civil disobedience had erupted again in India and several civilian British officials had been murdered. Only a few months after Lord Irwin's announcement of *eventual* Indian Dominion Status, nationalist extremists attempted to assassinate him.

Gandhi made it clear that he did not trust the British Government, and that only *immediate* Dominion Status was acceptable. After which Congress elected Jawaharlal Nehru as President. He ran a banner up a flagpole declaring full independence at midnight on 31 December, with the support of members of the Congress Party.

Lord Irwin was replaced as Viceroy and Governor General of India by Lord Willingdon in April 1931. In order to calm the situation in which more than 200 Indians were killed in clashes between Hindus and Muslims, and 30,000 were imprisoned for civil disobedience, Willingdon immediately imprisoned Gandhi again.[3]

It demonstrated one more time that Western democracy did not suit India – or perhaps any other nation consisting largely of illiterate masses. Certainly democracy was not wanted by their leaders, who preferred to establish themselves as nationalist rebels using the weapon of civil disobedience.

Violence in Germany

Churchill was still firmly opposed to the British Government's policy of disarmament, in view of Germany's ability to rearm. The rise of Adolf Hitler in 1930 had already resulted in huge increases in intimidation and street violence in that country, intended to overthrow democracy and a parliamentary system. Churchill believed the danger of dictatorship in a police state was imminent.

Only a year previously, the number of jobless in Germany had risen to nearly 3 million. By 1929 it was 7 million. It meant that one third of the wage earners in Germany were without an income. The Nazi Party grew in numbers and strength from the poverty and insecurity and fear that were created by the lack of a regular pay packet. The Nazi militant creed of authority and discipline through strength and power over others became more and more popular.

Elections were held throughout Germany in September 1930, while Nazi street fighters methodically encircled anyone who opposed them and beat them senseless. Bloodied bodies were left lying on the sidewalks. The Nazi Party polled 6.5 million votes, which was almost the same number as were unemployed.

Up until 14 September, the Nazis had only twelve seats in the German Parliament. After that date they had 107. Evidently their displays of violence had increased their popularity. It made the Nazi Party the second after the Social Democrats with 143 seats. The Communists won seventy-six seats, the Central Party only sixty-nine.

Proportional representation meant that, with numerous different parties, the votes became fragmented to a point where no party was powerful enough to oppose the Nazis. There was now the Catholic Centre Party (Zentrum, or Z), the Communist Party (KPD), the German Democratic Party (DDP), the German Nationalist People's Party (DNVP), the German People's Party (DVP), the National Socialist German Workers' Party (NSDAP-Nazi) and the Social Democrats (SPD).

Ten days later, Hitler announced that the Nazis would tear up the Treaty of Versailles if they took power. It would allow Germany to have a permanent army, navy, and air force again. He warned that 'heads will roll in the dust'. It was exactly what his dispossessed followers wanted to hear. And by now they knew he meant every word he said.

That alarming situation had come about only a decade or so after the end of the First World War, partly as a result of the unintended consequences of the Bolshevik Revolution in Russia and fear of it spreading across Europe, and partly because the Versailles Treaty had painted Germany into a corner. As Churchill had once warned in the Boer War in South Africa, a cornered rat will leap at your throat in desperation.

Churchill had no illusions about Britain's enemies, who had adopted a political veil to conceal their real intentions. Some made their cause a religious prerogative like a crusade or *Jihad.* Others faked a political creed like communism, nationalism, or national socialism. But he was not fooled by any of their fake titles. All they were intended to do was throw a cloak of mystery over their intentions. All possessed one thing in common with religion, in that they were cries of lamentation for a lost cause. Jews lamented the fall of their Bronze Age monarchy headed by King Soloman the wise. Christians lamented the crucifixion of Jesus by the Romans. Muslims lamented the collapse of their eighth century Caliphate ruled by the Abbasids.

It was about absolute power and they were determined to reverse history to take back what they felt should still be theirs. What made their loss of identity more painful was the knowledge that they had let power slip through their fingers by their own follies – generally a stubborn refusal to change with the times, or corruption. They wept for a lost Golden Age and looked for someone else to blame for their misfortunes. The yearning for a *Jihad* to restore what they liked to imagine was theirs would not go away, even if it were largely based on myths. Any sign of weakness in an adversary was seized as an opportunity to take revenge.

Hitler's situation was little different. Germany had built itself up to become the leading pre-war industrial nation – and then threw it all away by undertaking a war to demonstrate that their power over Europe was absolute. Their folly had destroyed the German Empire and toppled all the others like fallen dominoes by 1918, except for Britain.

As well as that problem, which would not vanish on its own, there were formidable challenges. There were other causes than the effects of unemployment arising from a severe global economic recession after the Wall Street crash, like weak leadership in Britain by Baldwin and MacDonald, who did only whatever pleased their constituents at the time. There was also the lingering despair at the losses of life in the Great War that was still remembered with sadness twelve years after it had ended. And there was the poor or even corrupt leadership of other European nations that were seen by Hitler to be weak. The result was that the Nazis had reached a stage where they could openly flaunt their power to encourage more recruits and also threaten their opponents. Each step that Hitler took was small and incremental, critical and unusually bold and irreversible.

On 11 March in the previous year, Sir Horace Rumbold, the British Ambassador in Berlin, had written to inform Britain's Financial Advisor of 'a hardening of opinion against the settlement of reparations on the basis of a large annuity'. A payment of 2 million German marks as reparation had been mentioned as an alternative. Rumbold had stressed that there might be huge protests in Berlin that could lead to fresh elections. The root of the problem continued to be Germany's refusal to pay for all the deaths and destruction caused by the Kaiser's war. Now that he was gone, they heaped all the blame on him.

From Reason to Madness

Opposition to the Nazi Party by an alliance between Social Democrats and the German People's Party was out of the question, although it could otherwise have created a strong centrist government. But there had been no common ground to form a bridge between them. And extremists on both sides were prepared to use violence to have their own way.

Communist rallies for the May Day celebration in Berlin by the fighting Red Front League had attracted large crowds. But a huge number of police charged suddenly into them on horseback and in armoured cars, using their firearms and wielding rubber truncheons. Barricades were erected by workers from the factories. Thirty-three people were killed. After which the government banned the League and also the right-wing ex-servicemen's organisation known as the 'Steel Helmet' (*Stahlhelm*).

The Nazi Party gained most ground in the 1929 street fighting between the extreme right and extreme left political parties, because of their deliberate extreme violence to gain more power. They flaunted colourful swastika flags and banners, which created an emotional impact like that of a violent fundamentalist religion. It demonstrated their loyalty to Hitler and encouraged recruits to the Nazi Party from university graduates and the lower middle classes.

The free-falling economy and increasing unemployment provided even more recruits for the Nazis. So did the insecurity of small businessmen, as it impacted on their livelihoods as much as it put factory workers out on the streets. Consumers no longer had enough money to buy goods or services, and inflation reduced the value of any savings.

Hitler's victimisation of Jewish business owners opened up opportunities to defeat trade competitors by damaging Jewish-owned property and scaring off customers to steer them into their own stores. The Nazi Party gained considerable support from small businessmen who supported Hitler because of his anti-Semitic policies.

Hitler was strong enough now to merge his Nazi forces with the most extreme nationalists of Germany's veterans associations, like the *Stahlhelm*, and Hugenberg's nationalists. The Nazis now had even more numbers and momentum to reduce the extent of reparations demanded by the United States. His rallying call now became 'No payment at all'. He began to accuse American Jewish bankers of being the enemy who profited from Germany's weakness.

Hitler and Hugenberg made a joint proposal to the government for a referendum against the 'war guilt' clause in the Versailles Treaty, and urged the trials of all German ministers and civil servants who opposed a referendum. Such a bizarre idea would formerly have been dismissed out of hand as reckless and without foundation. But he and Hugenberg now held ninety seats between them in the Reichstag and controlled a large percentage of public opinion, so they could no longer be ignored.

Despite this attempt at blackmail, the government felt obliged to respond. It did so with a firm answer that Hitler's proposal was based on 'a flagrant perversion of fact', resting on the 'crazy statement' that Germany's foreign policy had been based on an admission of Germany's war guilt and that denying it now would automatically free Germany from its obligations under the Treaty. In fact, the Weimar government spokesmen said, 'The German government has solemnly protested against this injustice.'

It was one of the last rational statements to come out of Germany for a very long time. The Weimar government declared that Germany 'has now to choose between reason and madness'.

Hitler and Hugenberg fully exploited the eagerness of millions of marginalised and jobless Germans to find and destroy scapegoats in revenge for their own failures. What the German mobs were demanding was violence and revenge on imaginary traitors and enemies of Germany, on the scale of the French Revolution. And Hitler was eager to provide it for them.

'By exploiting the fears of the German people, fears which he had nurtured so assiduously in his writings and speeches, Hitler gained a considerable number of local seats, and a new base of power and propaganda.'[4]

Hitler had risen far from having been the son of a minor Austrian customs official. He had left the provincial town of Linz to become an art student in Vienna, but failed to be admitted to art school. He had lived on money that his mother had sent him. When she died, he had lived on an Austrian orphan's allowance. As a provincial mediocrity, he was so overwhelmed by the splendour of Vienna that he had been too intimidated to apply for a job, even though he had possessed a written introduction to the theatre where he might have found work designing or painting scenery.

He had made a little money by selling postcards of his paintings, and working as a day labourer in Vienna, where he had become acquainted with the Christian Social Party, led by the notoriously anti-Semitic Mayor Karl Lueger. He had absorbed the Mayor's racism, together with a current of wild German nationalism. He detested Marxism, which he regarded as a Jewish philosophy. He had lived a lonely life in meagre men's hostels, and – as he would write later on – when the war was declared, he had 'dropped to his knees and thanked God', because he would no longer be lonely: he would have comrades. According to a student who had shared a room with him, Hitler's idea of comradeship was continually to bark orders that had to be obeyed immediately.

It is often wondered with incomprehension how he rose from such unlikely beginnings to leadership of the German people.

9

The Little People

'Hitler's Vienna is the Vienna of the "little" people, who viewed Viennese modernity with incomprehension and rejected it as "degenerate", too disconnected from the people, too international, too "Jewish", too libertine. It is the Vienna of the disadvantaged, of those who were living in *Mannerheime* [men's hostels], typically men full of fear and susceptible to obscure theories, particularly ideas that despite their misery made them feel like part of an elite, even to be "better than" other people after all.'[1]

Seeking revenge out of malice and spite for their own failures arose from ignorance clothed in arrogance that displaced their anger at their own helplessness on to others, beginning with all Slavs, Poles, and Italians who appeared to be better off. It was a common complaint that there were far too many of them.

Hitler was wounded on the Western Front in the First World War when he was a private soldier and a courier, and was awarded the Iron Cross for bravery. It meant promotion to the rank of corporal. He had settled in Munich after the war was over. There, he was in touch with a small nationalist and anti-Semitic group called the National Socialist German Workers' Party, which would become known as the Nazis after he became a member.

A new Nazi strategy and tactics came to Hitler's mind when he had obtained a following of other embittered ex-servicemen in Munich's beer halls. He became obsessed with a new world order espoused by the nineteenth-century occult group; the Bavarian Illuminati. Help came from a wealthy occultist named Baron Rudolf von Sebottendorf, who had founded the Thule Society after Germany's defeat. Its main objective was to combat the threat of Marxism. Those societies had taught Hitler how to present himself to the public as an orator rather than as a street corner rabble-rouser.

His first major political appearance had been towards the end of 1923. The first meeting of the Thule Society drew 1,500 members, before absorbing the German Workers Party, most of whom were unemployed, bitter, and suspicious of anyone whose finances were still intact after the war. Dietrich Ekhart was its trainer in mind control, who taught Hitler hypnotic speaking skills, and introduced him to Munich society as Germany's long-awaited saviour. It came about because of Hitler's discovery that he could arouse the wild emotions of audiences by his skills as a public speaker.

The German Kaiser had fled from Germany seven years previously, leaving a legacy of civil war and a leadership vacuum. The pale young man with his name officially changed to Hitler had applied to be released from his Austrian citizenship on 7 April 1925, and became a stateless person. He had erased his entire past life after isolating himself from family and friends and withdrawing into daydreams of primitive German mythology that would change his identity forever.

Envy and Hatred

Hitler had visited the magnificent city of Vienna for the first time as a narrow-minded teenager in 1906, and been overawed and fearful, because Vienna then was still the capital of the now-defunct Austro-Hungarian Empire. He had gawked at the elaborate and vainglorious Habsburg architecture on the Ringstrasse, and the Opera House. He was intimidated by the grand Baroque churches that represented pre-war Vienna; so much so that he was discouraged from looking for work by fear of rejection. How could he possibly compete for attention with all that Baroque nobility and the great history of the Habsburgs?

He had failed to understand the modern cultural climate that was beyond his experience or knowledge. What he couldn't help noticing, when he managed to obtain casual labouring jobs, was the visibility of the comfortably off Jewish families. That was because about 24 per cent of the population of Vienna consisted of Jewish individuals with families who had been drawn to the capital city from the provinces to find work, as he had been. Many had come from Galicia. They had found work or started up successful business enterprises, or become successful professionals, whereas he had not. The awkward young man had no skills to offer and no initiative, and had been withdrawn and apprehensive.

Envy and hatred evidently seeped into his soul in an attempt to flush out his feelings of inadequacy. But he was too dependent on charity to avenge his humiliation. After spending months lining up every night to obtain a bed in men's hostels, and deal with filth and lice, he was sufficiently reduced in spirit to change his opinion about the Vienna that had initially overawed him when he'd daydreamed about conquering it.

He would express an entirely different opinion of Vienna when he wrote *Mein Kampf* in prison in 1925:

> After the turn of the century, Vienna was, socially speaking, one of the most backward cities in Europe. Dazzling riches and loathsome poverty alternated sharply … Outside the palaces on the Ring loitered thousands of unemployed. And beneath this *Via Triumphalis* of old Austria dwelt the homeless in the gloom and mud of the canals.

His hatred of the city that had humiliated and rejected him, by forcing him to recognise his limitations and helplessness, would boil and bubble until it erupted. He had to find a suitable outlet for his own rage. But first he had to escape to

Germany and wipe the whole miserable experience of his humiliations in Vienna from his consciousness. Even when he did so, evidently the memories of successful Jewish families would always remind him of his own inadequacy.

Hitler was not the only one in Germany or Austria who felt demeaned and helpless in the face of circumstances that appeared to be out of their control. A young psychologist named Wilhelm Reich managed Freud's Psychoanalytic Polyclinic in Vienna, which gave shelter to mentally unbalanced vagrants and political agitators. Given the opportunity to study them at first-hand on a daily basis, Reich had produced a landmark book of psychological analysis and understanding that would become a pioneering classic. His monograph defined what he called the 'impulsive character'. He wrote his psychological character study entitled *The Impulsive Character* in 1925, at the same time as Hitler was writing *Mein Kampf* in prison for high treason.[2]

Now that Carl Jung had left Freud to practice on his own, and his brilliant pupil Otto Gross was dead, Freud was impressed with his new star pupil, because there were two reasons why Reich's study was such a landmark in psychology. The first was that it emphasised the importance of character analysis over the free association method that was commonly used in psychoanalysis. The second was that little had been written about such obsessively compulsive characters before, because they rarely turned up as patients in private psychiatric practices. Reich had plenty of opportunity to observe working-class patients, and impoverished ones like vagrants who could not afford private treatment. Treating such cases as casual day labourers and political and religious agitators who were not so very different from the young Hitler, led him to particular conclusions about their mental disorders and possible treatment.[3]

The purpose of his study was to analyse the 'impulse-driven psychopath' and the 'impulse-inhibited neurotic', and compare their personality types with normal character development, in order to define those three fundamentally different categories of the human condition.

The opening words in his introduction describe an unsatisfactory situation with psychiatry in 1925, which was still as incomplete as its theory. It was only in its infancy: 'We are, at the present time, without a single systematic theory of character rooted in psychoanalysis.'

Wilhelm Reich had become aware of a trend towards character analysis in his teacher Freud's discussions and writings; 'that the essence of analytic work does not lie in guessing a symptom's unconscious meaning and sharing it with the patient, but in the recognition and removal of resistances'. Resistance contains repressed material while also setting up resistance defences. The difference lies between analysing the manifested symptoms or their hidden complex cause.

Freud's other colleagues, Sándor Ferenczi and Otto Rank, stressed a need for 'dealing with the patient primarily in terms of his actions'. If that suggested neglecting the 'memory work' that Freud always put first, Reich maintained that, nevertheless, analysis of behaviour must lead to recollections of trauma or grief, since mentally unbalanced individuals allowed themselves to become prisoners of the past.*

Freud and his protégé Otto Rank observed the rise of the Nazis in Vienna, Berlin and Munich. They concluded that 'all instincts fall into one or two major classes – life drives and death drives'. Life drives involve procreation, social cooperation, and the instinct to survive. Death drives include aggression, lack of cooperation, risky behaviour, and suicidal and murderous tendencies. Those destructive features, they believed, arose from reliving a traumatic situation.*

Had the vagrant Hitler been one of his patients at the clinic, it is possible that he would have had an even better example of the 'unbridled, impulsive-driven psychopath', since, as Reich wrote, 'Grotesqueness is the hallmark of the impulsive character's symptoms.'

Repetition-Compulsion

Fragments of psychoanalytic 'characterology' first appeared in one of Freud's studies, which would be expanded by two other colleagues, Ernest Jones and Karl Abraham, in which 'Freud signalled the role played by drives in the formation of specific character traits: frugality, orderliness, pedantry, cleanliness, obstinacy, and so on …'

'The role of sadism,' he wrote, 'is a type easier to see characterologically. It is also difficult to explain why, in some patients, a compulsion to experience a given situation over and over again predominates as a character trait.'

There was nothing short of hero worship in Reich's attitude towards Freud's theories at that time, which were evidently a revelation to him. 'In *The Ego and the Id*,' Freud wrote, 'we find the groundwork for a psychoanalytically based theory of character. The process of identification holds the key to the characterological interpretation of personality.'

He then described the *Ego*, the *Superego*, and the *Id* – which are now considered controversial as symbolic descriptions for what actually takes place in the mind, but would become the basis for Reich's own formula for a three-layered mind – the *social* layer, a *perverse* layer, and *the core* of the self.[4]

What it meant fundamentally was that problems may arise with individuals who are in constant conflict with the outside world, and also those neurotics subject

* A prime example of the part that real or false memories play in unbalancing the mind was the rebellious 19-year-old Gavril Princip, who had assassinated the heir to the Austro-Hungarian throne and caused the First World War and the deaths of about 7 million innocent people. He was a Serbian Orthodox Christian from Bosnia. What had angered him to that point was a mental block, or repetitive fixed idea arising from an incident that had occurred in the thirteenth century. Apparently he had considered the assassination to be an 'honour killing'.

to typical repetition-compulsion – asocial types, occasional criminals, individuals who are grandiose or self-abasing, and those who remain totally infantile. They are gross caricatures.

DSM-V designations of today by the American Psychoanalytical Association describe a far greater range of mental disorders, symptoms and treatments than Freud or Reich had encountered at that time.[5] But 'the unbridled, impulsive types', as described by Reich, are in a special category. Even the *DSM-IV* definitions of violent types of criminals left something to be desired, because they are viewed as in a doctor–patient relationship.

Reich remarked in 1925 that such types are uncharted territory for psychoanalysis because they test poorly, and patients lack insights into their own illness. Unlike Freud, who avoided schizophrenics if he could – because, as he said, 'paranoia and dementia praecox, when fully developed, are not amenable to analysis' – Reich preferred treating them because he found them less inhibited and more candid in their responses.[6] He went on to relate, in his study, several cases of character neurosis that he had treated in the Vienna Polyclinic, and condensed for readers. To do so, he defined character as 'the specific, personalised expression of one's psychic attitude towards the world; the specificity itself [being] determined by one's temperament and life experiences …'

Grotesqueness

The neurotic character shows more or less gross deviations from reality in terms of goals, sex, culture and social adaptability. All types of neurotics possess conflicting experiences and inner turmoil leading to insecurity defined by their attitude and actions. 'Thus every neurotic symptom is built upon a neurotic character.' That seemed clear enough. 'The compulsion neurotic who seeks analysis because of an impulse to stab his friend in the back – compulsive symptoms – shows a compulsive character as well: he is pedantically clean, loves order, and is overly conscientious.'

Reich took pains to differentiate between the compulsive character and the acts of an impulsive character: 'Compulsive behaviour can be encapsulated, like a foreign body, in an otherwise stable personality.' In the case of the impulsive character, 'undisguised perversions are the rule': mainly sadomasochistic.

His primary goal was to clarify comparisons between the impulsive character and the impulse-inhibited character of the neurotic. 'Impulsives' do not perceive impulsiveness as an illness. But 'the overwhelming majority show all manner of symptoms, such as phobic and compulsive behaviour, compulsive rituals and ruminations.'

It was almost impossible to understand Adolf Hitler's fixations and where his extraordinarily bizarre and repetitive nature might lead him. But Reich's character analysis of a particular type of psychotic personality provided grounds for a better understanding. As the Nobel prize-winning author Elias Canetti wrote, after analysing two similar historic leaders in his *Crowds and Power*, 'people are irrelevant to them and easily disposable'. Canneti's special study was mob hysteria.[7]

Regardless of the means that Hitler chose to achieve his ends, it is enlightening to read what Churchill would write of him four or five years later, when he would assess the situation in 1935: 'When Hitler began, Germany lay prostrate at the feet of the Allies. He may yet see the day when what is left of Europe will be prostrate at the feet of Germany. Whatever else may be thought about these exploits, they are certainly among the most remarkable in the whole history of the world.'[8]

10

The Split-Minded Weimar Republic

'Under the old regime, Germany had placed too much trust in the authority of "blood and office",' wrote the new Minister of Reconstruction, Walter Rathenau... 'the crown, the church, professors, the army general staff and privy counsellors.'[1]

> Weimar was also a moment of great political as well as cultural achievement. The destruction of the old imperial order in war and revolution unleashed the political and social imagination. For a time, Germans created a highly liberal political order with very substantial social welfare programs. The lives of so many ordinary people improved greatly: the working day was reduced to a more humane eight hours, at least in the first year of the republic, and unemployment insurance seemed to herald a new era that would protect workers from the vagaries of the business cycle. New public housing offered better-off workers and white-collar employees the chance to move out of old tenements into modern, clean apartments with indoor plumbing, gas stoves, and electricity. Women won the right to vote, and Germany had a lively free press.[2]

But the power of the German army diehards had not vanished after defeat in the war. On the contrary, the army continually denied it had lost. According to the generals, they had merely run out of military resources. They insisted they had been betrayed by a mysterious array of forces at home. They appeared to be preparing to fight the war all over again. But where would they find the Howitzers and machineguns and tanks and aeroplanes? And where was the next generation of young combat troops? General Ludendorff, who had lost the war for Germany, was in a rebellious state at the conditions imposed on the Germans by the Treaty of Versailles, which prevented him from carrying on fighting a war that the German General Staff and the Kaiser had begun.

Rathenau was appointed Minister of Reconstruction before being invited to become Foreign Minister in 1922. His honest acceptance of Germany's obligation to pay war reparations annoyed the nationalists on the political right, including General Ludendorff. Rathenau's mother warned her son that he was risking his life by accepting the appointment in the face of the furious anger of political extremists who had no intention of paying a cent to France, Britain, or anyone else as war reparations. The Catholic politician who had signed the armistice agreement had already been murdered by the militia that now threatened Rathenau, because they believed the agreement had humiliated Germany.

Rathenau naively trusted in law and order when he refused bodyguards recommended by the police, while friends urged him to resign. 'You don't realise', Blumenfeld told him, 'A Jew should not run the foreign affairs of another people. You see only yourself. You don't realise that every Jew will be held accountable for your actions – and not only in Germany'.

'I am fulfilling my duty to the German people,' Rathenau replied with dignity. He felt obliged to reconcile Germany with her former enemies, convinced as he was that all the German people wanted was peace and quiet. He was wrong. In the eyes of General Ludendorff, Adolf Hitler, his propagandist Joseph Goebbels, and other leading Nazis, paying war reparations would be an admission of defeat, whereas the German Chiefs of Staff hotly continued to deny that they had been defeated.

General Ludendorff, who had lost the war for Germany and run away after a failed attempt at revolution, apparently thought he was still fighting the war. He returned to Germany and claimed that 'the Jewish prince' – meaning Rathenau - had sabotaged the war effort. Rioters had yelled, 'Kill off Walter Rathenau the greedy goddamn Jewish sow!'

Foreign Minister Walther Rathenau was murdered in the streets on June 24, 1922, when his car was overtaken by an open vehicle on the *Königsalle,* from which several pistol shots were fired. The bullets entered his chin and spinal cord and he died before a doctor could arrive.

General Ludendorff returned after fleeing from police, and claimed that 'the Jewish prince' had sabotaged the war effort by accepting the peace terms from the Allies. The assassination had been loyally carried out by his followers, the young and mindless sons of Junkers. Since the police, the judiciary, and state bureaucracy were on Ludendorff's side, little action was taken. As for Germany's young men, the universities were virtually controlled by the anti-Semitic student fraternities and Aryan dueling societies,

Rathenau was the 354th victim of political assassinations by right-wing extremists.[3]

The Weimar Republic was shaken, even though his murder did not have the effect that the Nazis had hoped; they had wanted chaos that would justify their quelling it and taking power. The assassins who were arrested were part of a terrorist gang called Organisation Consul. Since the universities were dominated by militant anti-Semitic fraternities in both Berlin and Vienna, a memorial service for Rathenau had to be cancelled at the University of Berlin as they were afraid of threats from right-wing students.[4]

Such was the regard for Rathenau by responsible Germans that his funeral was the biggest in German history, with two million mourners lining the streets in the rain. His mother could not take her eyes off the coffin mounted on a platform at the ceremony. She had done her best to dissuade her son from accepting the appointment, but he'd been proud to undertake his responsibilities for Germany, and there had been no one else with his ministerial abilities. The nation was split between the mindless military and its mass of supporters, and others who saw Rathenau's determination to serve Germany as a noble cause. The problem was that Nazi criminals were gradually taking over the streets of Munich and intimidating the population.

Whether or not Jewish families would be left alone to live their lives in peace and quiet depended on the extent of criminality and mob violence, and corrupt officialdom, in Germany.

Whereas Mrs. Rathenau's son had felt optimistic about the future of the Weimar Republic, an alarm signal warned her in her deepest survival instincts about the mindlessness of human nature and the terrible things it had always done to those who did not take enough care to assess the volatile mood of the rabble. At the core of the dilemma of Jewish immigration was a national legacy of primitive tribal jostling by the others, to survive against the entry of outsiders who might affect the buoyancy of the entire nation. Jewish immigrants were largely optimistic about the future, whereas the German population was not.

Demography was crucial to the destiny of German-Jewish families – just as it was with Jews in Hungary. The 'Jews out!' signal by closed-minded students had not been merely a sign of juvenile irresponsibility, it was a well prepared tactic to scare German-Jews into leaving. Most Jews had become accustomed to the rebellious nature and crudity of the German rabble, and took no notice of adolescent students. Professor Albert Einstein was one of the few who realised it was impossible to continue living in such an uncivilised country, and left.

Several days after Rathenau's murder, Maximilian Harden – the editor of *Die Zukunft* – was almost beaten to death with iron bars when attacked in the street. Not many years earlier, he had written, 'Freedom is an obsolete Jewish concept.' Here was more evidence of his cynical realisation that the more violent German rabble did not welcome an open society. One of the would-be assassins of Harden was a former army lieutenant, now turned pimp. The other had run away from home after a fight with his family. Both of the Bavarian political activists had been paid in cash by the Nazi organisers of the crime to beat Harden to death.[5]

Although Hitler still had only a small following of the far right, he and Ludendorff attempted to take over Munich in a coup on November 6, 1923. His most popular support came from the denizens of Munich's vast beer cellars who became emboldened and over-excited whenever Hitler made inciting speeches there. He proclaimed an end to the Weimar Republic, and the formation of a new regime which he would lead. He made an unsuccessful attempt to seize the city centre where the municipal government met. Police opened fire on him and his few thousand supporters, killing sixteen people. Hitler attempted to escape after picking himself up, but was caught and tried for high treason. His sentence was remarkably light, because the court sympathised with him and he was given comfortable quarters in Landsberg Prison, where he wrote the first volume of *Mein Kampf* with the assistance of his close friend, the Nazi Rudolf Hess, who was incarcerated with him.

The publicity worked wonders for him, and support grew for the Nazi Party. Ludendorff was released as a war hero, and Hitler was freed within eighteen months.

Jewish Hungarians

Where did all those energetic and brilliant Jews come from? It was a question they even asked themselves with some surprise, since centuries of their past had been lost in the fog of unwritten history since the annexation of the Jewish kingdom by Rome. Some Jews even joked that they must have 'come from Mars.' The brilliant Jewish Hungarian mathematician John von Neumann expressed the thought that 'It will be left to historians of science to discover and explain the conditions which catalysed the emergence of the many brilliant individuals from that area…' referring to the tiny Carpathian villages scattered across Transylvania in the Austro-Hungarian Empire, from which Hungarian Jews had emerged and become expatriates.

Jews had represented 'only about 5 percent of the Hungarian population in 1910.' and yet, Budapest's economy had burgeoned. It had been largely due to them, since the Hungarian nobility had kept a third of the Hungarians illiterate 'as late as 1918 and wanted nothing of vulgar commerce except the fruits.'[6]

By 1904 50.6 percent of Hungary's lawyers were Jewish, 53 percent of its commercial businessmen, 59.9 percent of its doctors, and 80 percent of its financiers. Jewish middle-classes consorted with the old nobility and monarchy, which wished to bestow titles on them for their contributions to the economy and society. George de Hevesy's entire family were ennobled, but most Jews were embarrassed at the excesses. When the Emperor Franz Joseph wished to reward Theodore Kármán's father for his fine job by bestowing an 'Excellency' on him, it was too much for him to swallow. He told the emperor he would be satisfied with a more modest 'von' in front of his name.[7]

Despite the emperor's magnanimity – or because of it – 'finally violent antisemitism drove them away.'[8] The Jewish dilemma was created, by and large, by the illiterate and semi-literate mobs. As Sigmund Freud would remark when they caught up with him in Vienna in 1936, 'All the fates are conspiring with the rabble.'

The expatriate Jews left the primitive Hungarians for the more scintillating social and intellectual environments of Vienna and Berlin. Even there, the extraordinarily large percentage of successful Jewish lawyers, doctors, scientists, intellectuals, writers, and businessmen prevailed as a consequence of the illiterate and semi-literate peasant masses with their envy and jealousies, grievances and resentments holding them back from progress.

> Von Neumann too wondered about the mystery of his and his compatriots' origins. His friend and biographer, the Polish mathematician Stanislaw Ulam, remembers their discussions of the primitive rural foothills on both sides of the Carpathians, encompassing parts of Hungary, Czechoslovakia and Poland, populated thickly with impoverished Orthodox villages.[9]

Among the vulnerable Jewish Hungarians who left to become expatriates were 'seven of the twentieth century's most exceptional scientists in order of birth,

Theodore von Kármán, George de Hevesy, Michael Polanyi, Leo Szilard, Eugene Wigner, John von Neumann and Edward Teller. All seven left Hungary as young men, all seven proved unusually versatile as well as talented and made major contributions to science and technology; two among them, de Hevesy and Wigner, eventually won Nobel prizes.'[10]

One of the problems of holding Jewish opinions was a desire to save the world – hence their most popular chosen careers in medicine, science and law – but it was neither understood nor appreciated by others. Science provided an anchor while they sought to discover how to preserve the world.[11]

11

The Jewish Dilemma

According to a German-Jewish historian named Peter Fröhlich, the high point of German-Jewish hope, until the outbreak of the Second World War, was during the decades of kings and emperors – in other words, when Jews were appreciated for their outstanding services to the nation. Evidently Fröhlich was inspired by wishful thinking, instead of being more sensitive to hostility from the rabble to envisage the peril of his position as a Jew in Berlin. Like most other German-Jews, he was proud to be a German citizen, an ardent admirer of German culture, and an enthusiastic German patriot. Most German-Jews were optimistic because they identified with Germany and believed that it was on its way to a new level of civilisation that imbued them with hope for the future. Fröhlich would remain in Germany right up until the very last moment in 1939, when the Nazis sealed off Germany's frontiers to prevent their victims from escaping.

It is difficult to know with hindsight how it was possible that he and his family could not have felt the threat from anti-Jewish hostility long before they did. After all, Protestants had previously been terrorised in many Catholic countries, to force them out. Catholics had been similarly persecuted in Protestant countries to encourage them to leave, and Christians and Jews had been attacked on numerous occasions in Middle Eastern countries forcing them to flee. There was nothing new in religious, racial and ethnic bigotry that resulted in persecution: they were all part of a long history of the jostling of tribes for dominance over thousands of years. German-Jews had plenty of warning that they were not wanted in the Weimar Republic, or anywhere else in Germany and yet, they had preferred to remain as German citizens.

Fröhlich's answer was that, whatever the residual pockets of antisemitism, and however persistent anti-Jewish prejudices were in business and society, assimilation had appeared to be proceeding. It gave them hope for the future.[1]*

* In Britain, by contrast, Jewish immigrants from Poland and Russia set up their own institutions to provide for their communal needs: 'The Board of Deputies, recognised by the government as the official representative body; the Beth Din, which administered religious law; the Board of Guardians, which coordinated relief and social services; and the synagogues, catering to the various classes of Jews…'[2] German-Jews, on the other hand, had become so culturally identified

It would turn out to have been no more than wishful thinking on his part, and an inability for him and other Jews to see themselves through the eyes of a huge and hostile class of people who envied Jewish successes in finance, the arts, academia, law, and medicine. Professional people had to compete with them, while the working classes were jealous of their dedication and superior skills – despite the fact that Jewish employers provided millions of jobs and finance to non-Jews. German–Jews, in their naïve desire to please, failed to understand the pettiness and spitefulness of Germans who felt not only challenged, but diminished and threatened by the success that German-Jews made of their lives. They were over-achievers who enjoyed their work, whatever it was.

Two factors may have been partly responsible for the demise of cultures and empires throughout history. One was the self-centered, powerful and menacing emotion of envy. The other was paranoia. But above all, it was the collapse of public order by the less intelligent and more violent masses. It had already begun in the Weimer Republic with paramilitary groups of terrorists and assassinations of Jewish government officials by the Nazis.

The very beginning of Germany's problem came about because their military had made a cardinal error in going to war on the basis of an imagined perception that they might otherwise be encircled by French and British armies. They were just as motivated by fear now the war was over, when they imagined they were threatened by the success of German-Jews. German nationals appeared to suffer from an erroneous worldview and faulty judgments at this time. Their persistent illusions created a dangerous situation in which the entire Jewish population was caught in a dilemma – to leave or remain? All that was needed for it to be turned into a catastrophe was a crisis in the economy leading to large-scale unemployment, for an ever-present danger to explode in their faces. Psychiatrist Carl Jung envisaged an even greater danger – that only a fine thread separated the entire postwar world from peril. It was the brittle balance of mind of Germany's leaders.

Jewish immigrants were welcomed in democratic Britain and the United States. Both knew from history that Jewish immigrants always created employment for others, prosperity and national stability. They also brought much-needed skills with them that improved all kinds of services from health care to the legal system, as well as commerce and technology. But to Peter Fröhlich – who would become author Peter Gay in his new life as an American after he escaped from Germany at the age of fifteen – Germany evidently represented something special. He was as optimistic about the future there as millions of other German-Jews. Their own

---

in their own minds with other Germans that they failed to differentiate, whereas German gentiles did. 'Why were Jewish immigrants so successful?' asked Beatrice Webb in an essay. 'And why was that success so resented by the Christians with whom they came in contact?'[3] Whereas she decided it was a combination of intellectual aptitude, moral rectitude, and physical stamina, others would argue that Jews and Asians were more dedicated.[4]

prosperity persuaded them that Germany would progress in a more optimistic frame of mind and leave its failures behind.

Even German-Jews who began to arrive safely in America and England would continue to admire German music, art and science, and give their children German names, like Siegfried. Whatever it was they admired so much in Weimar Germany they would cling onto after they were forced to flee. Even before then, there were people, like a Jewish writer in the 1890s, who wrote; 'I wanted to be German, to think, to feel, to work German. My heart leaped when I saw a German uniform, heard German military music.'[5]

Such deserters, who were carried away by the sight of steel helmets and the sound of brass bands, wrote Peter Gay, 'were often psychologically unstable and politically inconstant.'[6]

After Gay became an American scholar, he would write about the 'Berlin-Jewish spirit'. He would reflect on a progressive population of German-Jews who were eager to modernise society, while non-Jews continued to look back with nostalgia at their Prussian origins and bemoan their recent failure in war and attempt to deny it.

Later on in New York, former German-Jews were at the forefront of the 'Tinpan Alley' music industry, live theatre, literature, and the cinema that dramatised the hardships overcome by early settlers, and the opportunities available in contemporary American society for immigrants.

As well as the work-shy German Junkers, there was always a less well-educated section of the German nation who had difficulties maintaining a livelihood, and resented having to drive themselves to keep pace with continual improvements brought about by German-Jews. Change made them feel insecure, because they were not up to the innovations or effort required to meet new challenges. Their values and lifestyle differed from the lively and mindful, and more inventive Jewish community in Berlin, who eagerly accepted challenges. Many others in Germany resented being challenged, and wanted the Jews out, because Jews were eager for progress and modernity, which non-Jews did not want because they felt safer in the past with status, inherited privileges, entitlements and patronage from leaders of old families whom they knew.

'Today, our eyes sharpened by the Holocaust, we see the symptoms of underlying Jew-hatred far more plainly… to the smoldering, usually inarticulate resentment of many Germans against Jewish claims to speak for the German people, and the widespread readiness to project upon Jews whatever seemed most unpalatable in one's world…'[7]

To view the Holocaust in proportion it is useful to consider the phenomenon in company with the other victims of the Nazis – the Poles, Czechs, Slavs, even the French; all of whom were considered 'subhuman' or 'vermin' in the eyes of race-conscious and arrogant Germans who were Hitler's willing accomplices. Racism was an excuse for stealing whatever they wanted from Jewish neighbours and neighbouring countries.

'The Holocaust was a radical break with everything known in human history, with all previous forms of political practice. It constituted a set of actions, and an imaginative orientation that was completely at odds with the intellectual foundations of modern western civilisation, the Enlightenment, as well as the Christian and secular ethical and behavioural norms that had governed modern western societies.'[8]

Finding Scapegoats

The catastrophe that brought out all the worst instincts in the German people arose from the error of declaring war in 1914, when Germany had already become strong industrially and economically. Germany did not need a war when they were so successful in a wide range of industries, and exported their goods all over the world. But political and industrial leaders had become arrogant with their leadership in so many different industries. They led the world in chemicals and dyes, shipbuilding and armaments in the Krupp industrial empire. War was a bad choice, although it kept German industries like Krupp extraordinarily busy and profitable being the power behind the military regime. Unfortunately for Germany, the traditional Prussian generals and chiefs of staff blundered from the beginning, and continued to destroy German and Allied lives to no purpose other than to lose the war it had begun so recklessly. But military tradition, pride and arrogance overrode all other considerations, because of a paranoid delusion of vulnerability.

The German military had no excuse to offer for its incompetence, despite the bravery of its troops. It was much better to find scapegoats to blame for defeat, and behind whom they could hide their own mistakes which 'were resistant to detection by contemporaries'.[9]

The fragile partnership of German-Jews and their gentile adversaries in the Weimar Republic was short-lived when General Ludendorff and Hitler chose to conceal the mistakes of Germany's Chief-of-Staff after losing the war. Their intentions to shed the blame and transfer it onto German-Jews began to be gradually revealed in the hundreds of postwar assassinations by paramilitary terrorist groups.

Yet even then, the evidence remained ambiguous and the prognosis uncertain:

> German Jews continued to make contributions to German culture, to have non-Jewish friends and marry non-Jewish partners. Life for the German-Jew was problematic but not hopeless; significantly enough, Zionism, the most radical way out of the German dilemma, found, right down to the accession of the Nazis and even beyond, only limited response.

12

Hitler's Racism

Hitler's narrative owed a great deal to a number of authors who contributed to all sorts of his theories. Euthanasia, for example, was a popular subject of conversation among left-wing intellectuals at the time. Although most attempted to appear philosophically objective about getting rid of useless people, they were hardly unprejudiced. Judicial murder opened up malicious opportunities in their wishful thinking to destroy competitors by listing categories of people who wasted much-needed resources. A question sometimes posed was, who would choose who to eliminate?

Possibly the first full list of opponents to be put to death was made by Lenin in the Bolshevik Revolution. He had proceeded to carry out his intentions against priests, teachers, and other leadership categories to destroy all possible competition.

Hitler also read a wide range of anti-Semitic literature that had been successful in victimising Jewish communities in the past. All were based on fiction, superstitions, and libellous conspiracy theories. The Bible was another source for Hitler's more mystical ranting to enrapture superstitious Christians in his audience. He never talked about the books that impressed him most, as his research was only a means to create propaganda for himself and the Nazi Party.

'As a result, *Mein Kampf* contained little that was original. On the contrary, the two-volume work essentially summarised the things Hitler had said in countless speeches before November 1925, although it did maintain the pretence of systemising the highlights of Hitler's reading and presenting them as a consistent, coherent world view.'[1]

At the very core of his complaints were his theories about different races based on pseudo-science that categorised different levels of racial inferiority of different people, according to skin colour, shape of their skull or set of the eyes. All were biased according to preconceived notions that elevated the supposed 'Aryan' characteristics of the German nation to the status of 'Supermen' (*ubermensch).* It gave Hitler immense satisfaction to be able to raise himself above underlings. It was also a powerfully arrogant characteristic of the Prussian Junker class, and Germans who liked to indulge in self-aggrandisement. Races and social classes were the engines that activated Hitler's rise to power. The 'racial question' was, to him, the key to world history and Hitler's own aspirations.[2]

He developed a theory of 'racial purity,' despite the fact that evolution demonstrated there was no such thing. According to him, it could be argued that 'A fox is always a fox, the goose a goose and the tiger a tiger.' Thus, Hitler argued, mixing races was a violation of nature: it would result in decadence and decay of the race; he claimed it was why previous cultures had collapsed.[3]

None of his claims about the evolutionary process were true: the rise or fall of species was attributed to flexibility, or improvements in qualities that enabled them to survive in different circumstances. A popular influential book he might have quoted from and misinterpreted in *Mein Kampf* was *The Martyrdom of Man,* written by historian Winwood Reade and published in 1872. Reade described the rise and fall of civilisations very largely as Darwin had described the rise and fall of species through adjustment to new situations. It would have given Hitler an illusion of omnipotence, since the history of mankind was all about the victory of the strong over the weak.

It was by no means a new idea. German Chancellor Bismarck had believed in it absolutely before him. All that was needed to intimidate others was callous brutality towards unarmed or weaker people who, according to Bismarck, were only there to be used by the strong and kept in place by life or death threats.

According to Hitler in *Mein Kampf,* the ultimate goal was 'breeding towards perfection'. He claimed that, 'Everything we see today of human culture and artistic, scientific and technological achievements is almost exclusively the creative work of the Aryan.' That, he had said, in a speech in 1920, was 'Why we are anti-Semites.' Breeding so-called 'Supermen' was an important part of his wishes and declared intentions.

It hardly made sense as to who those so-called 'Aryans' were, other than in his convoluted mind, or when and how all of that was supposed to have taken place, Much of the ramblings in his book were a dense mystery buried in a mythological fog of the past. He felt obliged to elaborate on page after page about his Aryan theme, apparently in order to conceal the origins of the myths and legends of that and other fictions he raised, to make them appear to be part of recorded history. What it boiled down to, in essence, was that he did not accept Jewish people as members of his racial purity club.

It could hardly be described as 'White Supremacy', as he did not accept other nationalities whose skin was white; such as Slavs, Poles, Russians, Czechs, French, Belgians, or any other foreigners whose territory or property he planned to invade and annex. African nations, or any coloured race, needed no other justifications as far as he was concerned. All he needed to do was dehumanise them by labelling them as things, like 'vermin' that had to be destroyed before they polluted society.

It was his justification for every intended invasion or annexation of foreign territory, and every atrocity he intended to commit. He made it permissible because his victims were all 'subhuman', like the Poles, so they hardly deserved sentimental consideration. By linking Jews to the Bolsheviks with his phrase 'Jewish Bolshevism', he had already opened the door to invading Soviet Russia as 'living space in the east', He intended to use Russians as slave labour until he had colonised the entire territory as a Greater Germany.

His complex weaving of a number of ideas into a tapestry called *Mein Kampf* was the outcome of his labours during his prison term. Despite setting out his gruesome intentions when given power, his narrative was couched in such subtle terminology that it did not scare anyone who read it, because the West saw Hitler's Germany as a powerful barrier against Communism.

It seemed that nobody wished to penetrate his list of grievances to discover anything further than his threats against Soviet Russia. In any case, hardly anyone bothered to read it when it was first published. Otto Strasser would relate in his 1940 book, *Hitler and I,* that when he attended a Nazi Party conference at Nuremberg in 1927, he admitted to one or two others that he had not read all of *Mein Kampf.* 'He claimed that others, including his brother Gregor and Joseph Goebbels, acknowledged not having read it either.'[4]

It was no masterpiece, only a monstrosity of hatred against the world, with propaganda cobbled together for one purpose, which was to obtain total power for a mentally unhinged political activist.

Nevertheless, it would become the Bible of the Nazi Party by the 1930s, and Hitler made a great deal of money from its sales. Most people, like Strasser, would have found it too heavy-going to read in detail, and very confusing with all its complicated claims. There were far too many supposed justifications. When reviewed by the press, the Berlin magazine *Das Tagebuch* questioned the sanity of its author, and the *Frankfurter Zeitung* newspaper gave it as their opinion that Hitler was over and done with.

But the *Augsburger Neueste Nachrichten* claimed it was useful reading and Hitler was a highly gifted man, and a true fighter for his convictions. Sales exploded in ensuing years when more newspapers reviewed it. Perhaps the most realistic review appeared in *Die Weltbühne* in June 1932.

'Whoever had read Hitler's autobiography *Mein Kampf,* will ask himself in horror how a sadistic master of confusion could become the preferred leader of a good third of the German people.'

13

My Darling Clementine

1932

Clementine had always shown herself to be a self-confident and self-sufficient person with her own firm opinions, even before she had accepted Winston's proposal of marriage at Blenheim Palace when she was 23. She became more self-possessed and elegantly fashionable after she became his wife. She was the only person who could correct him if she felt he was wrong in his judgement, or if she thought he had behaved badly. She held firmly onto opinions of her own, and had no hesitation in speaking what was on her mind. According to her daughter Sarah's recollections of her childhood with her mother, 'She was an authoritarian figure with whom you could not argue.' Daughter Mary said that Clementine was 'a mixture of tenderness and severity'.[1]

With such a strong cast of characters dwelling at Chartwell, the growing children felt some pressure on them to appear just as intelligent as the general flow of conversation, and just as witty, to avoid seeming boring. It was considered to be a virtue at the time for upper-class English people always to appear unswervingly self-assured, or 'cool as an English cucumber' in any situation, however unexpected it might be. It was socially unacceptable to show signs of uncontrolled emotions or weakness.

Daughters were expected to behave like well-bred young ladies, and not disorderly teenagers. Correct social behaviour followed on naturally from being considerate to others. Just as Winston possessed a clear command of the English language, it was incumbent on Clementine and her children to express themselves clearly and unambiguously so that they could be understood.[2]

A sense of good manners was also a reminder to be candid, instead of being reluctant to speak the truth in case someone might feel upset. Controlling their feelings was *their* problem. Clementine had no qualms about expressing exactly what she thought, including her opinion of the Americans, whom she was convinced were taking advantage of Britain. The American President Calvin Coolidge was insisting, at the time, on Britain paying war debts to the United States for anything they had received to fight the war. His attitude reflected America's depleted economy after the stock exchange crash.

Private Lives

Winston's former lady-friend Violet Asquith had been unable to let him go, even when Clementine had her first child, Diana, at home on 11 July 1913, so he had written to her several days later, to tell her that his wife invited her to visit them to see the baby.

Violet had continued to be possessive for a while, at least, and spent a lot of time with him, rather than using it to pursue a prospective husband elsewhere, and Clemmie had felt neglected. Evidently put out by the arrangement, she had escaped to a cottage in the countryside, leaving baby Diana in London with Winston and a wet nurse. As it turned out, he was a doting father who spent more time with his baby daughter than was usual in those times, when a nanny possessed absolute rule over the nursery and did her best to keep meddling parents away.

It had been no easy task for Clementine to adapt her life to someone who already had a full life of his own. But both had appeared to be satisfied with separate arrangements that enabled them to be true to themselves. Sex was taken for granted, instead of being continually discussed or publicised as importantly as it would become with a new young generation some three decades later.

During Winston's years of military training at the age of twenty-one he had recognised the mental dullness that afflicted officers and men alike who were bound to the repetitive daily routines of garrison duties. In a sudden burst of energy he had resolved to educate himself in the absence of a university education. The books he had asked his mother to send him then were largely classics of history and philosophy and biology. Since Clementine had not attended university either, he set about educating her.

It was from such brilliant history books that he had learned of the global schemes of life. He realised that apart from their own will, human beings were little more than grains of sand on a seashore, where they were moulded by the waves of every incoming and outgoing tide. It was a view that enabled him not to take himself or others too seriously. The coming and going of so many different civilisations over the centuries and millennia had convinced him that nothing was of particular importance in the overall evolutionary scheme. On the other hand, every care should be taken to scrupulously ensure that everyone was responsible for their attitudes and behaviour.

Due to Winston's absorption in his career, Clementine discovered that politics was fascinating. While he was away with his constituents, she would write to discuss aspects of his political career in their frequent letters to each other. It provided an intellectual interest for her, since she lacked a thoroughgoing maternal instinct. As she wrote to him of her domestic life, 'My sweet Pug, I feel imprisoned here. I long to be in the thick of it with you.'[3]

It was not mere flattery, although she knew he loved flattery. It arose partly from her jealousy of any possibility that he might be away somewhere misbehaving with another woman. She was desperate to keep him for herself. He pointed out to her that his world did not admit small intrigues, but only 'serious & important affairs'. It was true that he saw life as a panorama of events viewed from a historic perspective.

Her emotional insecurity was due to the unfaithfulness of her own father to her mother, and the history of Lord Randolph Churchill's own unfaithfulness with other women. She possessed an impatient and volatile nature. Between her temperament and Winston's self-absorption, it was clear that their marriage would never be steady or dull or boring.

Since Winston's mother, Jennie, had already spent their inheritance from Lord Randolph, Winston and Clementine were obliged to finance their upper-class lives on the modest salary of a civil servant or politician. Fortunately, Winston was able to supplement it with a fairly steady income from his writing, which helped to stretch their household budget and enable them continually to entertain his friends and colleagues in style.

'Nevertheless, the prospect of financial ruin continually shadowed their lives. Clementine knew their future depended on his ability to churn out books and articles at a ferocious rate – and he constantly sent her drafts for her "deeply interesting" suggestions. Many assumed that the Churchills had a cushion of family money like other upper-class British politicians. They certainly appeared to live extremely well. But by the late 1920s his Irish inheritance had been exhausted by the cost of rebuilding and maintaining Chartwell.'[4]

By that time, Clementine had built up sufficient political confidence to be able to advise and influence him in several ways, like his attitude towards the very active women's suffragette movement.

Complicated legal reasons prevented women's suffrage. Only a quarter of the male population had the vote, because they owned property, and it was felt you had to have a stake in the country to vote responsibly. Women could not own property. A married woman's property belonged to her husband. Those legal hurdles had to be overcome first.

Sympathetic as he was towards the suffragettes, the general public were not. For one thing, the women's movement was soon joined and dominated by violent militant extremists who became more impulsive and abrasive in order to draw press and police attention to themselves.

Many men and women grew terrified of them. Their unpopularity prevented Winston from getting any helpful legislation passed on their behalf.

Gertrude Bell wrote of her own encounter with militant suffragettes on 28 March 1913, when she went to a party at the Glenconnors' at 95 Sloane Street in London:

> Just before I arrived 4 suffragettes set on [Prime Minister] Asquith and seized hold of him. Whereupon Alec Laurence in fury seized 2 of them and twisted their arms until they shrieked. Then one of them bit him in the hand till he bled. When he told me the tale he was steeped in his own gore.[5]

Clementine was particularly enthusiastic about Winston's work with David Lloyd George, who was then Chancellor of the Exchequer. Both he and Winston were determined to implement legislation to provide safety nets for the working classes so that they could live in dignity whenever they were unemployed, ill, widowed, or old. She thought it particularly heroic that he and Lloyd George were determined to uplift the living standards of the poor, since upper-class Conservatives looked upon Churchill's redistribution of wealth with disapproval.

In Clementine's Liberal eyes, the Conservatives, 'are ignorant, vulgar, prejudiced. They can't bear the idea of the lower classes being independent & free.'[6]

He and Lloyd George were known by the Conservatives as the 'terrible twins'. It is generally forgotten by now that millions of people in the UK were only a meal away from starvation on any day of the week before Churchill had several Liberal welfare reforms enacted to provide safety nets for widows and orphans, the elderly and unemployed. The National Insurance Act of 1911 was introduced by Lloyd George on 4 May when he was Chancellor of the Exchequer for Liberal Prime Minister Henry Campbell-Bannerman. It provided Britain's workers with insurance against illness and unemployment. It was Lloyd George who founded the modern welfare state, not the socialists who benefited from it. Winston was responsible for Part 2 of the Act, which dealt with unemployment:

> Winston Churchill and David Lloyd George were the two outstanding British politicians of the first half of the twentieth century. Their careers overlapped and interacted to a large degree. During the early years of the twentieth century, they formed a partnership as radical reformers that decisively affected the course of British history at home. Both during the two world wars, they were colleagues who seemed to be joint, or alternative, men of destiny. Their association began in earnest when Churchill left the Conservative Party and joined the Liberal Party.
>
> In the way Churchill chose to execute his change of sides in Parliament, he emphasised a specific intention to ally himself with Lloyd George. It was most fortunate for Britain, and perhaps also rather fortunate for the world, that Churchill and Lloyd George lived when they did and were willing, for some years, to deploy their talents and energies in concert.[7]

Young Randolph

Winston Churchill must often have recalled with sadness and regret his schoolboy admiration for the father he rarely saw. Now he did his best to spend more time with his own son than Lord Randolph had spent with him. Winston sent him to Eton as a boarder, the leading British public school that was as much derided as praised for claiming to educate Britain's future leaders. But Randolph was unpopular at school and uncontrollable at home.[8]

Winston had spent the Christmas of 1928 at Chartwell, where he had worked on his book, *World Crisis: The Aftermath.* His close friend Professor Lindemann visited him in the New Year and swiftly became drawn into a family discussion on Randolph's wish to go directly to Oxford University, although he had not taken the autumn entrance exam. Lindemann was an Oxford professor, and encouraged him to take up a place at Christchurch, where he had been educated himself. Winston was against Randolph leaving Eton so soon, and they argued about the relative merits of one choice compared with another, until Winston had finally agreed.

It had been a year later when Winston had decided to travel to Canada and the United States, and take Randolph along with him to broaden his mind about other lands and societies. His trip had no political objective, so that he and his son could enjoy each other's company.

Before leaving, Churchill was engaged in another dispute with the Conservative leadership, this time about their abandonment of imperial policy. To him, India and Egypt were prime examples of how British Imperialism benefitted its colonies and dominions with its 'constructive efforts'. He opposed the withdrawal of British troops from Egypt, warning that 'the whole quality of Egyptian administration will deteriorate' and damage Britain's prestige throughout the East. But his opinion was rejected.[9]

Randolph was eighteen when he accompanied his father to the 'vast open places of the Canadian countryside … with its "Scottish" burns and vast lakes of fish'. Winston wrote to Clementine with delight of Randolph's progress, and described him as an 'admirable companion', who made a good impression on all who met him. He felt proud of his son, who was in his 'Seventh Heaven'. Randolph also described his joy at being with his papa on riding trips.

'In each of his letters to Clementine, Churchill wrote of Randolph's progress. Never before had the two of them spent so much time together, and Randolph was even making short speeches at his father's side.'

'He speaks so well,' Churchill wrote, 'so dexterous, cool and finished.' He must have recalled how clumsily he himself had spoken on the few occasions when his father had visited him at Harrow and took him out to lunch. He added, 'I love him very much.'[10]

That relationship was not due to last. It had evidently not occurred to him how spending so much time with Randolph and indulging him with so much attention and praise might spoil him. Just as Randolph had interrupted his education at Eton to enter Oxford University, so now he left it unfinished again, after completing only a year at Oxford, to lecture in the United States. His fees for the lecture tour were intended to help pay off some of the mounting debts he had already run up at Oxford.

Winston dined him at Claridge's on his birthday, confiding in their guests that he had 'high hopes' of Randolph, and hoped he would work hard and diligently to develop his potential.

But, even though they felt a common purpose, the times they spent together began to end in 'fierce quarrels and angry disagreements'.[11] It demonstrated how Winston had unintentionally overindulged his son, causing him to be filled with a sense of self-importance and entitlement. One result was that young Randolph's lack of effort or discipline to concentrate on preparing his lectures, or any other work, in advance, usually ended in his not finishing whatever he started. According to Sir Samuel Hoare, Winston and his son fought like cats while drinking more champagne than was good for them.[12]

Clementine was particularly concerned about the effects on her son of some of Winston's closest friends, like the unmarried Brendan Bracken, who was a loner. He had separated from his family, who still lived back in Ireland. Bracken would often turn up uninvited in the Churchills' home, as if it were his own. Clementine was angry at the rumours that he was her husband's illegitimate son, and at his over-familiarity in calling her 'Clemmie', like Winston did. Sometimes he even called Winston 'Father'. It amused Winston, but Clementine disliked him intensely for it, although she eventually softened her position: 'She was rarely wrong about people and seldom changed her mind, yet with Bracken she did. He was not, as she had feared, another charlatan, using his connection with Winston for his own gain. Beneath his brash exterior he had a warm and generous nature.'[13]

F.E. Smith

Another of Winston's close friends, F.E. Smith – who became Lord Birkenhead in 1929 – also had problems with heavy drinking. She was afraid that he might lead her husband and Randolph astray. In fact, Winston – contrary to rumours – was not such a heavy drinker, compared with the manly custom of alcoholic consumption of the times. He was far too self-disciplined to allow his alcohol consumption to get out of hand. But the custom of joking about alcohol intake stuck like a Johnnie Walker label to Winston. In fact, he made sure that his drinks were heavily diluted with water, and made each drink last for hours.

Neither Randolph nor F.E. Smith possessed his self-discipline. Smith would die soon afterwards from the effects of alcohol.

Clementine's anxieties over Randolph continued as a consequence of what was often described as his 'pathological self-importance'. Winston finally felt he had to show firmness to counter his previous indulgence of Randolph's irresponsible behaviour. It must have been with a heavy heart that he wrote to him in 1929 – no doubt recalling with every carefully chosen word, the brutal letter he had received long ago from his own father, who had told him, 'You appear to be leading a perfectly useless existence.'

He told young Randolph that he was insolent and self-indulgent. 'I have tried – perhaps prematurely – to add to our natural ties those of companionship & comradeship. But you … give nothing in return for the many privileges and favours you have hitherto received. I must therefore adopt a different attitude towards you for yr own good.'[14]

Randolph continued to worship his father, and was intensely envious and jealous of anyone who spent time with Winston that Randolph considered should have been spent with *him*. Brendan Bracken was one, Clementine was another. Clementine's marriage to Winston was already turbulent enough, and Randolph created additional problems between them by his arrogant possessiveness, selfishness and rudeness.

Mary remembered her parents' bitter rows and recriminations over Randolph's abrasive ill manners and the subsequent chilliness in their relationship afterwards. There were even subtle suggestions that her parents' usual solitary vacations from each other could become permanent. But apparently Randolph was the only subject they ever really disagreed on to such an inflammable point.

Randolph was particularly brusque and ill-mannered when he drank too much, and Clementine found it hard to handle.[15] The Chartwell household was often filled with powerful egos, so that there were inevitable combustible sparks when they clashed. Randolph's sense of entitlement and resentment increased as a consequence of being in the huge shadow of a famous father whose gifts and skills he could not possibly match.

All the while, Winston and Clementine 'lived from book to book and from one article to the next' to enable them to pay their bills.[16] For his long-awaited biography of his ancestor John Churchill, he obtained an advance on royalties of £10,000.

Before the Second World War finally erupted, he would manage to write three more:

> 1933–38: *Marlborough: His Life and Times.* In four volumes (Harrap, London).
> 1937: *Great Contemporaries* (Thornton Butterworth, London).
> 1939: *Step by Step: 1936–1939* (Thornton Butterworth, London).

14

Inside Germany

The Ullstein Press launched a new Berlin afternoon newspaper named *Tempo* in 1928, the same year that author D.H. Lawrence had written a depressing letter about poverty in Germany. So evidently there was another side to Germany. *Tempo* appealed to German Jews who were always in a hurry for the latest news. Berlin's lively Jewish spirit was very different from the closed-minded and stiff-necked Prussian way that had caused the First World War and the post-war tragedy in the Weimar Republic. It was represented by Berlin's businesslike community, who looked for new opportunities rather than linger over past failures. That was the schism that divided Germany into two very different factions.

Tempo was read by the educated middle classes. The people without a pfennig that D.H. Lawrence had referred to were the unemployed working classes and ex-servicemen; the masses that Marx and Engels called 'the *Lumpenproletariat*'. They meant criminals, vagrants, and the work-shy unemployed. The post-war Weimar Republic was actually thriving according to the poet Gottfried Benn, who would later write that the stimulus of 'artistic, scientific, commercial improvisations … placed the Berlin of 1918 to 1933 in the class of Paris'.[1]

The Berliner was busy making things happen, whereas the masses of complainers in the huge beer cellars in Munich still reminisced over their beer tankards on how they had been let down in the war against the British, which they were convinced they had won. The Berliner was *schlagfertig* – meaning quick-witted, even 'sentimental about his lack of sentimentality, a born deflator of pomposity, self-importance, and empty grandeur', particularly of the Prussian kind:[2]

> Surrounded, especially during the Empire, by Prussian garrisons, deluged with colourful uniforms and solemn parades, the Berliner takes the tall, self-conscious, stupid, conceited Junker clotheshorse as an object for his entertainment and target for his wit. These tin soldiers are not heroes for the Berliner: his hero is the anti-hero – a comic figure like Nante, that mythical but living *Eckensteher* who finds all effort, except that of making jokes, too much for him.[3]

The clash of cultures, rather than being between Jew and Gentile, was between tribal *volkisch* primitivism and Berlin modernism. Among the post-war modernists were plenty of Jewish professional people, like lawyers, doctors and psychologists.

Most had grown up in small towns or villages before alighting on Berlin or Vienna or Budapest, to better themselves. Even Sigmund Freud in Vienna was a provincial at heart, but an achiever like the Berlin businessmen. The same could be said of young Wilhelm Reich, who managed the polyclinic in Vienna for Freud: he had originated in Galicia; or Alfred Adler, or Otto Rank. Each was unlike the other, and unlike the typical Berliner businessman. What they had in common was they were all quick-witted and ambitious to succeed. Those psychologists were intelligent rather than Berliner glib. Kafka, on the other hand, whose grim novels the western intelligentsia liked to take seriously, was always ridiculing the mediocrity of middle-European bureaucracies which were burdened with petty regulations that prevented anything from happening.

Jews were not *Eckensteher* – which meant street-corner loafers watching life around them with critical eyes from behind their coffee cups at boulevard tables. Habitués of street corner bistros, cabarets and brothels were more likely to be gentiles. It was German aristocrats who were the 'lounge lizards'; those wealthy Junkers who looked down their noses at everyone else and expected everyone to bow low before them and click their heels. The main goal of German Jews was financial success, in order to better the lives of their families. Many were leaders in all sorts of creative areas like painting, writing and composing light operas.

Creativity in Berlin was, perhaps, more refined by feminine influence that contributed 'an instinct for quality', in comparison with Prussian militarists in Bavaria who were suspicious of progress, and feared it. They liked military life and power just the way it had always been. It appeared to confirm Freud's and Otto Rank's distinctions between those who create and those who destroy. The clash of cultures in the Weimar Republic was an explosive combination. And, since Jews were drawn to the amenities of cities, the larger the city the denser the cluster of German Jews.[4]

Berliner Jews were more conspicuous than they were numerous, but 'their visibility aroused much comment'. Berlin-born or German-born Jews were just as conspicuous as foreign-born Jews from Russia or Vienna, because they were concentrated in visible professions that provided them with more prominent clients.

'Many of the publishing houses were located in Berlin and the biggest of these, Ullstein and Mosse, were owned by Jewish families. So were such distinguished publishing houses as Samuel Fischer's. Many of the journalists who wrote for their newspapers, many of the editors who edited their magazines, many of the authors who wrote their books, were Jews as well.'[5]

So were the drama critics and writers of editorials and sports columns. And the owners of the great Berlin department stores, like *Kaufhaus des Westens, Tietz, Wertheim.* Jews could be identified in such visible professions as bankers, lawyers, doctors, dentists, the garment and tailoring industries, salesmen and peddlers. The Weimar Republic was a tale of two parallel worlds that existed at the same time in Germany – one positive, the other negative; one with an enthusiastic interest in the future, the other with a gloomy but nostalgic longing for the past.

The prominence of Jews in Berlin went back at least as far as Moses Mendelssohn, who had arrived as a malnourished teenager in 1743. The early nineteenth century had been an era of Berlin salons, where Jews contributed to intellectual life, particularly in which Jewish women introduced a fresh stream of intelligence in selective private salons, with interesting and witty conversations of a more assimilated German or non-Jewish flavour, almost analogous to the more public newspaper and publishing industry. They initiated a flow of news and culture by word of mouth. Jews were visible because Berlin was a world city of commerce and industry that exchanged new and exciting international information daily and nightly:

> Debarred from owning land, kept out of civil service positions, the army and the universities, reminded of their pariahhood by persistent discrimination and periodic persecutions, Jews lived where and how they could … History made by non-Jews determined the course of Jewish life. It was not an inborn love of money or of glittering things that brought the diamond trade to the attention of the Jews: diamonds were portable, and for marginal men like the Jews, at best tolerated guests, at worst hounded victims, mobility – quite literally – was at a premium.[6]

Several new industries like 'chemical factories, metal works, electrical, smelting, and printing plants, and mills' were started up by Jewish entrepreneurs. 'They established the first German aircraft factory and department store chains and were among the first to introduce American production methods.'[7]

Berlin's population included many Jews who had converted to Christianity, Jewish Catholics, Lutherans, agnostics and atheists. Regardless of their religious conversions, they were still – like Conservative Prime Minister Benjamin Disraeli and Karl Marx in England – viewed as Jews. Zionist Chaim Weitzman despised the *Kaiserjuden* for their 'obsequiousness' and 'assimilationism'. He claimed they made themselves slaves in the middle of freedom. According to him, their impression of German power and efficiency 'had instilled in them a deep sense of inferiority, causing them to grovel and "deny themselves"'.[8]

Reason did not enter into the German attitude to Jews, because it was an emotional reaction towards something different from what *they* were. And they were far too self-righteous and humourless to question their own failings. Nevertheless, the ratio of Jews to non-Jews was far too small to exert the influence that the Nazis said it did. In fact, for any thinking individual, the question of 'Jewishness' – whatever that was or is – should have been settled by 1922, when H.G. Wells wrote *A Short History of the World.* He claimed in it that, on the basis of billions of marriages between Jews and gentiles over the centuries, most people in the world must be at least partly Jewish by now. A 1943 pamphlet printed in the United States and referred to by anthropologist Ruth Benedict, corrected his erroneous generalisation by stating; 'Aryans, Jews, Italians, are not races… Jews are of all races.' According to Benedict, Jewishness is a shared culture.*

Who could clearly trace their lines
To nearly prehistoric times?[9]

An investigation of the earliest appearance of Jews in the Old Testament shows them to have been 'a motley crew' of different types. What brought them together and made them different from others at that time were veneration for life and a desire for justice for all. Those two elements remained at the core of a shared Jewish culture.*

Spreading antisemitism revealed ignorance. It was a fallacy motivated by power politics that impressionable people had allowed themselves to be deceived by for centuries. But Hitler learned as an orator that if a conspiracy theory is writ large and repeated often enough, people without character or experience to form their own conclusions would believe him – and they did. Even before he wrote *Mein Kampf* in Landsberg Prison, Hitler was already testing out his big lies on audiences at Schwabing and in Munich's beer cellars, to decide which ones were more likely to incite them to violence. He learned very quickly to tell them what they wanted to hear.

A number of different theories have been produced to establish why he chose Jewish people as victims. It was because he could more easily exploit a tradition of antisemitism and abuse in Catholic areas like Bavaria, because primitive Christian superstitions went back two thousand years or more and had been ingrained almost from the rites of baptism. It provided him with a large audience. But they were not his only chosen victims, merely the easiest to attack. Far more of his victims would include all Slavs, Poles, Czechs, Gypsies, and people with dark skins; who were anyway distrusted, and always under suspicion as 'foreign'.

Hitler candidly described his plan to invade Russia in *Mein Kampf* at a time when the worst kinds of colonialism were accepted as 'normal'. He would use

* Motley might mean a band of workers with different coloured skins or clothes. It was long thought they had laboured on the pyramids in Egypt, but more recent archaeological finds suggest the turquoise mines as far more likely. 'The great demand for the mineral meant that the pharaohs sent expeditions of miners to Sinai to extract turquoise and copper, and bring it back to the more central Nile Delta region of the Kingdom. Wadi Magkara, Wadi Kharig, Bir Nasb and Serabit Al Khadim were the primary mining sites in antiquity' (Ref. The Stela of Seankhptah). Evidence includes 'mining tools and industrial installations for producing them as well as habitation sites and numerous inscriptions relating to royal expeditions to the Sinai region during the third and second millennia BC', says the Metropolitan Museum of Art. (Deborah Scharch, Department of Objects Conservation, The Metropolitan Museum of Art. April 2018).

its Slav population as slave labour until they dropped dead from malnutrition, exhaustion and disease, while he colonised the territory with Teutonic races. He explained his reasons for war in a very complicated way in *Mein Kampf*, apparently imagining that if one argument failed to convince readers, another three or four, or more, would. His air of desperation should have warned readers that his case was bound to be full of lies as he grasped at every possible straw.

He wrote about needing living room for the increased German population of over 70 million. He even added mystical reasons for his mission, when he claimed he was doing God's work.

Moreover, he invented an entire racial theory in which he claimed that German blood was superior to everyone else's; that Germans were 'supermen' or *ubermensch*. According to him, it justified destroying other races of people with 'inferior' blood in their veins. It was entirely false as science, since there are no pure races – all have long since mingled with others. He rambled on with other inventions and myths about a supposed common ancestry with so-called Aryan peoples. He was prepared to use facts or fictions and inventions to win any likely argument.

Some thought he wanted revenge on the Jewish people because the Jewish-owned Ullstein Press had ridiculed him when he had claimed to lead a New Germany. Others thought he was envious of successful Jewish families in Vienna when he had gone there for work as a poor student. Audiences he preached to during the depression in the economy in 1922 included unemployed ex-servicemen who genuinely believed that Hitler could save them from poverty, particularly as he was against paying war reparations that Germany could not afford. They believed whatever he said, because he invented excuses to justify their bad luck: they were glad to hear that the defeat on the battlefronts had not been their fault.

From 1880, a growing proportion of Berlin's Jews were foreign-born refugees from repeated Russian pogroms and oppression in Austro-Hungary. *Ostjuden* (Eastern Jews) were the main targets of gentile hostility. Their foreignness and poverty even embarrassed German-born Jews. They were the poorest of the poor. Although they numbered no more than 3,000, they grew to 11,000 by 1900. There were 43,000 by 1925.[10]

In short, Hitler protested far too much. A theory by a thirteenth-century monk named William of Ockham claimed that complicated excuses were more likely to be intended to cover up the real reason. It was the seductive attraction of getting away with crimes against humanity. If they wanted criminality, Hitler would give them the opportunity for it.

Total Force

The politics of Hitler's National Socialist Party were not as meaningless as his unscientific claims about race and blood. He had observed the success of Benito Mussolini's fascism, which justified using total force by the military and secret police, to impose order. There was plenty of chaos in Germany to make the same claim, even though the disorder was caused by Hitler's supporters.

Looking around him at his own countrymen and women while a teenage student in Vienna, Hitler had openly admitted to a friend that he could see how hard-working, prudent and successful German or Austrian Jews were. They owned material possessions and had savings that he and the Nazi gang could steal very easily if they seized power. All he had to do was withdraw their citizenship to make them vulnerable to confiscation of all their possessions. He would transform them into victims by propaganda designed to invent an excuse for persecuting them. Envy by predatory mobs would do the rest – as it had done in the French and Russian revolutions. All that was necessary was to whip up mob hysteria. Then he would turn his army on the Czechs, followed by the Poles and Russians, to steal their land and property, too. Hitler was convinced he had a winning formula.

The question often raised since those puzzling and tragic days was, 'Why did Hitler choose to murder the Jews?' The short answer is that Hitler did so because it found favour with the mass of Germans, and he was convinced that no one would stop him:

> We would rather talk about socioeconomic stresses and strains, political backwardness, group psychopathology, religious hatred, racism. All those things were indeed there, and Hitler was indeed affected by them – affected, not determined. Those things necessarily meant trouble for the Jews; they did not necessarily mean holocaust.[11]

His was such a simple, yet audacious plan, that no one realised what Hitler intended until it was too late to stop him, because he had become too powerful. He knew he could get away with it, because Lenin had done much the same thing in Russia between 1917 and 1923, and no nation had managed to prevent him. As Hitler claimed in the first edition of his book, the German nation was gullible enough to believe his lies. He deleted his cocky remark that 'Germans had to be gulled in order to be led' in the next edition.[12]

15

The Future of Civilisation

The German economy had collapsed on Black Friday in 1927. The Wall Street Stock Exchange had crashed soon after in 1929. It was the time when the German theoretical physicist, young Werner Heisenberg, was working on a theory that would result in the development of an atomic bomb. He wrote a paper that year on 'The Uncertainty Principle'. It was an appropriate title, since everything was uncertain from then on.

Apparently Sigmund Freud thought so too, when he sat down to elaborate in an essay what had been on his mind for some time. It was 'the probable future of our civilisation'. He called it *The Future of an Illusion.* It was about the human desire to return to childhood by seeking a father figure. At the end of his first paragraph he wrote: 'Finally, the curious fact makes itself felt that in general people experience their present naively, as it were, without being able to form an estimate of its contents; they have first to put themselves at a distance from it – the present, that is to say, must have become the past – before it can yield points of vantage from which to judge the future.'

In summarising the contents of his thoughts about where civilisation or culture stood at that particular moment, he focused on two aspects of which humankind had raised itself above the more typical life of other animals. One was all the knowledge and capacity that men acquired to control natural forces and extract its wealth. The other was 'all the regulations necessary in order to adjust the relations of men to one another', including distribution of the available wealth.

He completed his paper at the same time as the economic recession began. So he could not fail to observe the sad fate of the capitalist system. *The Future of an Illusion* would turn out to be a precursor to his *Civilisation and its Discontents*, which would be published in German in 1930 and prove to be his most widely read work. The conclusions he reached came about by analysing mankind's neurotic obsession with religion, or faith without evidence. He did so as if the whole of mankind was laid submissively on a couch in his consulting room to await psychoanalysis.[1]

He had felt it necessary to explain his negative attitude to all religions – in whatever form or dilution, as dogmas or cults – since discussions with his colleagues Ferenczi and Pfister in 1911. His thinking had followed the previous thoughts of the leaders of the French Enlightenment: Spinoza, Voltaire, Diderot, Feuerbach, and Darwin, as well as James G. Frazer and Havelock Ellis, Max Weber, and Emile Durkheim.[2]

It explained how everyone was 'necessarily exposed to disagreeable and difficult sacrifices, to postponements of wishes and deprivations of pleasure, all for the sake of the common survival'. It was the difference between living in a civilised society rather than living selfishly.

He analysed two typical types of people found in every society – the mob and the elite. He understood that the masses must 'have no love for the renunciation of drives'. They are not fond of work, 'and arguments cannot prevail against their passions'. While they choose to indulge their appetites, more cultivated persons 'suppress their natural urges'.

He found it only natural that the poor and deprived should hate and envy those who sacrifice far less; one could hardly expect them to internalise social prohibitions:

> It goes without saying that a culture which leaves so large a number of participants unsatisfied and drives them to rebellion neither has the prospect of maintaining itself permanently, nor deserves it.[3]

Culture 'must resort to coercion to enforce its rules'. Helplessness is the common lot, and the cause of religions, because 'the vulnerability and dependence of the child live on into adulthood'.[4]

Freud put the finishing touches to *Civilisation and its Discontents* early in July 1929, in which he explained the causes of the human predicament and the misery it entailed. The shock waves of the collapse of the New York Stock Exchange rocked all financial markets as it reverberated and spread into a great depression all over the world.

One of the problems that Freud had been pressed to deal with by French novelist and Nobel Prize-winner for literature, Romain Rolland, was a sensation of eternity that turned many people to religion. Freud argued that the 'oceanic' feeling might be derived at infancy. It created illusions of personal immortality. Freud felt it was simply a means to escape from the unhappiness of ageing and the prospect of dying. Whether people tried to escape through 'work, love, drink, madness, the enjoyment of beauty, or the consolations of religion, they are bound to fail in the end. Neither creation nor nature, or the evolutionary process, contained a plan for happiness.'

The pathetic quest for happiness, which is doomed to failure, had generated hatred of civilisation or hostility to culture. He viewed life in society as an insoluble predicament. Nobody who observed human nature at work, Freud remarked grimly, can claim that it is gentle, loving, or lovable. He had in mind the current situation in communist Russia, a regime that some deluded intellectuals continued to call the 'Soviet Experiment', even after the purges ordered by Stalin and the executions carried out by Dzerzhinsky's CHEKA torturers. Freud saw communism as a delusion as powerful as Hitler's. Both regimes knew that the only way to contain aggression was to focus it on selected victims. Hitler chose the Jews, whereas Stalin persecuted the middle classes. Freud remarked scathingly, 'One only asks oneself uneasily, what the Soviets will do after they have exterminated their bourgeois.' Who will they choose next?[5]

He had to travel to Berlin again for another consultation on his new prosthesis. He complained of heart trouble in November and December 1929, but had a moment to note laconically in his diary of his observations of Berlin: 'Anti-Semitic riots!'

The first edition of *Civilisation and its Discontents* sold out remarkably quickly. And suddenly, there was an unexpected revival of discussions on his 'Death Drive'. A second edition of *Civilisation and its Discontents* was planned for 1931. He had now written everything he had wanted to write, and seemed ready to die.

The Nazi Party had only just won a huge election victory in parliament in September 1930, when a Nazi named Wilhelm Frick became minister of State for Thuringia. The socialists won 143 seats, communists 77, and the Nazis 107.[6]

Freud had few illusions about what could happen. He had seven grandchildren to consider and was entirely pessimistic about life. He could offer no hope to anyone.

Only days after the election, Hitler was asked to describe publicly how he intended to come to power and what he would do. On the third day of a trial of three young *Reichswehr* officers, the defence called him to the stand as a witness. Several foreign press reporters had joined a crowd gathered outside to see the man who had now become 'the greatest hope of millions of Germans'.

An air of excitement rippled through the court when Hitler came to the stand. The judge warned him not to use it as an opportunity for an hour of political propaganda. Hitler began answering questions calmly, but very soon became excited when asked about his views about the state monopoly on legitimate force. He answered that the national army of the *Reichswehr* was 'the most important instrument in the restoration of the German state and the German people'.

He added that any attempt to erode it was insanity. If his party came to power he would ensure the military would once again become 'a great German people's army'. He boasted that the Nazi Party did not need to resort to violence, as it would be Germany's strongest party after the next election ... 'there will be a German national court, there will be retribution for November 1918, and heads will roll'.[7]

After Hitler's dramatic appearance in court, Goebbels was emboldened to ask, 'What do the authorities think they can do to us now?' If the Nazis won the next election they would be legal. Then they could do whatever they wanted.

Freud's despair at the flaws in human nature was echoed by the Austrian criminologist Hans Gross, who viewed behaviour in modern society from a somewhat different perspective. As a judge dedicated to law and order, he was most concerned, not with the average citizen, or with the elite, but with the subversive criminal mind. In essence, he asked himself, 'How can we keep criminality out of politics?' To answer it, he had to define what types of people deliberately committed criminal acts. No wonder his son, the respected psychologist Otto Gross, had rebelled against him – because his father's clearly defined criminal characteristics described his son Otto as a criminal type. It raised the question of whether society was going forwards or backwards. with the new liberal thinking of the younger generation that failed to consider the consequences of their actions.

Sociologist Max Weber missed a critical point when he chose to describe the Protestant Work Ethic in Germany at that crucial moment of unease when millions were facing unemployment, poverty and starvation. The core of the economic problem in German society now was animal passions bent on survival. The tipping point in Germany came in 1930 with the chaotic results from the momentum of growing unemployment from 1927 and the economic depression from 1929. Passions such as rage and criminality spilled over. The ensuing chaos demanded action to restore law and order.

Since the Nazi Party was a criminal gang of discontented misfits from the start, it did not want law and order, because it thrived on chaos. Whereas national leaders and the general public imagined that everyone wanted peace, in reality, the militarist Germany of Ludendorff and Hitler and their like was actively engaged in initiating another war for their own benefit.

That attitude was clearly demonstrated at the world premiere of a film dramatisation of *All Quiet on the Western Front.* It was screened at the *Mozartsaal* cinema in Berlin in late December 1930. Erich Maria Remarque's 1929 pacifist novel preached against war by depicting bleak battle scenes without glory, and only the daily monotony of butchering young men in battle. The author's pacifism was contrary to Nazi principles, since it might discourage support for Hitler. So Goebbels organised gangs of terrorists to descend on the cinema on Berlin's *Nollendarplatz.* The auditorium soon resembled a madhouse, according to Goebbels's diary entry: 'The police were powerless, and the embittered crowd turned on the Jews … "Jews out!" they cried. "Hitler is at the gates."'

II

THE GERMAN CRISIS

16

Hitler Unhinged

Prime Minister Chamberlain was nearing seventy when he first met with Hitler at the *Berghof* on 15 September 1938 to discuss the Führer's plan to annex the Sudetenland. He was in his usual urbane and diplomatic mood, in which he intended to avoid war at all costs. His assessment of his opponent was that he was common and an upstart. Chamberlain was prepared to walk out of the meeting instantly if he decided that Hitler was not serious about finding a highway to peace. Their meeting began in what seemed like Britain's favour, because Hitler welcomed an opportunity to deceive Britain about his intentions. They withdrew for talks into Hitler's office, with Foreign Secretary Ribbentrop waiting outside, ready to be called in if needed. Schmidt the interpreter watched them both.

Hitler began the conversation calmly, but, as usual, swiftly became over-excited and levelled several accusations against the Czech government in Prague. Chamberlain eyed him coldly and told him severely that if he had already decided to move against Czechoslovakia there was no point in continuing.

Schmidt realised it was a critical moment in a war of words. Chamberlain was composed while Hitler was not. But Hitler had instantly reassessed the situation and realised he had been too hasty. He was unaccustomed to opposition, and Chamberlain was immovable. Hitler instantly seized the moment to play a different role from his normal hot-headed and bullying one. Suddenly he was no longer the unpredictable power-hungry monster which Schmidt had previously been accustomed to, but a reasonable negotiator. 'If you agree that the principle of self-determination is the basis of the Sudeten question,' he said, 'we can then talk about how this principle can be put into practice.'[1]

Chamberlain responded by saying he must consult his Cabinet, and proposed another meeting. Hitler agreed not to attack Czechoslovakia in the meantime.[2]

The moment the Prime Minister had left, Hitler clapped his hands with glee in front of Ribbentrop. 'He felt he had manoeuvred this dried-up civilian into a corner.' Chamberlain would have to support the transference of the Sudetenland to Germany if he recognised the principle of self-determination. If the Czechs refused, Hitler would be justified in taking the German-speaking part of Czechoslovakia.[3]

Chamberlain wrote to his sister about his meeting with Hitler on 19 September: 'He looks entirely undistinguished. You would never notice him in a crowd and would take him for the house painter he once was.' But the Prime Minister had made a cardinal error in his judgement of Hitler as 'a man of his word'. He would regret that erroneous assessment for the remainder of his life.

According to historian Stephen Kotkin's explanation of Chamberlain's political strategy, the Treaty of Versailles could not last, since it was imposed on Germany without involving the Soviet Union when both nations were in no position to resist Britain and France. The Allies had won the war and could force the treaty through. France had suffered the greatest destruction from the German war. But what would happen when Germany's and Russia's economies grew? Hitler had defied the treaty in 1933 by building up Germany's combat forces. Stalin's motivation was to encourage a war against the two imperialist/capitalist nations so that Russia would come out on top by means of a socialist revolution in Germany. Hitler's motivation was the same as Chamberlain's in the UK, which was to recruit Hitler to his side. Each leader needed a partner.[4]

After Chamberlain's Cabinet agreed to support his next round with Hitler, the Prime Minister arranged cooperation with France, so that the French government sent an identical letter to the Czech President Beneš as the British. It demanded that Czechoslovakia cede to Germany the territories with a population of more than 50 per cent of German-speaking inhabitants. After initially refusing, the Czech government realised they had no choice and agreed on 21 September.

If Chamberlain thought Hitler would be pleased, he was wrong: Hitler wanted more than 50 per cent of Czechoslovakia – he wanted the whole of it. Chamberlain received an unpleasant shock at his next trip to Germany when he sat down with Hitler. After the development of the last few days, Hitler told him, he 'could no longer accept the deal'.

Schmidt the interpreter saw Chamberlain sit bolt upright, his face flushed with anger. Hitler showed him a map with new demarcation lines, and demanded that the handover must 'happen immediately'.

Chamberlain did not turn up for the continuation of the talks next day. He sent Hitler a letter instead, saying his demands were incompatible with what had previously been agreed.

The effect of the letter on the German delegation in the Hotel Dreesen was electric: they became edgy. American newspaper correspondent William Shirer saw Hitler up close in the garden of the hotel and concluded that 'the man is on the edge of a nervous breakdown'. According to him, Hitler had 'ugly black patches under his eyes', and a nervous twitching of his right shoulder. Negotiations had reached a dead end.[5]

Goebbels wrote in his diary, 'The whole situation is so tense it's coming apart at the seams.'[6]

Nevertheless, Chamberlain politely offered to act as a mediator between Berlin and Prague. The Czech government was given four days to hand over the Sudetenland to Hitler. But Beneš had mobilised his country's armed forces. At that point in the further negotiations, the room became silent, and the interpreter watched Hitler suddenly become conciliatory. He quietly agreed not to take military action if negotiations continued, and extended his deadline by two days.

According to Goebbels, Hitler did not think that Beneš would give in to the demands, and was already planning his revenge on the Czech president.

In the afternoon of 26 September, Sir Horace Wilson delivered a personal message from Chamberlain to Hitler that informed him that Beneš found the latest memo was completely unacceptable. Schmidt would recall afterwards that Hitler 'had a fit of a magnitude I never heard before or after in a diplomatic discussion'. Hitler's rage was no longer play acting. He had worked himself up into a psychotic condition as the Sudeten crisis headed towards a conclusion different from what he had intended, and he saw his plans of conquest slipping away.

He gave a speech that evening on 26 September at the Berlin Sportpalast, where – according to William Shirer – he built himself up by 'shouting and shrieking in the worst state of excitement I have ever seen him in'.[7]

Shirer sat in the gallery just above where Hitler stood, and watched his antics with amazement. It appeared that the German leader had completely lost control. After yelling with all his power, Hitler brought his hysterical speech to an end, and slumped in a chair from exhaustion.

Next morning, Hitler's hysteria veered from euphoria to wild fury and agitation, until Horace Wilson arrived with another personal letter from Chamberlain. It stated that Britain would guarantee that the Czechs honoured their commitment to evacuate the Sudetenland if Germany avoided violence.

Hitler's response was stubbornly to have his own way. He insisted his memorandum had to be accepted by 2 p.m. on 28 September. Otherwise the *Wehrmacht* would march in and take the Sudetenland on 1 October. He threatened to crush the Czechs. Sir Horace Wilson informed him he had another message from Chamberlain. If France felt it must engage in hostilities towards Nazi Germany, Britain would be bound to support the French.

Hitler believed that Britain was bluffing. He replied that if France and England wanted a fight they should go ahead: Germany was prepared. On the other hand, he recognised there might be war with France and England. Then an incident occurred that made him hesitate. He had glimpsed a motorised army division rolling down *Wilhelmstrasse* in what seemed to be a *Wehrmacht* demonstration of power. But instead of passers-by cheering the troops, they turned away silently and hurriedly avoided having to watch. He realised that the mood of the German people was against war. The lack of enthusiasm made him think again, and he reconciled himself to a diplomatic solution.

The question uppermost in people's minds was what might happen when Hitler's deadline elapsed? Hitler was in an agitated mood and repeated to Ernst von Weizsäcker that he wanted to obliterate Czechoslovakia.

Soon after 11 a.m. on the final day of his ultimatum, the French ambassador arrived. It was André François-Poncet, one of the few diplomats Hitler respected. He received him cordially. The ambassador advised him that an attack on Czechoslovakia would lead to world war. Why take the risk if you can get your demands accepted peacefully? Hitler listened patiently to the Frenchman's advice. Shortly afterwards, at about 11.40 a.m., the Italian ambassador arrived with an urgent message from *Il Duce.* Hitler left the French ambassador for a moment to welcome Bernardo Attolico. The British had requested the Italians to mediate, and Mussolini had agreed to do so.

Only two hours before the German ultimatum was due to expire, Hitler accepted Mussolini's offer. At the last moment, Britain's ambassador, Nevile Henderson, arrived at the Chancellery to deliver Chamberlain's answer to Hitler's previous letter. It was to suggest that Britain's Prime Minister could visit Hitler with a delegation from France and Italy to find a peaceful solution to the Sudetenland crisis. Hitler agreed.[8]

Regardless of the conclusion of a settlement, Hitler viewed the Sudetenland agreement only as an initial bribe to have him abandon a German attack. He saw it as recognition by France and England, and Czechoslovakia, that Hitler was the top dog. And he was quick to exploit the situation. He discussed it with Goebbels only three days after the agreement was signed in Munich. Goebbels noted afterwards, 'His determination to obliterate the Czechs is unbroken.'[9]

Hitler's obsession with the Czechs was only one example of how his impressions as a teenager in Vienna had created fixations in his mind. The Czechs had been a dominating minority of foreigners in Austria whom the Viennese had viewed as a threat. There had been others, like Poles, Slavs, Jews and Italians. It seemed that Hitler forgot nothing when it came to opposition. Revenge for the hurt to his sensitivity as a German speaker at the success of other nations ate into his heart.

Hitler decided to use bullying tactics towards Britain to get his own way again. He treated Chamberlain like an errand boy. It is possible that he had noticed Britain's Prime Minister patronising him, and he resented it. It had happened to him before from royalty in Rome and German aristocrats. He still cut a poor figure socially and knew they viewed him as a crude upstart of common origins.

Foreign policy was placed on the back burner for a while at the end of 1938 when Hitler spent more time on hunting, persecuting, and abusing Jews in Germany and Austria. But he needed victories to keep shoring up his prestige and provide him with self-confidence that drained away so easily when he fluctuated from bullying to being unsure of himself. The Czech problem had been only partly solved. He also had a problem with his officer corps, who considered that most of his actions were spontaneous emotional reactions and not strategically planned, as he kept insisting they were. He also returned obsessively in his talks to demanding more living space, which he felt his military commanders had not taken seriously enough. It was important to him that they should view him as a strategic politician and military leader.

He finally felt able to focus on preparations to annex the rest of Czechoslovakia. He had to find a way to circumvent his previous acknowledgment of Czech sovereignty, which the Munich agreement had guaranteed. The opportunity arrived when negotiations collapsed between Prague and Bratislava over Slovak autonomy. The new president, Hácha, who had replaced Beneš in Czechoslovakia, dismissed the Slovakian government and sent troops marching into Slovakia.

'This is a launching pad,' Goebbels noted gleefully in his diary.

On 10 March Hitler summoned Goebbels to the Chancellery at noon with Ribbentrop and General Keitel. His message to them was clear: 'On 19 March we'll invade and destroy the entire monstrous construct that is Czechoslovakia.' He issued orders accordingly to the *Wehrmacht* on 12 March.

On 14 March, the Slovakian parliament declared its independence. Hitler and Goebbels heard that Hácha, the new Czech president, had asked to meet Hitler. He turned up in Berlin that evening with the Czech foreign minister to negotiate with Hitler. But Hitler had no intention of doing any such thing, and kept the delegation waiting for hours in the Adlon Hotel, while he watched a movie in the chancellery. He would be satisfied with nothing less than capitulation.

It was past midnight before the Czechs were led through the chancellery and into Hitler's huge office. Hitler had lined up several of his supporters to outnumber and intimidate the two Czechs. They included Goebbels, von Ribbentrop and General Keitel.

Hácha had hoped to maintain Czech independence – at least some part of it. But Hitler was adamant: he would have his way and there would be no compromise. He already had the Sudetenland. He would turn the rest of Czechoslovakia into a German protectorate. The *Wehrmacht* would invade the territory at 6 a.m. He demanded that Hácha phone Prague and order them not to resist German troops. He told Hácha he would be doing the Czechs a favour to avoid bloodshed, since Goering threatened to bomb Czechoslovakia if Hitler's terms were not met.

Hácha reviewed their demands with his foreign minister in a private room before accepting Hitler's conditions. Both knew they had no choice:

> The significance of the destruction of Czechoslovakia for Hitler's war plans was considerable. The German Reich gained not only the largest armaments facilities, the Skoda factories in Pilsen and Prague, it also acquired enough weapons and supplies to outfit twenty further divisions. In addition to industrial resources, the German war effort gained access to Czechoslovakian copper, nickel, lead, aluminium, zinc and tin. The door was also wide open for Germany to penetrate the Danube and Balkan region economically. And in terms of military strategy, the Reich was now better positioned to launch campaigns to conquer further 'living space in the east'.[10]

Although Czechoslovakia was a relatively small country and an anomaly as a fragment of the old Austro-Hungarian Empire with its mixed religions and ethnicity, the British and French felt uneasy about the sell-out to Hitler. It was a final warning signal to the West that no one should believe a word that Hitler said. He could not be trusted. He was looking for more territory to conquer, if possible without wasting a bullet or a life.

German Expansion

Hitler's opinion that his seizure of Czechoslovakia would be forgotten in weeks was not borne out by subsequent events. Britain's Government finally realised that its policy of appeasing Hitler had been a mistake: they had been duped by him. He was no more than 'a criminal acting as his own judge'.[11] Ambassador Nevile Henderson was withdrawn from Berlin, and Chamberlain made a speech in Birmingham about Britain's change in foreign policy. His strategy had collapsed the moment he had finally realised that Hitler could not be trusted. Winston Churchill was brought into the Cabinet in an admission that no one in the Government knew more about war than he did.

The French supported British protests at German expansion, but the Nazi leaders were over-confident at their successes with Austria and Czechoslovakia without even firing a shot, and brushed them aside as hysteria, while they focused on the next territory to annex. They demanded the instant return of the Klaipeda Region, better known as Memel. The territory was relatively tiny. But Poland knew they would be next when huge German armies massed on their borders.

Chamberlain announced that Britain would declare war on Germany if Poland was attacked. The Second World War began when Germany invaded Poland on 1 September 1939.

It would have been almost impossible to find anyone in Britain or France, or anywhere else, who believed that Britain could win a war against Germany. And yet, men who could fight knew they had no choice if they wished to survive as a nation. Churchill claimed that it was better to die fighting than to become slaves. The French had already decided not to confront German troops, but hide their own forces in a concrete fortress on their border called the Maginot Line.

Most people in the British Isles comforted themselves with the old truism that 'Britain always loses every battle but the last'. The only small glimmer of hope was American President Roosevelt's judgement that it was impossible for a democracy like the United States to exist alongside a police state like Nazi Germany.

Status and Revenge

Three words – status and revenge – defined the entirety of Hitler's life. No wonder one of his contemporaries, the novelist Robert Musil, called him 'The man without qualities!' If Hitler was a half-wit – as Musil and some other onlookers evidently thought – then we would have to consider the mindlessness of those who feared him or supported him and put him in power. What type of individuals would conspire to destroy a workable parliamentary democracy in favour of a tyrannical dictatorship and police state? That question has continued to haunt historians, politicians, journalists, and the public ever since.

Literary critic and Pulitzer Prize winner Michiko Kakutani of the *New York Times* would refer to a recent biography of Hitler by Volker Ullrich in her 2016 review, in which she described Hitler's rise to power as 'from dunderhead to demagogue'. She attributed the Hitler catastrophe to 'the confluence of circumstances, chance, a ruthless individual and the wilful blindness of others'. She asked, 'How did Adolf Hitler, a "half-insane rascal", a "pathetic dunderhead", a "nowhere fool", a "big mouth" – rise to power in the land of Goethe and Beethoven? What persuaded millions of ordinary Germans to embrace him and his doctrine of hatred? How did this "most unlikely pretender to high state office" achieve absolute power in a once democratic country and set it on a course of monstrous horror?'[12]

17

The Nazi Power Grab

1932–33

The greatest danger to the entire world was posed by Germany when Hitler obtained 11 million votes against Field Marshal Hindenburg's 18 million in the German presidential election. The communists received only 5 million, which demonstrated that they were not the threat the Nazis had made them out to be. Hitler's share of the vote rose to 40 per cent in the second ballot on 10 April. As Hindenburg was old and far too ill to serve, Hitler became Chancellor of Germany on 30 January 1933.

A technical reason for the result might be that there were too many opposition parties, which fragmented the numbers opposed to the National Socialists and prevented enough voters from forming a more moderate government. It was a point of no return for the German people and the war against Germany that followed, in order to prevent the slavery and slaughter and devastation of Europe. The Nazis would never freely give up the power they had managed to seize by careful political manoeuvring and manipulation, in which they had seduced the electorate with their spiritual message of uniting the German-speaking people.

Hitler acted as swiftly as Lenin had done in Russia in October 1917 when he had seized the opportunity for total power. He amassed his troops in a torchlight parade in Berlin to entertain and deceive the population, while Goering hastily replaced senior public servants with his own dedicated Nazi followers on the following day.

Their next significant move that ended freedom in Germany was when the Nazis put through an Emergency Decree on 28 February, stating that 'Articles 114–18, 123–4 and 153 of the Constitution of the German Reich are for the time being nullified:'

> Consequently, curbs on personal liberty, on the right of the free expression of opinion, including freedom of the press, of associations, and of assembly, surveillance over letters, telegrams and telephone communications, searches of homes and confiscation of as well as restrictions on property, are hereby permissible beyond the limits hitherto established by law.[1]

It had taken Hitler only about five months to destroy parliamentary democracy in Germany. It was roughly the same time frame that Lenin took to obtain complete control of Russia. And all the while, perversely, there was enthusiastic popular support for disarmament in Britain.

There was something uncanny and sinister about the massive public demonstrations organised so efficiently by the Nazis as a show of their strength and dedication to white supremacy. And also an intimidating warning to anyone who might oppose them. It made a decisive impact, in particular on Churchill, when in 1932 he had undertaken a trip to Bavaria to tour the old battlefields on which his ancestor, the First Duke of Marlborough, had fought and won his famous battles.

Others who were similarly affected by what they saw included a young Cambridge student named Kim Philby, who influenced at least four other students to work with him in the KGB, because they realised the Nazis could be stopped only by a similarly powerful force like the Soviet Union. Winston shared their horror and revulsion, and thought so too, but it was not a suitable time to admit it. In the first place, Churchill's problem was how to convey the Nazi menace to the House of Commons and the British public, and warn them that once the German military machine was equipped for war they would use all the weapons at their disposal to achieve their aims, which were, 'Today Germany, tomorrow the world'.[2]

Churchill warned that Britons were underrating the seriousness of the situation in Europe. He was concerned for the future of his children and everyone else's. His article on the subject appeared in the *Daily Mail* on 26 May 1933, addressed to millions of well-meaning English people, cautioning them that, although he understood the horror of war, it was blinding them from recognising the blunt truth about what was going on beyond the English Channel.

He pointed out that each state sought its own security by holding on to its own armaments, while pressing the others to disarm. And what about smaller states like Finland, Latvia and Poland? How would they protect themselves from bigger nations on their borders like Russia and Germany?

He had taken Professor Lindemann with him to Germany in the summer of 1932, when they had spent three days in Munich on the way to the historic battlefields at Blenheim. Churchill's move indicated they had another item on their agenda. It was Ernst Hanfstaengl, a friend of Hitler, who attempted to arrange a meeting between Churchill and the German leader. However, the plan was aborted when Churchill raised the question of Hitler's anti-Semitic policy. Hitler would always abruptly cut off all conversation when anyone mentioned the subject. It appeared to be a mental fixation or blind spot beyond reason. When a German officer suggested to Hitler that he should meet Churchill while he was in Germany, Hitler dismissed the idea as a waste of time, since he said Churchill held no official position and no one listened to him.

After they had visited the battlefield as planned, Winston became ill with paratyphoid fever and spent a fortnight in a sanatorium in Salzburg. But he was not too ill to dictate twelve articles for the *News of the World.* He returned to Chartwell on 25 September, where he had a relapse and ended up at a nursing home in London, too ill to attend the Conservative Party Conference in Blackpool on 7 October.

By the end of the month, he had finished half of the Marlborough book and was planning ahead for his *History of the English-Speaking Peoples* in four volumes, for which he had already received an advance of £20,000.

When Churchill attempted again to warn Parliament of Germany's military build-up, he found himself isolated, with members of both parties deliberately leaving the chamber whenever he stood up to speak. *The Times* called him a Jeremiah and newspaper cartoonists made fun of him. He was shouted down whenever he began to speak. No one wanted to hear his warnings. They were bad news.

Equal Status

Germany had demanded equality of armaments with France in the summer and autumn of 1932. The French were its most heavily armed neighbour. Sir John Simon replied for Britain that Germany was still committed by the disarmament clauses in the Treaty of Versailles. Von Papen protested by drawing Germany out of the Disarmament Conference. Churchill was shocked to find public opinion in Britain on Germany's side, in a mistaken conclusion that a disarmed Germany would be in an unfair position against a more militarily powerful France.

Churchill supported Sir John Simon's firm stand in the interest of peace. And he pointed out that the German Minister of Defence, General Kurt von Schleicher, had announced that, regardless of what the Powers might decide, Germany would do what she thought fit in rearmament. Churchill's article in the *Daily Mail* in October warned of the danger of encouraging Germany in its misadventures.

As if to remark that the world was a dangerous place and that no one could do anything about that, Prime Minister Baldwin said in the House, 'I think it well for the man in the street to realise that there is no power on earth that can prevent him from being bombed.'

It was a fatuous remark. He sounded helpless with his fatalistic and defeatist attitude. Amery told Churchill about the 'incredible amount of sloppy nonsense' that was talked from every quarter of the House about disarmament while Winston had been on holiday abroad.

Churchill wrote another warning in the *Daily Mail* on 17 November 1932 that if disarmament negotiations failed in Geneva – which he expected they would – the National Government should increase the size and strength of the Royal Air Force so 'that it will not be worth anyone's while to come here and kill our women and children in the hope that they may blackmail us into surrender'.

As soon as he was well enough to travel to London, he spoke forcefully in Parliament on 23 November, warning that if Britain forced France to disarm, Germany would use her own numerical superiority to avenge its 1918 defeat.

He told the House of Commons that when he had recently visited Germany, he had seen bands of sturdy youths marching through the streets 'with the light of desire in their eyes to suffer for the Fatherland ... They are looking for weapons, and when they have the weapons, believe me they will then ask for the return of lost territories …' He warned that a war mentality was springing up in certain countries in Europe. Meanwhile, he said, there was a huge gap between what Britain's statesmen were saying and what was actually happening. They uttered pious platitudes to gain applause, without relation to the facts. 'I cannot recall any time,' he added, 'when the gap was greater.'

As if they had not heard a word of his warnings, MacDonald and Baldwin hurried on heedlessly with their plan for European disarmament, in which Britain would proudly provide an example for others by reducing its air force before anyone else did.[3]

At the age of 58, Churchill was still at work on his Marlborough biography at Chartwell, accompanied part of the time by Lindemann, who interpreted all sorts of scientific discoveries for the Churchill family, delivering on one day 'a treatise on the quantum theory', at which they all applauded him.

On the other side of the English Channel, Hitler promulgated a series of laws that secured his position in power by destroying parliamentary democracy and all political opposition in Germany. He opened his first concentration camp at Dachau almost immediately, on 22 March 1933, and arrested several thousand political opponents. The camp was designed to accommodate 5,000 prisoners. Heinrich Himmler, the police chief in Munich, was in charge of it. He was very precise about keeping records and making his powers clear from the beginning:

> The term 'commitment to a concentration camp' is to be openly announced as 'until further notice' … In certain cases the Reichsführer SS and the chief of the German Police will order flogging in addition … There is no objection to spreading the rumour of this increased punishment … to add to the deterrent effect. The following offenders, considered as agitators, will be hanged: anyone who … makes inciting speeches, and holds meetings, forms cliques, loiters around with others, who for the purpose of supplying the propaganda of the opposition with atrocity stories, collects true or false information about the concentration camps.[4]

Total power by the Nazis was now absolute in Germany, so that each individual was completely controlled. As Churchill had expected, there was a popular German demand for rearmament and a revision of the Treaty of Versailles, while Hitler prepared for the war he had planned all along, whatever might have happened.

The British Cabinet now discussed deficiencies in Defence, and Neville Chamberlain, as Chancellor of the Exchequer, warned of the 'financial and economic risks' of Britain rearming. He complained of the difficult financial situation at the present time, which he thought prevented it.

Churchill responded at Oxford on 17 February: 'I think of Germany with its splendid clear-eyed youth marching forward on all the roads of the Reich singing their ancient songs, demanding to be conscripted into an army; eagerly seeking the most terrible weapons of war; burning to suffer and die for their Fatherland.'

However vividly he attempted to describe the inflammatory situation in Germany it meant nothing to those who had not observed it themselves.

Randolph visited Oxford, too, in order to respond to the Oxford Union's declaration that 'this house refuses in any circumstances to fight for King and Country'. He hoped to reverse the Union vote, but it stood overwhelmingly as before. Britain had become a nation of pacifists. Meanwhile, Winston had to face hostility in the House of Commons when he opposed the Government proposal to reduce spending on the RAF for another year, and to close down one of its flying training schools.

Disarmament Proposals

Two days later, Prime Minister Ramsay MacDonald submitted Britain's disarmament proposals to the Geneva Disarmament Conference: the maximum period of military service in Europe would be eight months. 'France, Germany, Italy and Poland would be limited to 200,000 troops each; aerial bombardment would be forbidden; military aircraft would be limited to 500 for each country, with the German figure left open; any excess of aircraft would be destroyed, half by 1936, the rest by 1939.'[5]

The helplessness and haphazardness of MacDonald was shown in the sloppy and amateurish way with which he presented his scheme to the House on 23 March with the words, 'I cannot pretend that I went through the figures myself.'

Although apparently the Prime Minister had not thought it necessary to involve himself in the issue personally, Churchill had. He had read the reports of the Nazi demands. And he had read about their anti-democratic and anti-Jewish onslaughts.

He told the House of Commons, 'When we read about Germany, when we watch with surprise and distress the tumultuous insurgence of ferocity and war spirit, the pitiless treatment of minorities, the denial of the normal protections of civilised society to large numbers of individuals solely on the grounds of race – when we see that occurring in one of the most gifted, learned, scientific and formidable nations in Europe, one cannot help feeling glad that the fierce passions that are raging in Germany have not found, as yet, any other outlet than Germans.'[6]

Churchill added that the British Government had failed to redress Germany's grievances while they were weak, and should not urge France to disarm now they were strong. The Government's inaction had 'brought us nearer to war and has made us weaker, poorer and more defenceless'.

Members of Parliament on both Labour and Conservative benches angrily refuted what he had said by crying out, 'No! No! No!' They became even more furious when he told them that the Prime Minister was responsible for it.

As Churchill grimly insinuated, it cast serious doubts on the Government's ability to rule. But his remarks were rebutted by the Under-Secretary of State at the Foreign Office, Anthony Eden, who appeared to have modelled his own oratory on the smooth and sardonic wit of Winston Churchill.

'It was unfortunate that Churchill had chosen so serious a debate to practise his "Quips and jests",' Eden said. 'For Churchill to accuse MacDonald of being responsible for the deterioration of international relations,' he added, was 'a fantastic absurdity'. The causes of that deterioration went back to a time when Mr Churchill himself had a considerable measure of responsibility.

Eden was referring to the time when Churchill had held office as Chancellor of the Exchequer. But, in fact, Churchill had increased spending on the RAF in four out of his five budgets. And he had warned the Cabinet of German naval expansion and rearmament in 1929. Nevertheless, Eden continued to insist that unless France disarmed, 'they could not secure for Europe that period of appeasement which is needed'. Furthermore, he denied Churchill's allegation that Britain wanted France to halve her army. The ratio 'was 694,000 to 400,000'.

According to the *Daily Despatch*, 'The House was enraged and in an ugly mood – towards Mr Churchill.' But Admiral Sir Reginald Custance, who supported Churchill, claimed that he had been talking over their heads. It revealed Churchill's more dependable mindset, in that he had studied all the facts, whereas the Government evidently had not.[7]

Eden was still playing the honourable political game by loyally supporting his feeble party leader, as, no doubt, he had been taught in the debating societies where he had learned his polite rhetoric at Eton and Oxford, before the concept of appeasing the Nazis would become abhorrent to him; as it very soon would.

The Cult of Fascism

Since Churchill intended to speak again on the situation in Europe, he discussed the matter in more detail with his close neighbour and friend in Kent, Major Desmond Morton. Churchill had known him for more than ten years, since 1916, when they had both served in the army on the Western Front, and had brought him to the War Office in 1919 to undertake intelligence work. Morton now led the Industrial Intelligence Unit of the Committee of Imperial Defence. Armed with added knowledge of what raw materials for armaments were being manufactured by the leading European powers, Churchill went on to tell the House that Hitler's demands for rearmament when compared with MacDonald's insistence on disarming Britain and France (even Poland and other smaller nations who would not be able to defend themselves from attack) would mean 'a renewal of a general European war'.

For Churchill, it was not only the 'martial or pugnacious manifestations' in Germany. It was also 'this persecution of the Jews'. He appealed to everyone who felt that 'men and women have a right to live in the world where they are born, and have a right to pursue a livelihood which has hitherto been guaranteed them under the public laws of the land of their birth'. He warned them of the dangers of such odious and unjust conditions being extended to Poland by conquest.

He remarked on the Prime Minister's 'extraordinary admission' that he had not gone through the figures himself, and yet, he took responsibility for them. 'It is a very grave responsibility. If ever there was a document upon which its author should have consumed his personal thought and energy it was this immense disarmament proposal.'

On 10 May, the Nazis organised a public show of burning thousands of books in Berlin on philosophy and psychology, society and culture, which were contrary to their own policy and intentions. Their ideology was based on the principle that the strong had the power and the right to dominate and even destroy the weak. The burnt books were written by liberals, left-wing politicians, or Jewish authors. Some of the authors interpreted the Nazis' intentions correctly by realising that they themselves would be destroyed next, and hurriedly left Germany before it was too late. They were the fortunate ones who escaped in time.

Churchill understood the warning signs too, and the necessity of a vigilant defence policy. Meanwhile, the British Admiralty, the Air Ministry and the War Office warned the Cabinet of the grave shortage of war supplies.[8]

It has been said that perhaps the only difference between communism and fascism was that communists had plans or concepts in mind, even if they were unpractical, unjust and futile, whereas fascists were simply against things and people, like liberalism, democracy, Marxism, Jews, Slavs, Christians, minorities, and all ethnic groups. Fascism and the Nazis were about the glorification of power for those who had the initiative and ruthlessness to take it by force. Consequently there were few if any intellectuals of the extreme right.[9] Fascismo was a bullying state of mind manifested by Italian men strutting self-importantly in their uniforms, with Benito Mussolini as their role model.

Fascism represented a threatening macho and braggadocio culture without ethics or morality that would stop at nothing to be able to show off its power by bullying the weak. It was exemplified by Mussolini's delusions of grandeur to conquer Egypt and appoint himself its king or pharaoh, while Hitler's aggrandisement was demonstrated by his being glorified as a primitive warrior god.

Those who chose to follow them were largely third-raters who felt marginalised by the lack of opportunities resulting from their shortcomings, and could succeed only by destroying those who already filled rewarding posts in politics, science, commerce and industry, teaching and the medical professions. Others were ambitious for power or afraid of losing it.

The rise to power of the Nazis in Germany resulted from Hitler's anti-Semitic legislation. Every Jew who was fired, whether in government, universities or industries, had to be replaced by a non-Jew. Not only did it elevate mediocrities in their career and self-importance, and give them power over others, it also created a class of people who would show total personal loyalty to the warlord who had improved their circumstances.

Mussolini's 1938 Race Laws returned Italy to a form of eighth-century feudalism in which the commonality cringed to their warlords and obeyed them in return for part of the plunder. Hitler followed Mussolini's lead.

How Hitler Seized Power

1923: Failed attempt to seize power. Hitler imprisoned for high treason.
1926: Hitler builds up his power base. to impress and intimidate.
1927: Nazi Party now strong enough to threaten government.
1928: Nazis win 12 seats in parliament.
1929: Massive Nazi demonstrations intimidate public by taking control of the streets.
1930: Nazis win 107 seats in the Reichstag.
1933: Hitler appointed Chancellor in January.
1933: The Reichstag fire in February creates fear of a communist revolution..
1933: Nazis win 288 seats in March.
1933: Enabling Act to allow Nazis to pass laws without consent of Parliament.
1933: Nazis become the only legal party in July.
1933: Dachau murder camp opens in March to murder anyone who opposed the Nazis.
1934: Hitler murders opposition SA Brown Shirts in the 'Night of the Long Knives' in June.
1934: President Hindenburg dies in August.
1935: Nuremberg Laws passed to exclude Jews from citizenship, their jobs and all rights.
1938: Nazi attacks destroy Jewish businesses. Jewish homes and property confiscated.
1939: German troops invade Poland.
1939: Britain and France declare war on Nazi Germany.

18

A Sense of Resignation

Despite the political and military turmoil in Europe, family and social life in England continued at its normal leisurely pace, as if most of the population of the British Isles were resigned to yet another war between the tiresome and troublesome tribes on the other side of the English Channel, and an assumption that Britain would have to intervene once again to sort them out.

The very last vestige of an age of peace and innocence was vanishing as the Nazis brought back a determination for another world war. Its ideology of brute force with no recognition of human rights changed everything and drew a curtain across a tranquil period in England that was vanishing forever.

One romantic recorder of growing up at that time was novelist Nancy Mitford. She created an image in two of her novels that resonated with authenticity for anyone left who might remember it. Readers encounter her eccentric father, who had fought in the First World War and loathed all foreigners. Then there are the well-intentioned but dim-witted young sons of the upper classes who joined the Communist Party under an illusion and fought naively for justice in the Spanish Civil War. The successful romantic novelist knew the innocent young women of the times best, since she had five sisters herself, and her brother Tom. The six daughters were Nancy, Pamela, Diana, Unity, Jessica, and Deborah. No one had taught any of them about earning a living, or sex, or pregnancy. Their destinies, as the story would reveal, were simply to engage in an affair with a suitable or unsuitable man, and marry him before their physical attractions diminished. It reflected most women's lives at the time.

Their father was the aristocratic but hard-up Baron Redesdale, who was descended from the Norman conquerors of Great Britain.

The otherwise elegant and idiosyncratic Mitford sisters, who were much-admired cousins of the Churchills, appeared in Nancy's 1949 novels entitled *The Pursuit of Love* and *Love in a Cold Climate.*[1] The books provide an amusing and enchanting satire of pre-war English upper-class values, and were evidently based on the author's own childhood. Fanny tells us the story of her beautiful but innocent cousin and childhood best friend, Linda, who possesses a tender heart for the underprivileged and an altogether false conception of the world.[2]

As for the turbulent love life of Winston and Clementine, she had accepted an invitation on a four-month cruise to the East Indies by Lord Moyne, which held no interest for Winston. She wrote to her 'sweet and darling Winston', to tell him not to be vexed with her vagabond life: His Kat 'has gone off to the jungle with her tail in the air, but she will return presently to her basket and curl down comfortably'. Several days later she wrote, 'Oh my Darling, I'm thinking of you & how you have enriched my life.'

Her daughter Sarah wrote to her: 'Don't forget to come home some time. Papa is miserable and frightfully naughty without you! Your children however are model in every way.'[3]

The Simon Report on India

Since Sir John Simon's proposal for Indians to rule their own provinces was more or less what Churchill had been pressing for, he was suspicious of the Government's motives, and suspected that they had no intention of accepting the Simon Report, but were proceeding instead with a plan for self-government with full status as a British Dominion, with Hindus in the centre. Britain's Government cautiously announced what they considered to be safeguards for India's Muslims, and also for the Princely States. Sir Samuel Hoare described to the Cabinet how the British Viceroy would still retain complete control over Foreign Affairs and Departments of Defence, and a balance of power between Princely States and Muslims, of 30 per cent each of the votes in the lower chamber.

The Secretary of State for War, Lord Hailsham, cautioned that although they knew that Indians were very intelligent, they were not good administrators, and were often corrupt, because Muslims were required to look after their families and relations as a priority. 'Justice would be sold, the poor oppressed, and there would be a breakdown in the services.'

Sir Samuel Hoare was uneasy on that score, too. Despite that, the Cabinet agreed that the All-India Federal scheme would form the basis for the White Paper.

Churchill joined a meeting of fifty other MPs who had voted against the Government's policy on India. They formed the India Defence Committee. They believed, like Churchill, that it was far too soon for Indians to govern themselves, and unintended consequences would result in the oppression and murders of millions.

Notwithstanding their opposition, the Government issued its White Paper on India on 17 March 1935. It established that each province would be autonomous, while a Federal Government at the centre would provide for 'substantial Indian participation'. It had its third reading in the House, and received royal assent in August.

Since Churchill had opposed it and lost, it damaged his reputation so that he was considered unreliable. Churchill lost the sympathy of the House. He 'compounded his difficulties by his ungracious reception of his defeat'.[4]

Churchill wrote a protest to Hoare on 1 April, and again on 5 April, saying that he had watched with grief and indignation the process by which British responsibility in India would be abdicated to a central government. As he was outnumbered by those opposing his views who would endorse the White Paper, he had decided, he said, not to serve on the Joint Select Committee. He wished to separate himself from what he considered would be the unfortunate result if the White Paper on India was passed, namely the murders of millions of Muslim and Hindu men, women and children.

He felt that he and his friends were right to fight the White Paper scheme to the bitter end.[5] Churchill was impelled by his emotional belief that others felt the same way as he did, but he turned out to be wrong. J.C.C. Davidson remarked how Churchill stopped him in the House of Commons Smoking Room, told him of his plans for mass agitation against the India Bill and predicted that the Government would fall in a fortnight.

'I told him that I thought that the British public was much more interested in the size of their pay packet on Friday than by great rhetorical appeals to their loyalty to the British Empire. I told him that they might cheer him, but they wouldn't vote for him. He didn't like it a bit.'[6]

The link between Churchill's opposition to the Government's policy on India and its defence policies was that both demonstrated a weakening of British resolve.[7]

Even so, the Act was never enforced because it was opposed by the Indian princes.

Imperialism

It has often been claimed that Britain acquired its Empire by accident and not by intention – which is mostly true. It was the British East India Company that traded in India in the eighteenth century and recruited an army to defend itself and its property. The trading company appointed Warren Hastings as Governor General. It continued in that way until the Indian rebellion of 1857. By that time, the Company's powers were suspect by the British Government, which charged Hastings with corruption and impeached him. He was tried for mismanagement of funds. The trial stretched out in Regency England for seven years from 1788. Hastings was cleared in the end, and thanked by King George III for his services.

It did not mean there was no corruption in the Indian Raj. Bold adventurers who carved out empires expected to be rewarded for their efforts. Patronage had always existed. It meant that 'what a man wants – to win a lawsuit, to get a government contract, to be given a birthday honour or to get an official job – could be achieved by doing a favour for the man with power to give or withhold his patronage. The favour need not be a gift of money. It could be a gift of friendship and respect, lavish hospitality, or the gift of funds to a "good cause". Above all, it meant loyalty to the Raj.'[8]

As historian Eric Hobsbawm expressed it, capitalism and a bourgeois society provided 'the only model for those who did not want to be devoured or swept aside by the juggernaut of history'.[9]

The Indian rebellion had persuaded the British Government to take over the administration of India, which became known as the British Raj. It had sounded amusing and harmless when Prime Minister Disraeli had offered Queen Victoria the title of Empress of India, and she had accepted the offer jubilantly. Winston Churchill had been born seventeen years later and was expected to show loyalty to the British Empire into which he had been born.

He was not the only one to be shocked and appalled, as a young soldier, when he first discovered some of the awful Indian customs and traditions that abused other Indians, particularly their own women and children. They would not be considered acceptable in Victorian England. There was, for example, the callous attitude of some Indian princes towards their subjects, and the branding on the face of a huge Indian population known as the Untouchables, to ensure that everyone avoided them. Worse to Britain's Victorians was the traditional Muslim treatment of women and female children, with forced female circumcision and the selling of child brides as infant sex slaves.

English Victorian propriety was appalled when they heard that many female children were murdered at birth to avoid having to feed them. They were shocked to discover the Hindu custom of *suttee*, by which a widow showed her loyalty to her dead husband by burning herself alive on his funeral pyre.

There was also a huge tribe of criminal stranglers, or *thuggee* – a cult of professional assassins who preyed on travellers, which had existed on the Indian continent for over 450 years. Murder and robbery was their traditional way of life. No one was safe from being suddenly strangled with one of their silk nooses. Since they appeared to be no different from any other Indians, they would join groups of travellers and gain their confidence until the right moment arrived to strangle them without being seen. The victim would be robbed and buried. The word *thuggee* literally means the 'deceivers'.

On the plus side, when taking over the responsibility for governing India, some British officials delighted in everything exotic about the continent and its peoples; the new culture of Orientalism, the literature and religious beliefs of the continent. But most were horrified at the primitive customs and the lack of value of the mass of Indian lives to their Indian rulers.

Whether one approved of the British Empire that sought to eradicate injustices and abuses of human rights in India or not, no other empire was like it. And, 'No one can determine whether the accounts of empire ultimately closed with a favourable cash balance.'[10]

By comparison, the Kaiser told Churchill of the rebellion of the Herrero and Nama people in German South-West Africa, who had been badly ill-treated by the German colonial administration. German troops drove them into the desert, where 24,000–100,000 perished from dehydration. It was one of the first cases of genocide recorded in the twentieth century. In German East Africa it was recorded that 2,293 natives were sentenced to be flogged.

The truth was that for all its vainglorious posturing, the British Raj was a constant burden for Britain, and unlikely to have produced much in the way of financial benefits in the long run. For Britain at least, Empire was a losing financial proposition.[11]

Britain was more interested in obtaining strategic locations and ports that might protect them from potential enemies.[12]

Some historians, like Niall Ferguson and Thomas Sowell, argue that Britain's costly form of philanthropic colonialism was more likely to have shown a financial loss after they set up law enforcement to fight crime, kept enemies at bay with the British Navy and Army, provided new sciences and medicine to Indian and other colonial populations, as well as educating and uniting them by introducing the English language. Britain invested massive sums of money to build roads and railways. But discontented rebels continually inspired riots that prevented the ideal advancement of modernity and progress in most of Britain's territorial possessions.

As Churchill remarked with amused cynicism, the English had a habit of embarking on ventures only if it could be shown that there was no advantage for them in it. Typically, every Victorian act had to be made according to a moral principle.

A Just Society

Churchill's attitude towards the British Empire in which he grew up was very much a philanthropic one. When he visited or fought in countries that were not as advanced industrially or scientifically as Britain, or suffered from a high crime rate, or high rates of lethal illnesses that science and medicine had almost obliterated in England, he had the same attitude towards the underprivileged in countries like the Sudan, India, or parts of Africa, as he had for the underprivileged in Britain. If they needed a helping hand, he felt obliged to offer it. But such is human nature that – as previously mentioned in the Middle East – 'No good turn goes unpunished'.

His misgivings were reserved for human nature, as a result of his first experiences as a young army officer in India. As he wrote in *The Story of the Malakand Field Force*, about his misadventures with the Indian border tribes fighting the Afghani tribes, he recognised the pointlessness of punishing tribes who had committed criminal offences, and of continually putting down native uprisings, since similar situations would occur again and again afterwards to other British soldiers performing the same policing routines. Nothing was ever settled for good.

He often wondered whether it would be easier and more effective to annex territories and control the situation by training malcontents and bringing them into the British Empire, thereby establishing and maintaining peace, as Rome had done. But, as he remarked sceptically in the book on his early life, it was unreasonable to think that such areas of tribal conflict could be made as peaceful as Hyde Park.

For one thing, Britain never had enough money or troops to instil a permanent peace or develop a just society. As was often the case with British politics, there was an uneasy feeling that achieving perfection was impossible. Although certain situations were unacceptable for a civilised society, they nevertheless existed and there was no going back. The British Empire was propelled forward by a civilising purpose, but no one claimed it was perfect, as it was administered by imperfect human beings.

Prime Minister Lord Salisbury had read Winston's book on the Malakand frontier skirmishes, and found the information sufficiently impressive to remark favourably on it to Winston in 1898. He had felt it supported his own 'Forward Policy'. As the empire was a tool of civilisation and moved it inexorably forward, there had to be a practical framework to administer it.[13]

The Commander-in-Chief in India in 1897, Sir George White, had claimed that civilisation and barbarism could not coexist peacefully.[14]

It was the fundamental argument for maintaining the British Empire. The young Winston had already observed that the march of civilisation could not be stopped: it was impossible either to turn back or stand still. The idea was part of the Social Darwinism of the time, as expressed in Britain's Foreign Office by the injunction 'onwards and upwards'. And yet, here he was some fifty years later considering exactly the same dilemma about Nazi Germany; that 'civilisation and barbarism could not coexist peacefully'. It seemed that barbarism always flourished, and had to be crushed again.

19

Politics of Hatred

1933–35

The duel to come between Churchill and the Nazis in the not-so-distant future would be a fundamental one between Judeo–Christian ethics and the criminality of a Nazi death cult. A Nazi manifesto of March 1933 had made it clear by instructing organisations throughout Germany to publicise anti-Jewish propaganda among the people, since the Nazis deliberately rejected Judeo–Christian ethics and morals that were implicit in the Ten Commandments. Whereas Jewish ethics were based on the supreme value of life, Nazi ideology was founded on a political and psychological need to murder millions of innocent people to accommodate the Germanic tribes on vast tracts of their land that the Nazis intended to steal and repopulate.

Churchill had long been fascinated by the history of the Jewish people, and their land in the Middle East that had been stolen from them first by the Roman Empire. He found himself involved in their need for a Jewish Homeland and Jewish ethics aimed at living in peace with others.[1]

He had been captivated by Jewish ethics from an early age – no doubt from his father's personal friendships with Jewish leaders – and also their code of conduct with its human rights that had influenced the West in the direction of democracy. Their liberal but firm code of behaviour had persuaded him to switch his military career to that of a successful young Member of Parliament and fight for justice by establishing a more equal society – as his father had attempted to do in the House of Commons. Winston had even written an article on Jewish ethics that had appeared in the *Sunday Chronicle*.[2]

In it, he had rejected the idea that the biblical story of Moses described a mythical or legendary figure upon which the Jewish scribes had hung their moral and religious ideas. He credited Moses with being 'one of the greatest of human beings with the most decisive leap-forward ever discernible in the human story'.

He considered that Moses was the greatest of the prophets, and a national hero who received that remarkable code known as the Ten Commandments, 'upon which the religious, moral, and social life of the [British] nation was so securely fastened'.

He was particularly pleased with that article, which demonstrated his devotion to an ideal. And it was significant that he wrote it at the end of 1930, at the same time as the Nazis were rising to power in Germany and persecuting the Jewish people who represented Churchill's own views on the sacredness of human life.

'This wandering tribe,' he wrote, 'in many respects indistinguishable from numberless nomadic communities, grasped and proclaimed an idea of which all the genius of Greece and all the power of Rome were incapable.'

Churchill warned the House of Commons by adding, 'I cannot help rejoicing that the Germans have not got the heavy cannon, the thousands of military aeroplanes and the tanks of various sizes for which they have been pressing in order that their status may be equal to that of other countries.'[3]

He warned the Government of the folly of their commitment to disarm. Fortunately, he pointed out, Germany's barbaric behaviour had only been aimed at terrorising Germans – so far.

The much-admired scientist Albert Einstein visited Chartwell, to point out to him the opportunity for Britain to use Jewish scientists from Germany. Churchill immediately recognised the advantages for Britain and encouraged his friend Professor Lindemann to travel to Germany and identify Jewish scientists who could be found places at British universities.[4]

But he met narrow-minded and even racially prejudiced responses in some institutions in England, like at Bristol University, where Churchill had been honoured as Chancellor in 1929. The Vice-Chancellor of the university, Thomas Loveday, failed to imagine the advantages, not only of saving valuable scientists, but of the possibility of saving Britain in a race against possible extinction by the Nazis. Loveday was unwilling to cooperate. Instead, he sought to justify his refusal by writing that there had been 'a heavy rush' on entry to the Faculty of Medicine that year, 'and we have had to refuse applications for entry from all foreign countries and even from some of the dominions'.[5]

The Middle East

Winston took Clementine on a brief vacation in Palestine in the autumn of 1934. They were guests on Lord Moyne's private yacht. It enabled them to include Lebanon and Syria in their trip, as well as Palestine, Transjordan and Egypt. Their visits coincided with 'a spate of night-time Arab attacks on Jewish villages', often ending in destroying Jewish orchards and crops.

They drove from Beirut to Palmyra and Damascus. They crossed the Golan Heights into Palestine and visited Nazareth. Next day, they drove through Nablus to Jerusalem, where they stayed at the newly opened King David Hotel. They left the hotel the following day with Lord Moyne and drove to Jericho. After that they flew to Amman and to Transjordan, where they visited the old city of Petra in the former biblical territory of Nabataea – then across the Negev and Sinai deserts, the Suez Canal, and on to Cairo.

The Mufti of Jerusalem, Haj Amin al-Husseini, had been deliberately inciting riots by Palestinian Arabs against Jewish settlers for the past decade. His objective was to halt immigration to the Jewish homeland, fearing a Jewish majority in the land that the Ottoman Empire had taken after the collapse of Rome. The Mufti sought Arab rule and Sharia Law across the entire territory of the British Mandate. British policy was to cope with the thankless task of acting as a peacekeeper. One of the British High Commissioner's routine functions was to fine collectively if anyone rioted or caused damage.[6]

It was the second time in thirteen years that Churchill had seen Jewish efforts to develop a thriving agricultural economy in Palestine out of the formerly useless desert terrain. And, once again, he witnessed the obstacles placed in their way by Arab neighbours who were prepared to destroy whatever it was that they could not have themselves.

It appeared that destiny had reserved Churchill a special place in history as each of his major challenges involved him in fighting for justice against the forces of evil. First it had been against the ruthlessness of Soviet Russia, now it was against the power of pan-Arabism that sought to claim the entire Middle East as its own by destroying everyone else.

Blissful Days

Churchill's first volume of *Marlborough: His Life and Times* was published in October 1933. He sent a copy to Stanley Baldwin, who remarked that Winston's book would have represented years of work for a full-time historian who did nothing else but write: 'Well,' Baldwin remarked, 'there is the miracle.'

Baldwin was still urging the need for disarming Britain by limiting armaments as a priority. He continued to act on the irrational illusion held by pacifists that Germany would disarm its forces if Britain led the way. Baldwin knew his constituents preferred the comfort of illusions.

Churchill also sent an inscribed book as a gift to the newly elected American President Franklin D. Roosevelt, whose 'New Deal' policy Churchill admired. Roosevelt had been inaugurated as President, and commenced his first term in office in March 1933. Brass bands had played 'Happy Days are Here Again, the Skies Above are Clear Again'. The triumphantly smiling President was photographed with his firm chin jutting out and his habitual cigarette in a holder clenched between his teeth.

In spite of his cheerfulness, the United States economy that he inherited had an eerie similarity to what was happening in Germany. A quarter of the US workforce was unemployed. Jobless ex-servicemen arrived at a US Army camp in Washington to demand federal assistance. They were driven off, but threatened to return. America's banks had foreclosed on thousands of homes and farms. Thousands of banks had failed. Distrust of the safety of banks and the value of the dollar made many people resort to hiding their savings under the mattress instead of investing it.

Roosevelt told the public that he intended to keep the money changers at bay as a first step by taking the dollar off the gold standard. Then, to inject optimism into the nation, he began his radio 'fireside chats' that inspired faith in his New Deal.

Churchill supported a motion in the House by Lord Lloyd, who was concerned at the situation in which, 'We alone are growing weaker, while every other nation is growing stronger.' Although the motion won the support of Party members, it failed to influence Government policy.

As the British Government continued its quest to disarm, the Secretary of State for Air, Lord Londonderry, noted that Britain's air production had been halted in 1932. The halt was supposed to have ended in February 1933 in order to promote the aim of the Disarmament Conference, but the standstill had been voluntarily extended to the current year, despite the marked inferiority in Britain's air strength compared with other great powers. The cutback in manufacturing war material had set back completion of Britain's intended military programme by four years behind the original target.[7]

By that time, Churchill's research into the importation of commodities and the production of certain minerals on the continent of Europe revealed that imports of scrap iron and nickel and other war metals had increased considerably. As he told the House of Commons, 'The great dominant fact is that Germany has already begun to rearm.'[8]

To discourage the German desire for revenge, and to avert war, he believed that the League of Nations should be used to redress their grievances, instead of continuing to quarrel with them and haggle about details of rearmament that could never be effectively policed.

Churchill told his audience at a Royal Naval Division Association lunch that he had worked for peace before the last war, and yet he was constantly described as a warmonger. He pointed out that 'it was the Nazis who glorified war, who inculcate a form of blood-lust in their children without parallel as an education since Barbarian and Pagan times'.

He warned that there was no time to be lost. But the deluded Prime Minister Baldwin told Churchill he was convinced that if Britain disarmed, Germany would follow suit.[9]

Munich Rebels dedicated to destroy democracy in the Weimar Republic. April, 1924. Left to right: Heinz Pernet, Friedrich Weber, Wilhelm Frick, Hermann Kriebel, General Erich Ludendorff, Adolf Hitler, Wilhelm Brückner, Captain Ernst Röhm, Robert Wagner. (Source: German Federal Archives. Photo by Heinrich)

A pile of corpses of murdered victims by Nazis at Ohrdruf concentration camp. (Source: United States Memorial Holocaust Museum and Dwight D. Eisenhower Museum)

Left: Arab nationalist and pro-Nazi Amin al-Husseini became known as The Mufti of Jerusalem. He would be the leading figure in Hitler's "Plan Orient" to destroy all non-Muslims in the Middle East.

Below: Amin al-Husseini with Adolf Hitler who would allow him to study Nazi murder camps in return for oil.

Vienna, March 1938: Members of the League of German Girls wave Nazi flags in support of a German takeover of Austria.

Sigmund and daughter Anna Freud opened his first psychiatric clinic in Vienna in 1886. (Permission from Freud Museum in London)

Left: Nazi propagandist Julius Streicher, editor of the anti-Semitic *Der Stürmer*.

Below: Corpse of anti-Semitic Nazi Julius Streicher, hanged as a war criminal at Nuremberg, 16 October 1946.

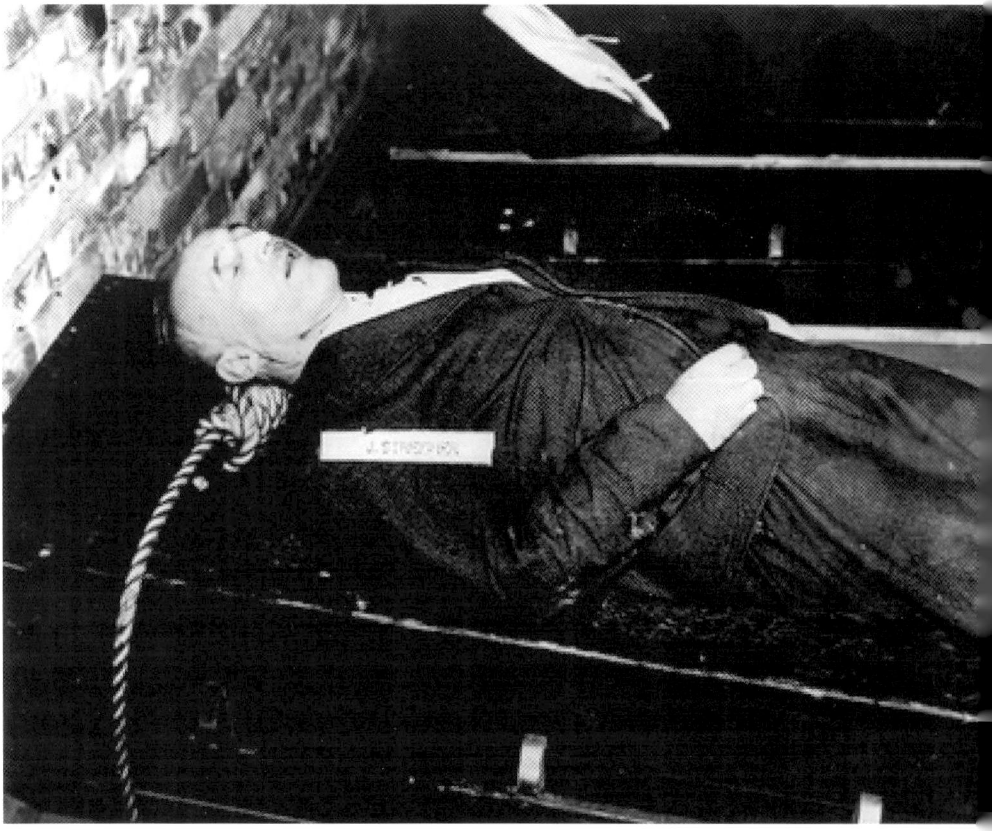

Britain's bemused Foreign Minister Lord Halifax (left) entertained in November 1937 by Hermann Göring on his hunting estate.

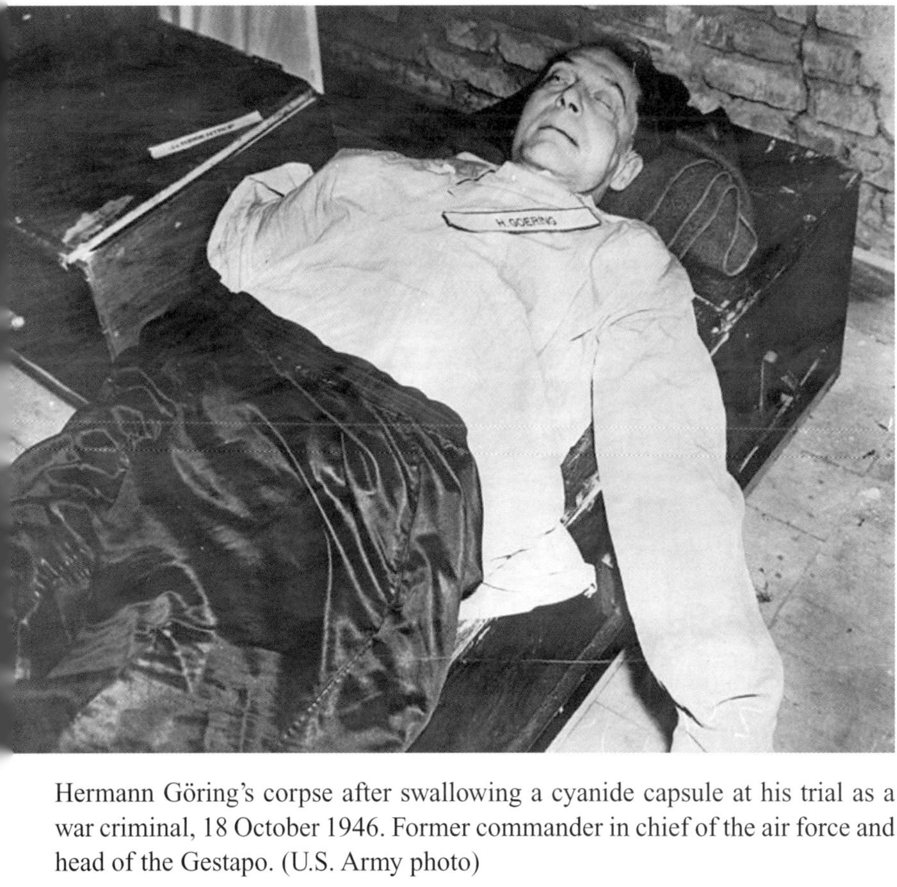

Hermann Göring's corpse after swallowing a cyanide capsule at his trial as a war criminal, 18 October 1946. Former commander in chief of the air force and head of the Gestapo. (U.S. Army photo)

Left: Austrian-American psychoanalyst Wilhelm Reich who treated patients he described as "The Impulsive Character" in Vienna's polyclinic. (1922).

Below: The need for psychoanalysis in Germany and Austria. Front row: Psychoanalysts Sigmund Freud, G. Stanley Hall, and Carl Jung. Abraham Brill, Ernest Jones, Sándor Ferenczi standing behind. 1909.

Above left: Psychotherapist Otto Rank was Freud's closest colleague for 20 years. "There are people who create and others who destroy."

Above right: Sociologist Max Weber was an enemy of Germany's authoritarian bureaucracy and its Prussian militarist society (1918). (Source: Canadian Britannica)

The "New Woman" of the Jazz Age: Marlene Dietrich in *The Blue Angel* in 1931. (Source: National Board of Review Magazine for January 1931, Volume VI, Number 1, page 10)

Left: Foreign Minister Walther Rathenau, assassinated in June 1922.

Below: Munich Conference, 29 September 1938. Neville Chamberlain on left, beside anxious French Premier Deladier. Hitler in centre beside Mussolini and son-in-law and Foreign Minister Count Ciano. (Source: German Federal Archives)

Left to right: Field Marshal Hindenburg, the Kaiser, and General Ludendorff at German GHQ. They controlled all German forces in World War 1.

Heinrich Himmler visiting Dachau Murder camp on 8 May, 1936 as propaganda for the so-called "Master Race" and its so-called "concentration camps".

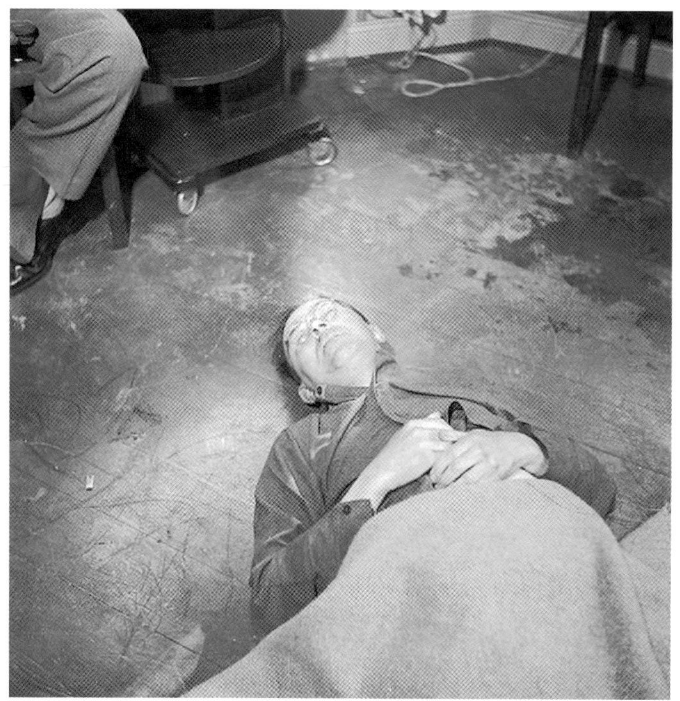

Left: Himmler's corpse after taking cyanide to escape hanging as a war criminal, 24 May 1945.

Below: Typical victims of the Nazis: Hungarian women and children sent to Auschwitz death camp in Poland to be murdered in May 1934. (Source: German Federal Archives)

Reinhard Heydrich was in charge of all Nazi murder camps and slave labourers. Munich 1934.

Heydrich's Mercedes-Benz after assassination by Czech secret agents in British Intelligence's SOE. 27 May 1942. Jozef Gabčík and Jan Kubiš were hunted down afterwards by the Gestapo. They killed themselves to avoid torture.

Captain Ernst Röhm led the SA Brown Shirt Storm Troopers in 1924. Hitler ordered him murdered in Dachau death camp.

Right: Chief Nazi racist theorist Alfred Rosenberg in 1934.

Below: Rosenberg's corpse after he was hanged as a war criminal, 16 October 1946.

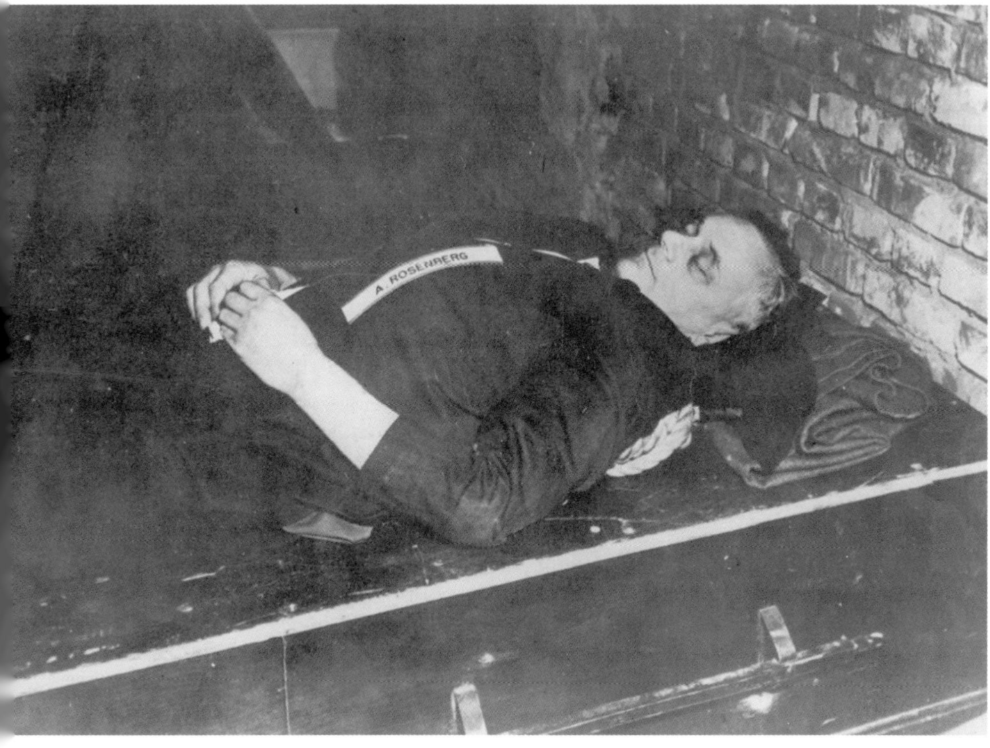

Rudolf Hess, Deputy Führer of the Nazi Party in 1933, had championed Hitler from the start. He was thought to be deranged. He hanged himself in his prison cell. (Source: German Federal Archives)

Britain's ineffective prewar prime ministers. Left to right, Ramsay MacDonald, Labour (1923); Stanley Baldwin Conservative (1920), Neville Chamberlain Conservative (1937).

Winston Churchill confided his anxiety to Foreign Secretary Lord Halifax, prior to the Munich Agreement with Hitler in 1938.

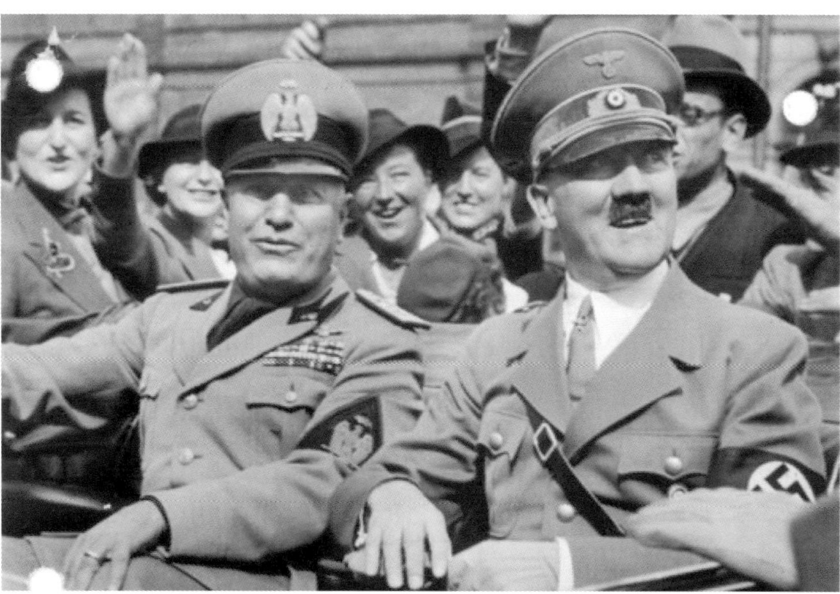

After tricking everyone, Hitler and Mussolini drive triumphantly through cheering crowds in Munich on September 29, 1938, to sign an agreement that would keep Britain and France out of a German war to invade Europe, North Africa, the Americas, and then the whole world. The Munich Agreement would lead to World War Two and the Holocaust.

Mussolini was machine-gunned to death with his mistress by anti-Fascist partisans. His body was stoned by a mob who wanted to end the war. Their corpses were hung upside down in public with other Fascists on 29 April, 1945.

"Peace in Our Time." September 30, 1938. Britain's Prime Minister Neville Chamberlain waves his useless agreement with Hitler for the media, while Foreign Secretary Lord Halifax in bowler hat, modestly stands back to show who is responsible for the sell-out.

20

Germany's Iron Cage

Churchill turned fifty-nine on 30 November 1933. On reflection, it seemed that there was nothing more he could do. He spent much of the time over the winter months working with Maurice Ashley on the second volume of his *Marlborough* biography. Nevertheless, in a broadcast on 16 January 1934 he talked of the need for alliances to prevent a return to war, not only with former Allies but also neutrals including the Netherlands, Denmark, Norway, Sweden and Switzerland.

That was not all. He also wrote fifty articles, which were published in newspapers and magazines, and made more than twenty speeches during 1934. Their main line of reasoning was the need to defend Britain. At the same time, he urged on the House of Commons the necessity of aiming for Britain's air superiority, and to begin reorganising civil factories to switch speedily to war purposes. The responsibility of the Government, he said, was to lead, and not wait for public opinion to wake up to the danger when it was too late.

Prime Minister Baldwin appeared to be listening to Churchill's warnings for the first time when the Government pledged on 4 March not to let the size of the Royal Air Force fall below Germany's.

Despite that, the leader of the opposition Labour Party, Clement Attlee, declared on 8 March that there was no need to increase air arms, while the Liberal Party's spokesman, Archibald Sinclair, called it a folly to accumulate armaments.

Churchill attempted to convince them of the reality of the situation, no doubt remembering being told that members of Parliament were ignorant of the facts. They also lacked imagination. He warned them that the 'air sports' segment of the aircraft industry in Germany was capable of developing a powerful offensive and defensive air force very rapidly. Their autocrats were in full control. In only a year or eighteen months, that gifted nation could have the means to threaten the heart of the British Empire.

Three days later, Churchill wrote to Sir Samuel Hoare, 'No time should be lost in doubling the Air Force.'

On 21 March, he recommended to the House that a Ministry of Defence should be created to coordinate the supply and planning needs of the Army, Navy and Air Force under a single Minister. The Cabinet rejected both of his proposals, jeering at him that it would be impossible to find anyone big enough to handle such a huge responsibility – although it was one he had undertaken successfully himself as Minister of Munitions in the previous war. Nevertheless, they continued to mock him.

One of Churchill's closest friends, F.E. Smith, had died four years earlier. Now Winston's cousin, Sunny, a close friend since they were children, died of cancer. Their deaths caused Winston to admit that, for the first time in his life, he had begun to feel old. He was immediately told off by Lady Lambton, who said that he was letting them all down, and that he was still 'a promising lad'.

He was deeply affected when, 'On June 30, Hitler ordered the murders of his senior rivals in the Nazi Party, as well as the killing of a former Chancellor, General Schleicher, and several prominent Catholics.'

The whole matter of Germany now gave off a ruthless, lurid, and uncanny image of a sinister tyrannical state in which Hitler now held the powers of both Chancellor and President, and had obliged all German armed forces to swear a personal oath of 'unconditional obedience' to him as their Commander-in-Chief, like a medieval warlord.

Hitler's complete control over the life of every single individual in Germany, with their consent, resulted from Prussian military traditions to command and expect immediate obedience.

'Closely linked with the army as a central institution in German life was the Civil Service.' Even as early as 1910, sociologist Max Weber saw in it the future rule of western civilisation and 'the death of spontaneity and freedom'. His brother Alfred Weber demonstrated in an essay 'that Germany then had 150,000 bureaucrats to 500,000 workers' in commerce, and 800,000 bureaucrats to 8,500,000 workers in industry. Practically every German was 'controlled in an iron cage'.[1]

Perhaps the point was close when Churchill may have realised that Adolf Hitler possessed a psychopathic and antisocial personality – if he had not already done so. Germany's dictator behaved like a sleepwalker who had convinced himself that his mental delusions were real. He had already stepped over the line into a state of hallucination, encouraged by having the entire German nation willing to place their lives in his hands. But, on an objective historical level, Churchill was evidently mesmerised by Hitler's extraordinary achievements. He did not know exactly what to make of the situation, because he had no idea of Hitler's grotesque plans. All that Winston could attempt to ensure was that, at least, the British Isles were protected from the expected Nazi onslaught.

Air Power

Churchill's priority now was the air defence of Britain, since it was abundantly clear to him that air power trumped every other type of war on land and sea. He spoke of it to his Epping constituency on 7 July 1934. He had recognised by now that Britain's air force had to be an overwhelming power to succeed. He wanted the Government not only to double its size, but then to redouble it.

Herbert Samuel accused him in the House of Commons of 'running amok'. And the always well-mannered Eden, who had just recently been appointed Lord Privy Seal, was still calm and polite about the situation, explaining where he differed – with respect – from his Right Honourable Friend the Member for Epping, in that 'he seems to conceive that in order to have an effective world consultative system nations have to be heavily armed. I do not agree.'

Labour leader Clement Attlee followed by remarking dismissively of Hitler, 'I think we can generally say today that his dictatorship is gradually falling down.'

Both opinions expressed in the House of Commons were examples of how uninformed and complacent both the Government and the opposition parties were at such a critical situation taking place on the other side of the Channel. They were accustomed to bizarre European antics and had become indifferent to them. Evidently they still had no idea what was happening in Europe. Their ignorance might well have arisen from the budget reductions imposed on Britain's intelligence services at the end of the war in 1918. Churchill had argued against cutting off the flow of important information when the world was in such chaos.

Lord Londonderry wrote to warn Baldwin of the danger of a weak air force. The RAF could neither deter aggression, nor adequately defend the British Isles. There would be nothing to stop enemy bombers from concentrating their maximum destructive force against London and continually bombarding it until they had achieved their aim.[2]

On 18 July, the Cabinet accepted a plan whereby Britain would have 1,465 first-line aeroplanes by March 1939. Desmond Morton informed Churchill that it was not enough, and gave him a list of the air strengths of Britain and Germany, and the Air Ministry's estimate of aircraft production capacity in Germany. As a result, Churchill was able to advise the House that Britain was only the fifth or sixth air power in the world and – at the existing rate of production – would be worse off in 1939 than now.

He went on to tell them that the German Air Force would be almost equal in numbers and efficiency to Britain's by the end of 1935. But if Germany continued to expand at this rate, their air force would be substantially stronger than Great Britain's in 1936. In addition, German civil aviation was three times the size of Britain's, and designed to be converted easily for military purposes. Germany possessed 500 qualified amateur glider pilots who could quickly be trained for military actions, whereas Britain had only fifty. Only if Britain's air force was strong in the air, and allied with that of France, could it act as a deterrent against German aggression.

Sadly for English Democracy, Churchill was desperately trying to do exactly what Prime Minister Clemenceau had attempted to do with France's Government when the First World War had loomed – convince them of the reality of a situation they wished to deny. Their denial had made it impossible for Clemenceau to 'create an indomitable will to victory'.[3]

It was a typical example of how human nature continually repeated its mistakes as a consequence of wishful thinking, instead of facing facts and reacting positively to them.

Few of Britain's politicians, if any, appeared to have read history and learned its lessons. Nor did they seem to have seriously studied the politics of foreign affairs or world events. Had they done so, they would have recognised, as Churchill did, the recurrent repetition of similar situations which could have been avoided if the Government had been better informed. It was extraordinary to Churchill that governments chose not to believe bad news because they were incapable of handling it.

Several speakers were scornful of Churchill's arguments and explanations. Herbert Samuel compared them to a gambler doubling his bets and redoubling 'for terribly high stakes'. Churchill must have felt like *Alice Through the Looking Glass*, where everything was viewed the wrong way round. But he stubbornly refused to be deflected from his argument. He would continue to assemble all the facts he could and press the Government for more vigorous action.

He felt increasingly anxious. But since Churchill was not in the Cabinet, he did not have the authority to do anything more. And yet, he never gave in. His persistence when confronted by rejections was extraordinary, but he knew he was the only individual who understood what stared them all in the face. A three-week holiday he took in the south of France in September 1934 presented an opportunity for him and Lindemann to visit Baldwin, who was on vacation in Aix-les-Bains.

It was typical of Churchill's impatient and persistent nature to create opportunities for things to happen favourably, instead of waiting hopefully for something to occur of its own accord. Randolph accompanied them. So did a great deal of material for Winston's third volume of the *Marlborough* biography. 'Mrs. P' was, of course, essential for taking down his daily dictation for the new volume, and also twelve articles for the *News of the World.*

Churchill, Lindemann and Randolph left Cannes to drive to Grenoble on the old Napoleonic road. It reminded Winston to write to Clementine, who had remained at Chartwell, 'I really must try to write a Napoleon before I die.'

Their visit to Baldwin was an opportunity to discuss the need for a more active air defence policy. And they stressed that a special effort was needed to meet the challenges of air attacks, even if it involved increasing spending. As a result of their persuasive tactics, Lindemann was appointed to a new Air Defence Research Sub-Committee in which he could present ideas for new scientific methods to defend the British Isles.[4]

21

The Old Grim Choices

Churchill prepared a speech for a BBC broadcast on 'The Causes of War' on 16 November 1934. He was assisted by Orme Sargent, a Foreign Office official who shared Winston's anxiety about what Germany intended to do. The broadcast was heard by over a million listeners. He took the opportunity to lay great stress on 'the most brutish of all the evils of Nazism, which was forcing the submission of races by terrorising and torturing civilians'.

But, he pointed out, much as Britain would have liked to detach itself from Europe, it was physically impossible.

He warned that Britons would soon face the same grim choices our forebears had to face – whether to submit to stronger nations or prepare to defend our rights of liberties and our lives. If we decide to prepare, it must not be too late. And if we submit, our choice will involve also the acceptance by other, smaller countries, like Norway, Sweden, Denmark, Holland, Belgium and Switzerland, who will be dominated, perhaps even enslaved by Germany. He assured them that, although war was horrible, slavery was far worse.

Unknown to him at the time, the Government had finally become aware that the British public was impatient with their complacency and idleness. Churchill's cousin, Lord Londonderry, had warned Ramsay MacDonald that it was no longer possible to talk about disarming.

Back in 1922, Churchill had described the twentieth century as a terrible one in which things could only get worse. He had not changed his opinion by 1933, at which time most people's hopes for the future had been left unfulfilled.[1]

Trotsky had remarked that it was a bad time to be born in. The United States, which had hoped for prosperity, was still struggling to emerge from the Great Depression with its large-scale unemployment. Western Europe was facing military domination by a rearming Germany. Czechoslovakia was struggling to hold on to its democratic way of life. Yugoslavia was attempting to maintain a reasonable standard of living under King Alexander, who had chosen to become a sole dictator. Manchuria was ruled by armed Japanese forces. The Nationalist Government of China had just established itself in Nanking after considerable bloodshed, while Chinese communists prepared to regain the military initiative they had only recently lost.

From a purely historic perspective, nothing had changed for thousands of years, since life still involved the continual jostling of tribes to determine which would win and which would lose ground. It was an altogether gloomy situation.

Those empires that had collapsed by the end of the First World War had been replaced, with few exceptions, by unstable kingdoms or dictatorships. Stalin ruled Soviet Russia even more brutally than most of his predecessors including the Romanovs, and kept his forced labour camps in Siberia full of people he wanted to get rid of. Mussolini had eliminated parliamentary democracy in Italy, and his armed fascist thugs had taken possession of the streets. Hitler possessed total power over a militarised Nazi Germany and was building more death camps for murdering anyone who disagreed with him. Austria's fascists were waiting with open arms to embrace a merger with Germany. Piłsudski was still Dictator of Poland. Dictator Primo de Rivera ruled Spain as President of the fascistic Falangist Party. Mustafa Kemal ruled Turkey as its sole dictator. All were kept in power by their military and the secret police. Among them all, perhaps Marshall Piłsudski was the only one who could be described as a 'benevolent dictator'. All the others were tyrants.

Ireland was terrorised by lawless young gunmen of IRA militant squads who threatened anyone who disagreed with them. The Irish republican Army had transformed idealistic heroes into murderous hooligans. France and Britain were among very few parliamentary democracies left. Even though France possessed more armed forces than any other European nation, its leadership and organisation were in a shambles. Britain's own leadership and management was little better. The overriding question was, 'What would happen next, and how awful would it be?'[2]

Air Superiority

To celebrate Churchill's birthday on 30 November 1934, Randolph organised a dinner dance at the Ritz in Piccadilly two days earlier, where, 'The whole Churchill family was resplendent and beautiful,' wrote one of his aunts. And 'dearest and noblest of all, your beloved Papa, who certainly didn't look sixty'.

Clementine felt she had to get away from all the pressures and demands for her attention. She left soon afterwards on a four-month cruise to the Dutch East Indies.

'I miss you very much,' Winston wrote to her, 'and feel very unprotected.'

By 1935, Churchill believed that at last his concerns and those of the Foreign Office were now 'almost identical'. But Ralph Follett Wigram's study of the Air Ministry's most up-to-date intelligence report revealed Germany's substantial superiority over Britain's and France's aircraft production.

Wigram was a Foreign Office official who was anxious to warn of the threat of German rearmament. He helped to prevent Churchill from being cut off from knowing what information the Government possessed about Germany's air strength. Churchill now estimated that the German Air Force would far exceed Britain's air strength by 1936, and dominate Britain in the air.

According to the *Daily Telegraph*, German industry could now produce a minimum of 100 military aircraft every month. Sir Christopher Bullock at the Air Ministry informed the Foreign Office that the total number of front line British aircraft was 453 as at 5 April, without reserves, compared with 690 German military aircraft, and another 160 in reserve. It meant that German Air Force superiority was about 2:1.

The British Ambassador in Berlin put the number of German first-line air strength at 800–850. As well as the implications of weakness in the event of war, the disparity also reduced the possibility of Britain taking an independent foreign policy at the present time. The balance of power in Europe was in favour of Germany. Apart from the crucially important threat of German air superiority, the question was what Hitler intended to do with it.*

Wigram sent a twelve-page memorandum to Churchill on Hitler's territorial claims. What they did know was that Nazi Germany did not intend to keep its present eastern frontiers fixed with Poland or Czechoslovakia. Nor did it accept Austria's independence.

Meanwhile, Stanley Baldwin replaced Ramsay MacDonald as Prime Minister on 7 June 1935, although Baldwin had been doing most of McDonald's work anyway. Sir Samuel Hoare became Foreign Secretary. Eden was appointed to the Cabinet as Minister without Portfolio and responsible for League of Nations affairs. The new Secretary of State for Air was Sir Philip Cunliffe-Lister, who would shortly be known as the Earl of Swinton.

By 4 December 1935, Foreign Secretary Sir Samuel Hoare had come around to the same view of Germany as Churchill, and was anxious at how slowly Britain's defensive arrangements were moving; in particular, anti-aircraft ammunition.

If anyone was both impressed and afraid of Germany's military strength it was Lord Rothermere, the owner of the *Daily Mail*, who kept phoning Churchill daily. 'His anxiety is pitiful,' wrote Churchill. 'He thinks the Germans are all-powerful and that the French are corrupt and useless, and the English hopeless and doomed. He proposes to meet this situation by grovelling to Germany: "Dear Germany, do destroy us at last!"'

---

* Lessons had not yet been learned from the Spanish Civil War because the bombing of Guernica, when a third of the civilian population would be killed or wounded, was still two years into the future.

22

Implacable Enemies

1935

Neville Chamberlain remarked on the advantage a dictator possessed to get essential things done several years sooner than a democracy could manage by having to obtaining a majority vote in the House of Commons. Churchill agreed that democracy was not perfect, but it was still the best system, and they had to make the most of it and protect it, even though they were often hampered by it. He must often have deplored the necessity of having to persuade collective thinkers in Parliament to pass Acts that he regarded as simple common sense to meet the most obvious challenges, while they argued about it among themselves or chose to follow a contrarian party line instead.

Churchill had spent years warning about the necessity of air supremacy and urging the need for more aircraft production. And yet, he was still warning that it was not only London that would be at risk from enemy bombers, but also major industrial cities like Birmingham, Sheffield, and other great manufacturing centres that were essential for making weapons and ammunition. Dockyards, oil storage depots, and railway junctions would also be in danger of bombing. His military training also firmly established in his mind the need for offensive actions as well as the more obvious defensive ones, since only offensive strategies won wars.

Dispersing industries would not be enough preventative action before a state of war occurred. Total war of the type that dictators undertook meant attacking unarmed civilians, particularly women and children.

This would be the year when Italian forces were gearing up to attack Abyssinia (now Ethiopia). Anyone who had been under attack from aircraft would be conscious of the threat. There were no effective mountainous retreats for protection in the British Isles. Nor could large populations be moved from areas where they depended on their livelihoods, like London's dockyards or the Thames Estuary.

Churchill pressed the Government not to neglect scientific technology that could be used against attacks by enemy aircraft. In particular, he argued, Britain had to possess the power to inflict as much damage 'simultaneously upon the enemy' as the enemy could inflict on Britain.

He urged the House to double, or even treble, the amount of money now being spent on RAF expansion.

On 8 March 1935 he wrote to Clementine that the Government, 'tardily, timidly and inadequately have at last woken up to the rapidly increasing German peril'. German counter-espionage had just beheaded two women.

As a consequence of the Government announcement that Britain's sudden heavy increase in expenditure on armaments was due to Germany rearming, Hitler flew into a violent rage and refused to receive Foreign Secretary Sir John Simon, who had planned to visit him in Berlin. As Churchill observed, all the frightened nations were beginning to huddle together at last, because if they wanted to live in peace, they would have to join together for mutual security.

On 16 March Hitler reintroduced compulsory military service to bring the existing German army up from 500,000 armed men to double or even triple that number. Three days later, Secretary of State for Air, Philip Sassoon, announced in the House of Commons an increase of over forty RAF squadrons in the next four years. He aimed for 50 per cent air superiority over Germany. But no one knew if they had four years left.

Churchill feared that the moment had passed when Britain might have had a secure margin for air dominance, and claimed that Britain was in an extremely dangerous position. To Sassoon's assertion that 151 aircraft would be added to Britain's front line in the coming year, Churchill pointed out that the Germans were adding at least 100 to 150 *a month*, and that German personnel were already trained and their aerodromes ready.

According to Hitler – who finally received Simon and Eden in Berlin – Germany had reached parity with the RAF. But, soon afterwards, Churchill came by more accurate information from Ralph Wigram, who was head of the Central Department of the Foreign Office, that German aircraft factories 'are already practically organised on an emergency war-time footing'.

A week later, Wigram sent Churchill more information that minimum German first-line air strength had reached 800 aircraft, compared with Britain's 453. Wigram was shocked at the problems of defending the British Isles. He provided a memorandum on 19 November showing that the strength of the regular German army was now 300,000 plus reserves under training. They were also building more aerodromes. One of Wigram's points was that German production was more and more geared to war materials, whereas Britain's was not.

As Churchill explained later, 'He saw as clearly as I did, but with more certain information, the awful peril which was closing in on us.'

He wrote to Clementine, 'Germany is now the greatest armed power in Europe.'[1]

Wigram was a semi-invalid. He had been a victim of infantile paralysis before and since he had become First Secretary at the British Embassy in Paris. Churchill was impressed by his courage as well as his intelligence and dedication to his job and to Britain. At one time, it had seemed he would not survive his condition. Now it was considered that any further illness would be likely to prove fatal.[2]

Wigram worked hard to help Churchill change Government policy. He urged that Britain should consider the industrial and commercial aspects; transforming factories to manufacture war material and building up stocks of raw materials. Once Germany freed itself from the Versailles Treaty, he believed it would absorb Austria and invade Central Europe. He maintained that one reason for the British Government's inertia was that his political chief, the Foreign Secretary Sir John Simon, 'did not really want to know uncomfortable things'.

That became more evident in a debate in July 1935, when Simon's main purpose in ending it quickly was to avoid being questioned by Churchill. They could not avoid him, but they could evade him. As far as they were concerned he was still bad news.

The tide turned in Churchill's favour when, on 3 May, the *Daily Express* apologised to him in print for having ignored his warnings of German air strength in the past. Nearly 2 million readers must have been jarred by the admission that Churchill's gloomy warnings had been true after all. Then on 22 May, Stanley Baldwin admitted to the House of Commons that he had been 'completely wrong' in his estimates.

'Speech successful,' Churchill telegraphed his son; 'but Government escaped as usual.'

Nevertheless, on 31 May, he persevered by drawing the attention of Parliament to the pro-Nazi movements created by German-speaking populations in Czechoslovakia. He warned that they and Austria, Hungary, Bulgaria, and even Yugoslavia, were now viewing German strength with admiration. His friend Morton wrote to him afterwards, 'You alone seem to have galvanised the House.'

Regardless of recognition, Churchill's friends and supporters were disappointed that Baldwin had not appointed him to his new administration. The reason for this was implied by Samuel Hoare in his first speech as Foreign Secretary on 11 July, when he spoke of those who 'seem to take a morbid delight in alarms and excursions, in a psychology, shall I say, of fear, perhaps even of brutality …'

A Danger of War

Two weeks later, Baldwin asked Churchill to become a member of the Air Defence Research sub-Committee. Winston learned there of the recent success of locating enemy aircraft by radio-location, known later as radar.

As each month passed, the dangers of war appeared to grow closer. In August, Mussolini threatened to invade Abyssinia. Churchill urged immediate reinforcement of the British Mediterranean Fleet, arguing that collective action was necessary against Italy, commencing with economic sanctions by the League of Nations.

'Where are the fleets?' he asked Hoare. 'Are they in good order? Are they adequate? Are they capable of rapid and complete concentration? Are they safe? Have they been formally warned to take precautions?'

In September, a letter from the editor of the *Observer,* J.L. Garvin, reached Churchill while he was painting on vacation near Cannes in the south of France: 'On India you couldn't have more than a quarter of the Unionist party with you.

On Defence you can have three quarters of it at least with you for good, and change all – by stating the case as you alone can state it. I see no other hope.'

Churchill had been talking about Abyssinia to a guest at Maxine Elliott's château. 'It's not the *thing* we object to,' he had remarked, 'it's the *kind* of thing.'

His prescience was always at work, knowing what actions would inevitably lead to unfortunate consequences. Churchill recognised them immediately while other prominent politicians did not even notice them. 'The world had progressed,' he said. The aim of the League of Nations was 'to make it impossible for nations nowadays to infringe upon each other's right'.

Returning to Chartwell at the end of September, he corresponded with First Sea Lord Admiral Chatfield, hoping that a show of strength in the Mediterranean by the British Fleet might discourage Mussolini from doing anything drastic. He also spoke to Conservative businessmen in London on the need to warn Italy against attacking Abyssinia. And he made a widely reported speech on the growth of German rearmament, adding: 'We do not wish our ancient freedom and the decent tolerant civilisation we have preserved in this island to hang upon a rotten thread.'

One of Churchill's vociferous past critics, the poet Osbert Sitwell, suddenly wrote an apology for his past stupidity and said that he spoke for numerous people. At last the truth that Churchill had been speaking all along was recognised – or so it seemed.

Mussolini launched his expected Italian military attack on Abyssinia on 3 October 1935. Churchill reacted by urging the Government to organise British industry for immediate conversion to improve the defence of the British Isles, and to make a new effort to achieve air parity with Germany.[3]

The *Strand Magazine* published one of Winston's articles that described Germany as a country pock-marked with concentration camps in which thousands of Germans were caged and cowed into submission by the totalitarian state. It was a picture of which most people had been unaware, and many thought exaggerated, but one that Churchill now knew to be true. What he did not know then was that they were not merely prisons. The purpose of the camps was to murder anyone who opposed the Nazis.

Implacable Enemies

Hitler was well aware that Churchill was his implacable enemy, and feared that he might be appointed Minister of the British Navy. Others mentioned a possibility that Baldwin would bring him in to the Cabinet as Minister of Defence after the general election in November 1935.

In the event, the Conservatives obtained 432 seats, compared with 151 for Labour, and only 21 for the Liberals. Churchill gained such an increased majority that Beaverbrook greeted him by saying, 'Well, you're finished now. Baldwin has so good a majority that he will be able to do without you.'

Churchill waited at Chartwell for six days for a call to come from Baldwin, but none did. Instead, Baldwin wrote to Davidson, 'I feel we should not give him a post at this stage. Anything he undertakes he puts his heart and soul into. If there is going to be war – and no one can say that there is not – we must keep him fresh to be our war Prime Minister.'[4]

Churchill knew nothing about that, and felt disappointed and frustrated at what he took to be rejection by the Prime Minister. He was now sixty-one. He decided it was time for a long working holiday, in which he would paint in Majorca and then travel to Morocco with Clementine. They took a train from Paris to Barcelona, where Professor Lindemann joined them; then a boat to Majorca.

While Winston was away, an extraordinary event took place in Paris in December between Sir Samuel Hoare and French Foreign Minister Pierre Laval. They reached an agreement between the two of them that Mussolini would be allowed to keep his territorial conquests in Abyssinia. The Italians had invaded and easily taken almost a fifth of the country by then. The arrangement was intended to be a trade-off for an agreement by Mussolini to stop the war, which his modern Italian army was conducting with machine guns, tanks and poison gas against half-naked African warriors armed only with spears.

By entering into what amounted to a private agreement, Foreign Secretary Hoare had flouted the League of Nations's aim of collective security. Hoare had openly appeased and encouraged the Italian dictator by rewarding him with a large piece of Abyssinia, whereas the League should have mounted sanctions against the Italians to stop them.

Mussolini had now shown himself to be not as relatively harmless, compared with Hitler, as originally thought when he'd claimed sovereignty over Abyssinia and warned he was intent on war. Hoare had apparently recognised that sanctions would have been useless against Italy, compared with what Mussolini would gain in territory and plunder by this agreement.

The public indignation at the 'Hoare–Laval Pact' was so great that, ten days later, the British Cabinet renounced it, and Hoare wept in the House of Commons at his public humiliation. He offered his resignation. It was accepted. He was replaced as Foreign Secretary by Anthony Eden. But the impression of Britain's weakness when confronted by the Italians was not lost on Hitler.

Winston was thoroughly fed-up with the Government shenanigans, and remained in Tangier, while Clementine returned to England for the Christmas holidays at Blenheim. He wrote to her that the Italians were throwing away their wealth, since Mussolini had asked all married women for their wedding rings, to be melted down for munitions for his shameful adventure in Abyssinia. Winston was unsure whether Eden was up to his new job. He signed his letter, 'Your wandering, sun-seeking, rotten, disconsolate W.'

But nothing discouraged Winston for long. He still hoped for a Cabinet post, and hurriedly wrote to Randolph, who had become a journalist, to caution him against printing anything that might reflect badly on him, like 'attacking the motives and characters of Ministers, especially Baldwin & Eden'.

23

The Endless Repetitions of History

Churchill spoke in the House of Commons on 2 May 1935 about the current situation of foreign affairs. 'There is nothing new in this story,' he said, "... It falls into that long, dismal catalogue of the fruitlessness of experience and the confirmed unteachability of mankind, want of foresight, unwillingness to act when action would be simple and effective, lack of clear thinking, confusion of counsel until the emergency comes, until self-preservation strikes its jarring gong – these are the features which constitute the endless repetition of history.'[1]

All of that, he said, led to the principal matter of Britain's national defences, and on Britain's foreign policy. Things had got much worse, he warned the House. But they were now much clearer. Germany had worked continuously to rearm on a scale that gave them military dominance in Europe, in order to reverse the results of the last war. They had acquired mastery in the air, under which protection they may also develop land and sea forces that would dominate Europe.

For forty years since 1921, Churchill had been deeply involved in three huge and profoundly complicated spheres of political operation; the Middle East, Soviet Russia, and Nazi Germany; even one of which might have discouraged a lesser civil servant. But his own sense of responsibility and justice demanded that he dedicated himself wholeheartedly to the depressing tasks.

Nine months previously he had urged the Government to double and then redouble the size of the Royal Air Force without delay. Unknown to him, the new Secretary of State for Air, Lord Swinton, had shared his fear that the RAF was falling behind Germany in strength and numbers.

At the same time, the situation in Soviet Russia was just as dismal. After Sergei Kirov's murder by the secret police in Leningrad at the end of the past year, and other death sentences had been carried out by the NKVD – like the trial and execution of three people who had questioned Kirov's death – there were the death sentences of Zinoviev and Kamenev. A direct appeal to Stalin from Lenin's widow led to their sentences being commuted to prison terms. But it was only a temporary measure for public relations purposes, after which they would be taken out and shot a few years later when everyone had forgotten about them.

The public intellectual and novelist H.G. Wells showed himself to be particularly naïve about communism, by imagining that frank discussion with Stalin could achieve what Wells wished for; whereas all it did was provide propaganda for the Soviet Union. Stalin published an interview he had given to Wells in 1934. 'Isn't your propaganda old-fashioned?' Wells had asked him, calling it 'the propaganda of coercive methods'. Stalin had replied that communists 'cannot count on the old world leaving the scene of its own accord, they can see that the old order is defending itself with force, and therefore the communists say to the workers, "Be prepared to answer force with force."'

Stalin went on to say, 'What's the good of … an army leader who does not understand that the enemy will not surrender and that he must be finished off?'

It was precisely the point that Winston had continually made to Britain's Government about Hitler. Both dictators found it easier to get rid of people who disagreed with them. Stalin relished the phrase, 'to finish off'.[2] It demonstrated how to deal with all opposition. He called for those who opposed him, or the remnants of the exploiting classes, or the kulaks, the degenerates, the double dealers, spies and terrorists, to be *finished off*. And he *did* finish them off, as well as his rivals.[3]

There were three show trials of 103 innocent Russian generals and admirals whom Stalin feared might otherwise have drawn followers to them and competed with Stalin for power. The 1934–39 trials were fabricated by the new head of the NKVD secret police, Genrikh Yagoda. All would be found guilty of treason and eighty-one executed. After which, 'Yagoda was charged with having been one of the closest accomplices of Zinoviev, Kamenev and the other Bolsheviks; the very men he had tortured and executed.'[4]

Now it was Yagoda's turn to be 'finished off' and quietly buried.

Ivan Uksusov, the Russian author whose books had been burnt by the Nazis in Berlin when they were being praised wildly by the Soviet authorities, was now accused of being a spy. He was arrested on 5 April 1935 and severely tortured in prison for sixty-two days. His torturers continued to ask which country he was spying for.

Uksusov was sentenced to so-called 'administrative exile' in Siberia. He was transported eastwards in a prison train comprising five goods wagons, with about thirty-seven men packed into each car, and about two hundred prisoners in total. Not one of them said a word throughout the train journey, because they all assumed that everyone else must be guilty. Between Sverdlovsk and Omsk he 'saw other freight trains full of prisoners from all over the country'.[5]

At Tobolsk, he watched a column of 100–150 old men and women, as well as younger women with children or carrying babies. They were relatives of men who had been arrested by the NKVD, like himself. They had been forced to walk 320km from Tyumen to Tobolsk, because there was no railway track. He described how a woman reached a stream and drank thirstily. One of the Alsatian guard dogs leapt at her and ripped off her left breast. As she lay dying, her body was picked up and dumped at the end of the column.[6]

Crimes of Parents

On 7 April, a decree was announced that all penalties, including death, were now extended to all Soviet citizens as young as twelve. It was part of Stalin's coercive propaganda to convince all opponents who had children, like Kamenev and Zinoviev, that the sins of the parents would be avenged on their children. Word was spread that thousands, perhaps tens of thousands of foreign spies, saboteurs, criminals and enemies of the people had infiltrated the Soviet Communist Party over the previous years.[7]

Most types of statistics featuring outstanding achievements by Russian railway men and other workers that appeared in newspapers, were aimed at showing the world how Stalin's Russia was meeting its industrial goals, like loading 86,742 trucks in one day of production from Soviet factories. Realising that cinema could be their most powerful propaganda medium, Soviet authorities also planned Russian film studios in the Crimea. One of Eisenstein's films justified a son betraying his father.[8] Another youngster was declared a hero for telling the authorities where his father and grandfather had hidden grain. In Airograd, a man shot his best friend when discovered to be a traitor; in another, a wife shot her husband as a hidden enemy of the State. It was how social re-engineering worked by educating others and the next generation in spying on their own family and betraying them to the secret police. No one was safe.

Much of this was known by British socialists who averted their eyes from it in the interest of spreading socialism in England. Loyalty to the Party was considered to be more politically correct than loyalty to family, friends, or truth. Denunciations were an opportunity to settle old scores. Socialism was more important than people.

Sidney and Beatrice Webb in England wrote, as if for a child's book of fairy tales, how some 'foreigners are apt to think of [Stalin] as a dictator, being merely principal secretary of the organisation, a post from which he could at any moment be dismissed by the highest committee'.

That they would deliberately suppress the truth about the dangers of Marxism to mislead the British public made them the Pied Pipers of socialism, who played a liberating and seductive tune to captivate their followers while leading them into the trap of a totalitarian state under a ruthless dictator. The disillusioned socialist H.G. Wells described the Webbs as 'short-sighted, bourgeois manipulators'.[9]

The Bourgeoisie

Ordinary people remained puzzled at the mystery of why so many left-wing intellectuals detested the middle classes, when most of them came from middle-class families themselves. Lenin had been brought up in a comfortable middle-class home in the respectable city of Perm. Trotsky, Karl Marx and Friedrich Engels came from similar backgrounds. Freud claimed that those who rebelled against authority were the same juveniles who had previously rebelled against the authority of their father. He had seen and heard it all from his emotionally unbalanced patients, and was convinced that it was childish resentment against a father's discipline that produced rebels against the nation and the world.

Historian Tony Judt wrote, 'The notion that what is wrong with bourgeois democracy is the adjective rather than the noun was a truly brilliant innovation on the part of Marxist rhetoricians.' Co-author Snyder added, 'The bourgeois-democracy association always seems to me a brilliant Freudian adaptation on the part of the Marxists; it means that you can be against the lawyer-father or the banker-father while remaining at liberty to enjoy the privileges of childhood and childish rebellion.'[10]

If Marx was the first public intellectual who had managed to disparage the so-called 'bourgeoisie', from which he himself stemmed, it was Lenin who had managed to fill the word with contempt by the way he used it. Both condemned numerous categories of people to have them exterminated. Lenin was possibly the first influential public figure to use identity politics to dispose of competitors. Since he could not control a parliamentary democracy like England, he would criticise its actions contemptuously as '*bourgeois* democracy'.

The Soviet Revolution was Lenin's invention, and he was determined to control it when he arrived back in Russia by train. It, and everything else he invented, was an egocentric projection of himself. It was not his ideology that won over his followers: they did not understand it. It was his powerful self-confidence that prevented them from arguing. He sneered at nations that Soviet Russia lost to other ideologies, as '*bourgeois* republics'. Self-determination of countries that opposed him became '*bourgeois* self-determination'. He was a master of propaganda in the way he added special meanings to words, according to his approval or disapproval.

The phenomenon of widespread communism is not easy to explain, except to say that it promised all sorts of seductive benefits that no one could deliver. For many recruits it was an escape from grim reality into a fantasy that offered hope. The communist fantasy was as delusional as the fantasy of the Nazis. Both were fictions. And each used propaganda instead of evidence for their theories.

Most recruitment took place typically when young candidates were still growing up and searching for an identity, when they were still naive and suggestible. Neither doctrine had to fulfill the promises it made to impressionable young recruits. Like Sartre did, they were told to 'judge communism by its intentions and not by its actions'. The end justified the means.

24

Dead Past and Unknown Future

1936

At this stage in Winston Churchill's life, according to one biographer:

> He was now well into his fifties and had acquired a more impressive presence than when he was younger … his face was fatter, readily delivering the chubby, saucy looks which encouraged the impression that he was always good humoured and nice to everybody. In fact, he was not always nice to everybody. He could put on a good show of benevolence in public, but the truth is that he didn't enjoy mixing with people he didn't already know and, unless embarking on a well-prepared for public occasion or in the House of Commons, he much preferred being in private with familiar faces around him. Without thinking about it, he had grown into the style of taking servants for granted. He had and he would retain a way of looking at subordinates and inconsequential strangers described by them variously as staring, scowling or glowering; sometimes, if there was a group of them, facing them down one by one. He was bossy and demanding, good humoured and genial so long as he wasn't thwarted. He couldn't cope without a manservant or valet and he was unselfconsciously accustomed to having himself fussed over and looked after, and to living well. Winston, said his bosom friend F.E. Smith, 'is a man of simple tastes. He is always prepared to put up with the best of everything.'[1]

Criticising Churchill became a sport, with the result depending entirely on the personal opinions of his judges. But, most importantly, it was what people chose to do that mattered, and not their personal quirks. Churchill was little different from other men of his status at the time. Some biographers might define it as autocratic, but it was just as characteristic of the late-Victorian and Edwardian upper middle class who found it prudent to mix only with their own kind. It was still a time when one of the most important social virtues was to show respect for the privacy of others. People of all classes learned not to intrude in other people's private affairs. As for strangers with abrasive manners who were a disruptive force and required correction, they might receive a reproachful glare from a busy older person, to remind them to behave, and sometimes even a stern reprimand of 'Manners!'

Those who were not alive when Churchill was would be unlikely to know that he was not exceptional in that regard, since codes of behaviour in England were more formal than they are today. They changed with the reinterpretation of democracy. Social customs became more relaxed around the time he died, in what became known as the permissive society. It began with ridiculing authority figures. Prior to that, and during Churchill's middle age, gentlemen preferred their own clubs to avoid mixing with strangers who might not share their values. With new public transport systems, like buses, trams and trains, new forms of courtesy had to be invented and adopted when meeting or sitting beside strangers, so as not to offend them. Separating oneself from others or remaining silent avoided a great deal of embarrassment.

Even among their own kind inside their private clubs, members took care, as a matter of gentlemanly consideration, not to interfere with the composure of others. Hiding behind an outstretched newspaper was one means of escape. Another was to follow the club rule of absolute silence. Private dinner clubs were, after all, a refuge for former officers who could never forget the horrors of war. They were an escape from all that.

Churchill's own composure had not been at all ruffled by the scandalous gossip about the young heir to the throne who had taken up with an American tart – as some described her – who apparently did not know her place and managed to offend British society. Churchill had served Queen Victoria, King Edward and King George loyally and was generally comfortable with the charismatic but limited powers of the monarchy in a parliamentary democracy. And now he tarnished his political record by supporting the debonair Duke of Windsor, with whom he had always been on friendly terms, and who was now involved romantically with the American divorcée Mrs Wallace Simpson.

When she and the heir to the throne became a media scandal, because she was about to divorce her second husband, Winston stood by them, while others recognised that she appeared to have mesmerised the new king to a point where he might insist that she should be his queen, or he would abdicate the throne.

The royal dilemma was settled largely by public opinion, which was heatedly against the idea of any intrusion into the royal line by a woman who was suspect in the eyes of most of the population of Great Britain. Evidently she had a hold over the king, which those in the know recognised was a sexual one.

Churchill erred in his judgement by taking up Edward's cause in Parliament, largely because he had been encouraged by his close friend, the media baron Lord Beaverbrook, and his influential newspapers, the *Evening Standard* and the *Sunday Express*. Winston had misjudged popular opinion, which was revealed when he attempted to speak on the new king's behalf in the House on 7 December. He was astonished to find himself shouted down from all sides. His views on the liaison encouraged his opponents to claim he had poor judgement.

The Drift to War

Most people in Britain were still unaware of what was really happening on the other side of the English Channel, particularly in Germany. Their *laissez faire* attitude was fairly typical, and continued with a feeling that nations had to resolve their own internal problems, providing they did not stir up turmoil in Europe. Churchill, who did know what was going on, was deeply committed to prevent any threat to Britain.

He refused to keep silent. But even with his tempestuous nature, he knew that Britain was not strong enough to threaten or even negotiate diplomatically with the Nazis and expect to succeed.

When Britain finally began rearming at his instigation, he was reassured by the strength of the Royal Navy's fleet of battleships in the Baltic and the Mediterranean. What he did not anticipate was the threat by Japan in the Far East.

He still viewed the Japanese as traditionally cautious, conservative, sensible and prudent, and failed to take into account the effects of their industrial rebirth. They had, after all, previously been Britain's ally. In any case, he felt that the British Navy was 'virtually immune from destruction'.[2]

Dominance of the seas still meant world dominance. But the arms race had stimulated an energetic increase in the effectiveness of new weapons of war and technologies to outwit and outfight enemies, whether with submarines or detection finders, or the mechanisation of cavalry regiments with light and heavy tanks. As for fighter and bomber aircraft, and new military skills, inter-service rivalries had prevented the Royal Navy from coming to terms with the superiority of air power. But it had certainly not escaped Churchill's attention, although at this stage no one understood how dramatically air power would change war. They would not have to wait much longer to find out, when the Spanish Civil War commenced on 17 July 1936.

The most important of Britain's allies at the time was France, which was submerged beneath its frequent bouts of pessimism, fatalism, and defeatism – three ingredients destined to cause disaster and defeat.

Nevertheless, with his confidence in the navy and his steady new focus on British air superiority, Churchill had been strategically prescient, and believed that Britain could win a war against a German air assault on the British Isles. He had been one of the first to recognise the value of air power in the previous war. Now he realised that London was a sitting target from the air, and Britain's defences against the most powerful air force in the world were 'a scandal' of unpreparedness.

Despite the contributions of Professor Lindemann's imagination, ideas and innovations, the Air Defence Research Committee thought them unrealistic and thereby limited themselves to a conventional and lukewarm approach. Lindemann was well ahead of them scientifically, and Churchill was far ahead of them intellectually, so the Cabinet could not understand either of them.

To those sophisticated enough to recognise the dangers, Churchill emerged as a 'prophet from the wilderness'. Even then, the Government continued to distance itself from him. It was partly due to Baldwin's indolence. The Prime Minister's reputation had dropped sharply. He was not an imaginative man, and might be described as little more than a time-server, like Ramsay MacDonald. He had recently been obliged to take time off to stem a nervous breakdown in the summer. Other members of the Government and civil service, too, kept their distance from Churchill, for fear of risking him 'stirring things up'.

As Baldwin's reputation suffered, Churchill's blossomed.

Even so, unknown to Churchill, the Cabinet had decided against setting up a shadow armaments industry, because it might prevent normal trade and adversely affect the economy. But there was growing demand by the media and in Parliament for a Minister of Defence. Hankey and Admiral Fisher were the two most prominent advocates. 'What I want,' wrote Hankey, 'is something that will work and not upset the psychology of the whole machine.'

It was typical of the cautious compromises and hesitance of the Foreign Office, the War Office and the Admiralty, which pleased no one. What they did not want was a disruptive influence. Fisher wrote to Neville Chamberlain on 15 February, that the future minister should be a disinterested type of individual with no personal axe to grind and no ambition to make a significant career for himself. He suggested Lord Halifax, who had already made a place for himself in history as Viceroy of India. He was a solemn high-church Christian gentleman dedicated to serving his country.[3]

Some others, like Austen Chamberlain, who had turned down the job, felt that the ideal man was Churchill. But he hardly fitted the job definition.

Sam Hoare met Baldwin on 23 February, and then told Neville Chamberlain that the Prime Minister did not intend to appoint Churchill as Minister of Defence. When Churchill wrote to tell Clementine, she replied, 'My darling, Baldwin must be mad not to ask you to help him.'

The Right Man

Winston had other supporters apart from his devoted wife. Harold Macmillan and Lord Castlereagh had begun a whispering campaign on Churchill's behalf. Even Neville Chamberlain remarked to a friend, 'Of course it is a question of military efficiency; Winston is no doubt the man.'

Hoare certainly was not, if only because of the way he had embarrassed the Government over his initiation of the Hoare–Laval Pact, which they had been hastily obliged to scrap. Kingsley Wood did not want the job; he wanted to be Chancellor. Sir Robert Horne had no intention of giving up a lucrative directorship in the City for it. As for Churchill, despite his previous experience in munitions, he knew the position would be a burden because Britain was so far behind in defence, and Germany's capability to produce more aircraft was demonstrable.

Even when Hitler's forces invaded the Rhineland, which had been demilitarised by the Allies in 1919, Labour Minister Clement Attlee opposed the Government's new Defence White Paper intended to expand the British Army, the Navy and the Air Force. Attlee, a mild man, thought the defence proposals were 'too bellicose'. Churchill praised them as a belated step in the right direction. But he added that, even with the intention of manufacturing an increasing number of armaments, Britain was unsafe, due to the fact that it lacked 'the expansive power of the industrial plant'.

He wished to counter the delusion that Britain was catching up on Germany. On the contrary: 'All this year and probably for many months next year Germany will be outstripping us more and more.'

Ironically, Herbert Fisher's new history of Europe had been published in three volumes at the beginning of the year. In it, he stated that: 'The fact of progress is written plain and large on the page of history; but progress is not a law of nature. The ground gained by one generation may be lost by the next.'[4]

It was very largely what Churchill had been warning in the House and in his press articles for years. American journalist John Gunther remarked on how the civilisation on which Europe had been built was now being overshadowed by Hitler and Stalin, both of whom were now taking an interest in influencing Spain, which was struggling between the dominance of the extreme left and the extreme right parties.

It had begun to be suspected that Germany was run by 'a handful of desperadoes'. The idea of a Nazi-controlled Europe, or England dominated by Nazi criminals, was repugnant to Churchill. It did not mean diplomatic relations were out of order: on the contrary, they were essential to avoid war. The last chances for peace were fading. But negotiating from a weak position was bound to fail. The main question now was how many people in Britain had the stomach for a fight, if it came; since the chronology of events was leading almost inevitably to war.

Churchill wanted a coordinated plan led by the League of Nations, to help France challenge Germany's invasion of the Rhineland. But any attempt to resolve situations by diplomatic means was weakened by the military deficiencies of those nations who might participate, including Britain. It caused them to pause to recognise that diplomacy was useless without the power to carry it out. And the British Government found itself cornered by restraints that limited its action.

Churchill's article in the *Evening Standard* warned of 'the horrible, dull, remorseless drift to war in 1937 or 1938'. According to him, there was only one way to stop it: by putting together an overwhelming moral and physical force in support of international law.

In the end, the Government chose Attorney General Sir Thomas Inskip as Britain's new Minister for Co-ordination of Defence. The appointment was described by the retired Admiral Sir William Goodenough, as 'a mountain giving birth to a small mouse'. The Government had aimed at modesty on purpose, to avoid shaking up anyone or upsetting any department.

As Chamberlain confided to his diary, the invasion of the Rhineland had created an excellent reason for getting rid of both Winston and Samuel Hoare, because both had reputations in Europe that might be dangerous if they were in the Cabinet, whereas: 'Inskip would create no jealousies. He would excite no enthusiasm, but he would involve us in no fresh perplexities.'[5]

25

Hitler's Territorial Ambitions

Before invading the Rhineland, Hitler met with his General Staff and listened equably to their objections and fears, and warnings that the French would react strongly against the invasion. Brushing aside their objections, he replied with complete self-confidence, 'France won't move an inch.'[1]

He instructed the German forces to return if there was any resistance from either French or British troops. They found none when they entered it on 7 March 1936 and duly annexed the territory without a shot having to be fired. Hitler offered to negotiate afterwards, to settle any Anglo-German differences.

The Rhineland had been part of Imperial Germany before the Great War and was demilitarised in accordance with the Treaty of Versailles, because France had been apprehensive at German troops too close to its border. Sending German troops into the zone now was a violation also of the Locarno Treaty, which Germany had freely signed with Britain, France, Belgium and Italy eleven years previously, when the Weimar Republic wanted to cooperate with the rest of Europe.

The question that Churchill posed in the *Evening Standard* was: 'now it was remilitarised by German troops, would the League of Nations take the opportunity to re-establish international law in Europe and end the stockpiling of weapons in every European country?' France had already appealed to the League. If the League proved to be powerless and could provide no means to put the fears of Belgium and France at rest, then the entire system of international law would collapse and invite chaos and destruction.

Britain's government indicated to Churchill that evidently he was at odds with their own attitude, which was 'governed by the desire to utilise Herr Hitler's offers [to negotiate] in order to obtain a permanent settlement'.[2]

Uppermost in Churchill's mind when he spoke in the House of Commons on 26 March was the question of whether Austria would be next on Hitler's list of conquests. And would Britain take the lead to organise a union of states threatened by Germany?

Churchill invited Soviet Ambassador Ivan Maisky to lunch, after obtaining Sir Robert Vansittart's approval. His personal relationship with Maisky was very close. Maisky was more worldly and urbane than his more provincial Russian colleagues – most of whom had never been outside Soviet Russia – and had deliberately established a personal friendship with Churchill.*

On 6 April, the House of Commons debated whether to continue economic sanctions against Italy in retaliation for Mussolini's war against Abyssinia. All that sanctions had done so far, said Churchill, was make Italy more antagonistic. It had not saved Abyssinia. One result was that Britain would need costly naval budgets to maintain larger forces in the Mediterranean in future.

In his view, sanctions obscured the real problem, which was the Nazi threat to Europe since Hitler had torn up the treaties and put German troops in the Rhineland. Its 'line of fortifications would enable the German Army to attack France through Belgium and Holland'. Once France and the Low Countries were dominated by Germany, the situation would threaten Britain's own security. Then, he warned, the desperate position of Poland, Czechoslovakia, Yugoslavia, Romania, Austria, and the Baltic States, would oblige them to commit to Germany, or be incorporated into Germany by threats and force.

Hankey wrote to Inskip after lunching with Churchill, to tell him of Churchill's plan, which he thought fantastic. It was to send part of the British Fleet to the Baltic and base it in a Russian port, to display permanent naval superiority over Germany. Churchill had asked Inskip to collect all information about Russia's military capacity as a possible ally. He had also invited Reginald Leeper to Chartwell. Leeper was head of the Information Department of the Foreign Office. Churchill wanted him to speak out in public against German propaganda. But Leeper was a civil servant and had been directed by the Government to 'get on good terms with Germany'.

Nevertheless, Inskip spoke in the secrecy of the Cabinet to support Churchill's request for a new Ministry to prioritise increasing supplies of armaments to protect the nation.

Churchill agreed to speak for the Anti-Nazi Council, which was supported by the trade union movement and prominent members of the Labour Party.

He knew how greed inspired some people to profit in anticipation of war, and suggested measures against profiteering when addressing Parliament on 23 April: 'You will not get the effective cooperation of the working people unless you can make sure that there are not a lot of greedy fingers having a rake-off.'

Churchill wanted the government to set up a Ministry of Supply or a Ministry of Munitions. If the factories for making guns, shells, and aircraft could not be created under peacetime conditions, the government should introduce emergency powers in place of wartime conditions.

A gap was finally opening up and widening between members of the Government who believed that Hitler had no aggressive intentions, and those who recognised

* Churchill's relationship with Maisky was so close that, some years later, Stalin would have Maisky arrested, imprisoned and interrogated in Moscow's Lubyanka prison on a charge that he was Churchill's spy.

a pattern of aggression in the making, similar to the way that the power-hungry Napoleon had become a general and a dictator in careful stages, and then a self-glorifying Emperor who wanted to conquer the entire world. Most of those who did not have the intelligence or imagination to realise it before now finally recognised that Britain's security was at risk.

The Traditional Balance of Power

Some still wavered in spite of that. Lord Londonderry had just returned from meeting Hitler in Berlin. He wrote to Churchill that he would like to persuade Winston against any strong anti-German obsession in his mind. Churchill replied that Londonderry was wrong in thinking that there was any such 'obsession'. He explained that British policy for four hundred years was to oppose the strongest European nation by allying with others to face off the bully. If it were France, he would equally oppose the French. That was how Britain had managed to keep its liberties and maintain its lifestyle for so long. He added a vision of what might come, which was extraordinarily accurate – the Nazis would confront Europe with a series of military outrages and 'ever-growing military might'.

But, for some people like Londonderry – who was Churchill's second cousin – the lesson would come too late.*

Fortunately, many officers shared Churchill's views and his sense of urgency, and submitted various confidential information and ideas to him at great risk to their careers. They involved notes on the workings of the Fleet Air Arm and its problems, such as the lack of training facilities, and the disruption of conflicting systems of Naval and Air Force discipline; inadequate aircraft from the Air Ministry; the inferior performance of aircraft; and the critically far too slow machinery of Admiralty and Air Ministry controls.

He spoke at the first of a series of luncheon meetings organised by the Anti-Nazi Council, where worthies of the Labour Party were present, and felt the public should know that all classes of men shared a common attitude when it came to 'resisting dangers and aggressive tyranny'.

As Churchill's views gained him a greater following, Prime Minister Baldwin evidently resented Churchill's newfound popularity and interpreted it as criticism of his own leadership. He shared his personal annoyances with friends and colleagues, including Thomas Jones, a former member of the Cabinet secretariat. 'One of these days I'll make a few casual remarks about Winston,' he threatened. He would explain why Winston was born without judgement or wisdom and, 'while we delight to listen to him in this House, we do not take his advice'.[3]

* Lord Londonderry's anti-Semitic prejudices muddled his thinking about Germany. He came under attack from anti-Nazis and proved to be unreliable when he attempted to explain his German position in 1938.

Churchill's friends advised him to stop criticising the government if he wanted to be brought back into its influential hierarchy. He answered them and his constituents by saying that his conscience was more important to him than obtaining political office.

But fear was mounting at what was happening on the other side of the English Channel and the deficiencies in Britain's defences. Another anxious serving officer came to Churchill with more information on 25 May, showing that not enough was being done to prepare the RAF for war.

Peter Pans and Wendys

Churchill completed the third volume of Marlborough's biography that summer at Chartwell. He was helped with its considerable historical material by Bill Deakin, an Oxford don, who remarked that Churchill was organised like a clock, with formidable concentration, a ruthless timetable, and the maximum use of available time. He would talk animatedly on an entirely different subject at lunch, and then cut himself off from politics and writing in the afternoon. He would spend time with his family in the evening, then entertain guests at dinner and sit up with them until midnight, without in any way referring to the work he was doing. He would start work again as soon as his guests had left, and not finish until three or four o'clock in the morning.

When Sarah Churchill decided to abandon her career as a dancer in provincial theatre productions to join the Viennese comedian and dance band leader Vic Oliver in the United States, Churchill arranged to meet her and speak with her for about half an hour to explain why he was anxious about her proposed marriage. She understood his concern but was adamant about marrying Oliver, because she was in love with him. But her father insisted on pointing out to her the dangers of losing her British passport and being bound by an Austrian one.

'Do not marry him until he is an American citizen. Otherwise you will be married to the enemy, and I would not be able to protect you once you lose your passport.'

Sarah claimed afterwards that she was left spellbound. She did not doubt for a moment that her father knew what was about to happen; that war with Germany and Austria was imminent – so she gave him her promise.

What was far more worrying than the military build-up on the other side of the Channel was the naive attitude of some Britons on this side of the water who were pacifists. They had the nonsensical idea that everything would be all right if Britain disarmed to show it was no threat to anyone. Novelist Beverley Nichols was a typical example of that shallow state of mind, against which it was useless to argue. He was a popular romantic novelist with juvenile wit and adolescent ideas about life. He had no desire to grow up. He was one of the permanent Peter Pans of England. He remarked to an interviewer: 'I am coming to believe that to follow

Christ all the way is the only way. There is much to be said for the conduct of the Quakers. One must be prepared in the last resort to submit to Force. It is no use resisting Force with Force.'[4]

Nichols was one of many people in Britain who lived a life of romantic isolation from the real world beyond the close-knit circle of his intimate friends. Some, like the poet Auden, professed similar sentiments, largely because the only Germans they knew were their clandestine homosexual lovers.

'Why not Great Britain disarm completely?' Nichols said glibly. 'One nation must make the first gesture in the world. Great Britain should make it. There is, of course, no harm in keeping a few boys in red tunics to march up and down in front of the Palace.'

Another popular attitude at the time among undergraduates and other uninformed classes, was: 'Let the Germans come and rule over us if they will.'[5] Some juvenile pacifists imagined that war would be a bit of a lark that would not affect them in any way. Their adolescent reaction to war provided an example of how estranged many people were from reality at the time, like many immature students at Oxford University. Their view of life was learned at West End cocktail bars and elegant restaurants that resounded with witty gossip, rumours and petty scandals, where the opinion of a bartender or the head waiter formed their world view.

Reality was being faced more seriously and courageously by some intellectual students at Trinity College in Cambridge, who began to wonder what they could do to reshape a world that was evidently falling apart. Baldwin was not the only person who – as he confided to a friend – hoped that if there was going to be a war it would be between the Nazis and the Bolshies.

Emergency Powers

As Winston had expected, Inskip was soon frustrated in his new appointment. On 11 June, Churchill argued for emergency powers. It would permit him to make particular factories switch to wartime production. But Samuel Hoare, who was now Home Secretary, and Neville Chamberlain, were against it. Chamberlain was almost confident that Germany's next move might *not* bring Britain into a war. It was typical of the different attitudes expressed by politicians and diplomats compared with the military who would have to fight a desperate war when it had been left too late to win.

Churchill continued to demand that industry should turn to manufacturing armaments and other war material compulsorily. But the wish not to ruffle the economy was higher on the Cabinet's priority list.

Churchill told his constituents that he had done everything he could to warn the Government of what was happening overseas, and of the dangers of doing nothing about it. It had been a thankless task. Three weeks later at Birchington in Kent, he quoted Inskip as saying that Britain had reached the planning stage, whereas

Churchill pointed out that Germany had completed its planning stage three years previously.

He continued to vary his fortnightly articles in the *Evening Standard* on the same theme. It enjoyed a circulation in London of some 3 million copies. Although they annoyed members of the government who differed from him, he reminded the House sarcastically that the complacent Conservative Party machine had many more channels to spread calming messages to lull the public into imagining there was no urgency and they were doing everything necessary, whereas he intended to stir them up to the dangers of inaction.

In a secret defence policy meeting on 28 July with Baldwin, Austen Chamberlain and Amery, Churchill pointed out that the months were slipping rapidly by. He referred to intelligence material brought to him by, among others, Anderson, Morton, Wigram and Watson-Watt. They showed a need to improve the training of pilots, to make provisions for London's defences, as well as other major industrial cities; to protect the nation's oil supply depots against attack, and to accelerate the work on radar.

He explained that Germany was focusing on training pilots and practising night flying under wartime conditions. He wanted to know if all the squadrons listed for the RAF were up to full strength. He emphasised that: 'Everything turns on the intelligence, daring, the spirit and firmness of character of the Air pilots.'

He had heard that one squadron had only thirty airmen instead of the 140 on the list. Others, he felt sure, were well below their listed numbers. Some had their aircraft being serviced and were therefore not operational. Then there was the gap between planning an aircraft design and its actual time of delivery, and the delay in providing spare parts, since an aeroplane that was not operational was nothing but rubbish.

A State of Emergency

Churchill had been through it all before in the First World War, when he had been Minister of Munitions, providing aircraft, tanks, guns and shells for the Allies. First he had had to set up factories to make them. 'I say there is a state of emergency,' he insisted: 'We are in danger as we have never been before.'

At a second meeting next day, he listed the many items needed. They included ammunition, tanks, lorries and armoured cars, machine guns, bombs, poison gas, gas masks, searchlights, trench mortars and grenades. But even at that stage the trade unions were unhelpful, because they had no idea of what was happening in Europe, and the socialists voted against the estimates.

Churchill still believed that if the true position were placed before the public the situation could be eased enough to prepare the country for war. How could he impose 25 to 30 per cent of industry to making war material with no support, and even opposition from the trade unions?

Unknown to Churchill, Inskip had also requested special emergency powers because of a shortage of building material. The Cabinet had turned him down. The biggest problem was Neville Chamberlain's belief that emergency powers or controls aimed at switching industry from making peacetime products to war products would have an adverse effect on Britain's economy. He feared it might even collapse. Chamberlain was more fixated on balancing the nation's budget ever since it had been his job as Chancellor of the Exchequer.

On 24 September 1936 in Paris, Churchill made one of the most important speeches of his political career about always being vigilant to protect democracy. He said that democracy was a heritage of Britain, France, the United States, Switzerland, Belgium, Holland, and the Scandinavian countries. What really mattered, he explained, was that when we have differences with each other, we can discuss them among ourselves, because we are free; because 'thought is free, speech is free, religion is free; no one can say the press is not free. It enables us to improve conditions and correct abuses, since we are all aware of the shortcomings in our civilisation.'

However, Baldwin was still not entirely convinced of the German peril, or the possibility of Britain being drawn in to a war. He was afraid, as Prime Minister, of not being able to convince the electorate of the danger. As he explained, 'I have never quite seen the clear line by which you can approach people to scare them but not scare them into fits.'[6]

Just as Chamberlain's primary concern was balancing the nation's books, the Prime Minister was more concerned about his own popularity. As for his opinion about Hitler's military ambitions, Baldwin was convinced that Germany wanted to move east. And if he did, 'I should not break my heart. I do not believe he wants to move West because West would be a difficult programme for her.' He added hopefully, 'I am not going to get this country into a war with anybody …'

26

The Hitler Menace

1937

Churchill was hungry for intelligence information after his close friend from the Foreign Office, Ralph Wigram, died. Wigram had provided him with useful information and encouraged him to persist in his attempts to warn the British Government, the news media, and the public of the German threat to the nation's survival. He continued to seek out intelligence reports, and discovered more omissions in the preparations for the defence of the British Isles. Among his sources of intelligence now was Sir William Beveridge at the Board of Trade, and Sir Eustace Tennyson d'Eyncourt, the co-inventor of the tank.

He had tired of continually warning Parliament of the same dangers, and being repeatedly rebuked as a warmonger. He was only a poorly paid Member of Parliament who carried little influence where it counted. But he continued to maintain his correspondence to encourage others to volunteer information.

He wrote a letter to Inskip about what he thought was the Government's indifference to the machine industry. There was no system of controls. England showed itself to be remarkably amateurish when it came to industry, compared with more efficient German industrialists. Now he heard that the armament industry as a whole was behindhand. Most important for Churchill at that time was the aircraft industry, since he was certain that only air superiority could protect Britain in the event of war. Battleships had become sitting targets for bomber aircraft and even fighter planes. The British Isles were a sitting target, too.

Inskip was doing his job to the best of his ability without full government support. He hopefully assured those at the Air Debate on 27 January 1937 that the current programme was proceeding well. But he did not possess the information that Churchill had acquired. When Inskip claimed that nearly 120 of the 124 squadrons promised would be ready by July 1938, Churchill pointed out that, in fact, only 100 would actually be completed. And of those, twenty-two were in no condition to be operational in wartime. Churchill pointed out that 'we have not got the parity which we were promised'.

Two days later he received a memorandum from Group Captain Lachlan MacLean of No. 3 Bomber Group that confirmed his fears by criticising, in particular, 'long-distance navigation, maintenance work and pilot training'.

A Change of Leader

Winston wrote to tell Clementine – who was cruising in the West Indies – that Baldwin would probably resign as Prime Minister after King George VI's Coronation in May. He explained that Neville Chamberlain, who was already doing Baldwin's job, would be likely to replace him officially. Chamberlain became Prime Minister on 28 May 1937. The greater responsibility swept aside Chamberlain's previous reluctance to increase defence spending. Now he sought ways to increase taxes to fund the cost of defending the British Isles.

If Churchill had seemed obsessed by the threat from Germany, he was not the only one. Geoffrey Dawson, the editor of *The Times*, admitted that he 'made continuous efforts not to offend the Germans'.

One of the most efficient skills the Nazis possessed was public relations and propaganda, since they were committed to a game of bluff in which inflammatory words were more effective in getting their way than bullets. Their hypnotic promotional rallies were professionally organised and highly effective in stirring up the emotions of young German men and women, to bind their loyalty to the Nazi Party and dedicate their lives to Hitler personally. Rallies of thousands of uniformed Nazis encouraged cheering crowds of Germans to give the fascist salute and hail their leader. They also impressed and influenced the more conservative British news media in their favour. Newspaper editors became imbued with the potential power of the Nazis to unite the German people against Soviet Russian communism, which they considered was the bigger evil.

Dawson wrote to a friend: 'I should like to get going with the Germans. I simply cannot understand why they should apparently be so much annoyed with *The Times* at this moment. I spend my nights in taking out anything which I think will hurt their susceptibilities and in dropping in little things which are intended to soothe them.'[1]

Soothing meant appeasing Hitler, by those who were unaware of the reality concealed behind the facade of Nazi pageantry and lying propaganda. Even now they failed to understand Hitler's intentions. Among the ignorant and gullible were influential members of the Government and the Foreign Office who were anxious to give the Germans the benefit of any doubts. So was the news media. Hitler, his diplomats and his publicists, shared a keen ability to deceive and manipulate them, so that they unknowingly acted as publicists for the enemy. *The Times* was the most influential Conservative newspaper, read regularly by gentlemen and conservative club men and leaders of the Church, who were still blithely in favour of accepting Hitler's demands.

Churchill was not one of them. He knew that the Nazis were a danger to peace and progress.

Three days after evidence of bias towards Germany by the editor of *The Times*, Prime Minister Chamberlain also looked for ways to conciliate Germany. His primary aim was to save Europe from the brink of war by negotiating a settlement of Germany's grievances.[2]

The insular Chamberlain was unaware that it was already too late. He had become accustomed as a civil servant to the gentlemanly courtesy of diplomacy, instead of the cut-and-thrust rapier-like traditions of international politics.

Deception has always been considered essential for victory by the greatest commanders, since it could avoid the needless waste of troops and arms and ammunition in battles. But Chamberlain's idea of bluffing an enemy was by using the gentlemanly game of diplomacy to reach a compromise in order to maintain peace. However, it was not in Hitler's nature to compromise. Nor was he interested in peace. What he wanted was war. But he was not ready for it yet. His only use for bluff was to buy time to outwit Britain and lull Europe into defeat without firing a shot.

A War of Deception

Chamberlain was too honest for his own good. So was the editor of *The Times* and his like. Their attitudes were evidence that Hitler had already won the war of deception by saying what he knew the British Government wanted to hear. Nazi public relations campaigns had provided comfort for the consciences of pacifists, cowards, and appeasers in Britain.

Unknown to the Allies, German authorities had managed to evade arms restrictions imposed at the Versailles Treaty by having them manufactured in Soviet Russia behind the smokescreen of their propaganda, which had lulled Europe's leaders into a deep sleep, while Germany prepared at full speed for war. They had managed to rearm without discovery for years, and had now built up a huge stockpile of weaponry with which to threaten the West. Their Russian connection had been maintained throughout the inter-war years, as each enemy nation used the other to its own advantage:

> The help took the immediate form of *Freikorps* officers, munitions and in due course industrial expertise in building new war factories. The last point was vital to the Germans, who under the Versailles treaty had to dismantle their armaments industry.
>
> By secretly coaching the Bolsheviks in arms technology and developing new weapons in Russia they were maintaining a continuity of skills which, when the time was ripe, could once more be openly exploited back at home. Thus a strange covert alliance was formed, which occasionally broke surface, as at the Rapallo Conference in 1922 and, still more sensationally, in August 1939, but which for most of the time was carefully hidden: a working relationship of generals, arms experts, later of secret police, which was to continue in one form or another until 22 June 1941.[3]

Chartwell

As Clementine had feared from the beginning, the continual costs of entertaining, heating, maintaining and improving Chartwell had drained Churchill's finances. In spite of what he earned from his writing, he was short of ready cash to pay the bills. He had enjoyed enlarging and improving the house and estate to make it suitable for a man of destiny who had been born in the grandeur of Blenheim Palace. He had so far staved off the possibility of having to sell it, but was now forced to recognise the damage to his finances resulting from the worthlessness of his investments on the New York Stock Exchange.*

He reassured Clementine that they still had a year or two to consider offers. Their children had grown up and left the nest, and his life was probably reaching its final decade. But, 'No good offer should be refused.'

Perhaps Chartwell had already served its purpose by being an impressive home for entertaining world leaders and those who influenced them. And it had become a centre for the exchange of intelligence information from all over the world.

Another close friend, Austen Chamberlain, died on 16 March. They had shared their thoughts together on the form that the Hitler menace might take. Now Inskip wrote some gloomy news to Churchill in private. Since Winston was a Privy Counsellor, Inskip felt he had a right to know that ten of the RAF squadrons would be under strength in aircraft, and some of the others would not be up to standard. Churchill passed on the information in confidence to Captain Lachlan MacLean, and recommended to Inskip how the deficiencies should be dealt with.

He advised him to make a list of all items that a regular squadron required to be operational – pilots, machines, spare engines, spare parts, machine guns, bomb sights, and so forth, with reserve equipment. He suggested that Inskip should make personal surprise visits to squadrons, to cross-examine officers and go through their lists to see how ill-prepared they were.

There were plenty of mixed emotions and mixed signals regarding Britain's response to the upheavals in Spain that had brought it into a civil war between the extreme political right and the extreme left. The British Navy refused to support British ships attempting to deliver food to the Republicans, while Britain's Labour Party condemned the Admiralty for not helping the revolutionary communists attempting to prevent the trend to fascism.

Churchill supported the government line of non-intervention and neutrality towards Spain. He told the House that Britain should not become partisans of either side, neither the communists nor the fascists. He saw the conflict in Spain

---

* Contrary to perceptions of the past in today's consumer society, most people were short of money and prudent about buying new clothes or anything else. His bodyguard remarked on the condition of Churchill's clothing, 'His striped trousers were threadbare at the knees.' It and frayed shirt collars would barely be noticed by others who were also hard up for ready cash.

as part of a scheme in which 'we seem to be moving, drifting, steadily, against our will, against the will of every race and every people and every class, towards some hideous catastrophe. Everybody wishes to stop it, but they do not know how.'

However the Spanish Civil War might end, he wrote in the *Evening Standard* that 'the violence, and cruelties', and the help of outside forces like Soviet Russia and Nazi Germany – for whom it was a rehearsal for something bigger – would only contribute to the rise of Nazi power.

Churchill's reputation had risen in recognition of his broad and insightful world view, while most other politicians were mired in insularity because of their lack of knowledge and understanding, and their disdain for foreigners. Mixing only with people who shared their own views had isolated them from what was happening in the real world outside of their narrow circles. A common wish at the back of most minds was to leave the Nazis and the communists to fight it out.

Among the new Cabinet appointments in Chamberlain's Government was Duff-Cooper as First Lord of the Admiralty. Inskip stayed as Minister for Coordination of Defence, Sam Hoare was appointed to the Home Office. And Leslie Hore-Belisha was now Secretary of State for War. It was thought that Chamberlain would not have to call a General Election until 1940. No ministerial offer was made to Churchill.

Churchill assured the House with equanimity – which he did not feel – that he would take a benign, philosophical and avuncular interest in Britain's new Government, and feel free to speak as a Member of Parliament without the restrictions of being in ministerial office.

Waiting for the Call

Churchill's sources of new information broadened even more that summer to reveal the gap between war supplies needed by Britain's three armed forces and the amount actually being manufactured. He provided suitable information to senior officers in air defence and the Home Fleet. The conclusions of the Committee of Imperial Defence turned out to be the same as his own, that necessary supplies of war material would not be ready by November 1939 as intended.[4]

Despite his absorption in the problems of defending Britain, Churchill was always fresh and ready to take up work on the final *Marlborough* volume, since he still desperately needed money to pay off his debts. Deakin, his researcher, and Grace Hamblin, his secretary whom he dictated to, would be ready for him at ten o'clock at night after dinner, when he would greet them cheerfully and become entirely immersed with his book until two or three o'clock in the morning. He enjoyed their company, which often included Lindemann or Brendan Bracken.

Miss Hamblin remarked that despite being a driving force and a hard taskmaster, she enjoyed 'the beauty of his dynamic, but gentle character'.

But all the time, said another of his secretaries, Kathleen Hill, he was 'waiting for the call to serve his country'.

He wrote an article for the *Evening Standard* on 17 September that appealed to Hitler to stop persecuting Jews, Protestants and Catholics. He ended on a note of conciliation that fell just short of appeasement, by referring to him as a patriot. But he knew that Hitler was only after his own ends, rather than having any consideration for the German people or anyone else. People were there to be used by Hitler. Even so, the events that followed came as a shock.

Wigram had been convinced that Germany was following a policy that would lead it to invade smaller nations on its border: 'slay them and take their farms and houses for themselves'. If Germany wanted British goodwill, Wigram had remarked, it would not commit such crimes. It showed they did not care.

However, still dominating Churchill's mind was Britain's lack of air preparedness; particularly when Group Captain MacLean surprised him by writing to him about an imminent visit to England by a German Air Mission, at which Air Chief Marshal Edgar Ludlow-Hewitt had remarked that the RAF would have to comb the country to find sufficient aircraft for a sham-show to make it appear that Britain possessed an air force.

Forecasts of numbers were one thing, but there were too many ifs and buts to substantiate their actual existence. The moment of truth came at a time when some Government circles had been panicked by a secret document circulated to the Cabinet by Swinton, which revealed that by December 1939 Germany's first-line air strength would be 3,240 aircraft, compared with only 1,736 British aircraft. In addition, Britain's anti-aircraft artillery and searchlight defences would be nowhere near complete until 1941. Britain was in a position of 'grave inferiority'.

Notwithstanding the latest bit of bad news, Churchill refused to despair. He even claimed that Britain's spirit was reviving: 'The working classes are ready to defend the cause of Liberty with their lives.'

But they would not succeed without enough weapons.

At that critical time, Clementine's much-loved niece, Diana Mitford, greatly admired the Nazis. In October 1936, she had married for the second time at the age of twenty-two. Her new husband was the debonair Sir Oswald Mosley, leader of the British Union of Fascists. They chose to marry in Germany in the home of Goebbels, so that Hitler could be the guest of honour. Diana's young sister Unity was so wildly enamoured of Hitler that she did her best to get his attention. And he did attend on her, until she realised he was not interested in women, and she attempted suicide by shooting herself in the head. The bullet would leave her in an infantile condition for the rest of her life. Bizarre though it might seem, there were others in England like the Mosleys.

When Churchill stood up again in the House to denounce Chamberlain's toadying to Hitler and calling it friendship, Winston's local political party began looking elsewhere for someone more amenable to represent them who toed the Party line. He was now in danger of losing his seat in the House. His unfortunate impetuosity might well have been because Clemmie was not there at his side to restrain him. It seems that they might have quarrelled. He missed her deeply. She was cruising in the Caribbean on Lord Moyne's yacht when Winston wrote to her. 'Do you love me? I feel so interwoven with you that I follow your movement in my mind at every hour & in all circumstances …'[5]

Clementine was so moved when she arrived in Jamaica and found herself greeted as the 'wife of the future prime minister of England', by jubilant crowds, that it acted to restore her faith in him, as she realised once again the exciting life that Winston had brought her.

27

Pro-German Feelings

1937–38

Churchill was uncomfortably aware of the effectiveness of the insidious German propaganda that was planned to lull the British into a state of complacency, resignation, even submission, and of the pro-German feelings emerging in Britain in 1937. He had done his best to combat it. But, according to Tom Jones, the previous Cabinet Deputy Secretary, conflicting opinions had arisen in the previous year to encourage all kinds of Germans to be on friendly terms with the British. There were thought to be at least 200,000 known influential British leaders actively working to encourage the nation to ally itself with Germany.

There was also a clash between pro-French factions in Britain who wished to ostracise Germans, and pro-Germans who were indifferent to the French. To counter the latter, Churchill wrote more than a hundred articles in that year alone on Nazi tyranny and Hitler's territorial ambitions. They were published in the monthly *Collier's* magazine in the United States, and fortnightly in the *Evening Standard* in London; also weekly in the mass market *News of the World* with 4 million readers.

Despite his prodigious print coverage of current affairs, the newspapers and the public continued to be far more interested in what Hitler, the leader of a successful nation, said, than what an outsider like Churchill said or did. Many were completely taken in by Hitler's lies. Some were flattered by Hitler's offers of friendship to Britain, and to hear that he admired the British Empire and considered that Anglo-Saxon England was akin to the Germans.

Churchill's cousin, Lord Londonderry, had not changed in his support for Hitler, and now argued that Anglo-German friendship was possible because of Hitler's admiration for the Empire. Churchill told Londonderry that it would be wrong to buy immunity for Britain at the expense of the smaller countries in Central Europe. Nor would it be possible for British people, or the Americans, to allow Nazi tyranny to dominate countries that were democratic.

Despite these beliefs contrary to his own, Churchill did not lose faith in the recovery of Britain's will to resist, or in the British spirit to revive and defend the cause of liberty with their lives, as a consequence of his broad historic view of Britain's destiny.

America was different, and even more divided than Britain. In spite of the traditional isolationism of the United States, President Roosevelt had been making overtures to meet Prime Minister Chamberlain and discuss what could be done to end the conflicts on the Continent of Europe. Anthony Eden supported United States involvement. So did Churchill. But Chamberlain opposed it. More and more, he wanted to undertake a one-man show of conciliation to Hitler. He was supported by his confidant, the insidious Sir Horace Wilson, who played a key role in appeasing the Nazis as Chamberlain's closest advisor. Wilson enjoyed power. And so, evidently, did Chamberlain.

Eden disliked Wilson's influence, and even referred to him privately as 'Creeping Jesus'. Since Eden had been working for closer relations with the United States, he was disconcerted by Chamberlain's rebuff of any help offered by the American President.

Horace Wilson was a long-standing civil servant. He had been Chief Industrial Adviser to the British Government, in which capacity he had helped Chamberlain when he had been Chancellor. Now that Chamberlain had become Prime Minister, what he really needed was moral support for his pro-German stand and his determination to reconcile Britain with Germany and Italy. What he did not want was the Americans getting in his way.

Wilson occupied a room adjacent to the Cabinet room, so that he could slip in and out instantly whenever Chamberlain needed him to restore his equanimity after arguments with Eden or Lord Vansittart over foreign policy.

Wilson advocated close and private talks with German officials, without the French being present. He supported Halifax's visit to Germany, which was supposed to be only an informal social call to join Goering on a hunting expedition on one of his estates. But hunting was only a cover for the long talks that Halifax had with leading Nazis and Hitler.

A Very Bad Time for Us

Halifax reported back to the Cabinet on his return to London on 24 November, and described his German visit. He claimed that he had found friendliness and a wish for good relations between the two nations. Goering had assured him that 'not one drop of German blood would be spilt in Europe unless it was forced on them'.[1]

Lord Halifax, who was always scrupulously honest, had the good grace to admit that his judgement could be wrong, since the discussions had taken place through an interpreter and his visit had been short and limited. But he claimed that all would be well with Czechoslovakia if it treated Germans within its borders well. Since there had been no question about that before, it presented something of a paradox, a question mark, even a possible warning of things to come.

Hitler had dismissed talk of a catastrophe and claimed that the world was not in a dangerous state. It seemed that, in summary, Halifax had been relieved to find what he had hoped for, and considered Germany to be a non-threatening and well-ordered country.

Chamberlain agreed with Halifax's first impression and told the Cabinet that he took the same view as Hitler. The visit to Germany restored confidence in the desire of the British Government to appease Hitler's demands.

As it would turn out, the judgements of both Halifax and Chamberlain about Hitler's personal friendship with them were entirely wrong-headed. Hitler would remark of them later on with contempt. 'Our opponents are little worms,' he told his German High Command at Obersalzberg on 22 August. 'I saw them in Munich … Close your hearts to pity. Proceed brutally.'[2]

Britain's military took a different view of the situation than the politicians. Churchill pointed out to General Ironside at Chartwell that German strength in Europe would be double that of France in 1940. Ironside agreed that 1940 would be 'a very bad time for us'. He was worried about shortages of war material and thought that Churchill should be appointed as Minister of Supply.

During the debate on Germany in the House of Commons on 21 December 1937, Churchill raised the matter of the persecution of the Jews in Germany, which evidently Halifax had not confronted Hitler with during his visit to conciliate the Nazis. Churchill was uneasy about Halifax's visit, because of the sensitivity of the situation in which it might be thought by smaller nations that Britain was seeking special terms with Hitler at their expense.

In fact, there had already been 'widespread commotion' at Halifax's visit from those who disagreed with the Government's stance of appeasement. Churchill told the House that it would be wrong for any nation to give away any territory as a result of Hitler's territorial demands or military threats. He repeated his consistent theme of closer relations with France as the keystone to Britain's security. He believed in the combined forces of France's large army and Britain's naval fleet.

Then Churchill discovered to his amazement that the British Government was now going in an entirely different direction from the one he had proposed, and that Chamberlain did not agree that air parity with Germany was essential.

Sir Thomas Inskip was happy to think that there seemed to be no good reason to believe that Germany would break her word about honouring Belgian neutral territory. Inskip insisted that, since a policy of collective security through the League of Nations had failed, it had to be replaced with something else. Chamberlain and Inskip now considered it to be more important to maintain Britain's credit facilities and its balance of trade. They justified their conclusion by stating that economic stability should be considered as 'a fourth arm of defence' with Britain's army, navy, and air force.

Inskip thought a helpful policy would be 'the appeasement of Germany's economic conditions'. Otherwise, he insisted, there was now no other course than announcing emergency powers and placing Britain on a war footing.

While Eden and Duff-Cooper were in favour of a war approach, Sir Samuel Hoare thought it would cause immense upheaval. And the Secretary of State for Dominion Affairs reminded his listeners that there was a strong opinion in Britain that friendship with France prevented them from coming to terms with the dictators.

Chamberlain was still more concerned with balancing the budget than placing Britain on a war footing, and insisted that Britain needed a clear policy to preserve its finances. He proposed 'changing the present assumption' as to Britain's potential enemies. Halifax agreed with his escapist notion and concluded that they should make more progress to improve Britain's relationship with Germany.

Churchill was dumbfounded at the Government's complete change of direction for the sake of a delusion. After returning to Chartwell from a holiday in the south of France, he found a letter awaiting him from MacLean. It was about training problems in Bomber Command. And, at the end of January, Group Captain Frank Don gave Churchill the latest information on German air preparations.

Regardless of all that Churchill had been attempting to do for the past five years, Chamberlain put forward an entirely new proposal at a Cabinet Foreign Policy Committee meeting. It was for Germany to become an African colonial power. He believed that an offer to Germany of new territories would answer the dictator's call for more living space for a Greater Germany. He also intended to win over Mussolini with a similar offer. He appeared to imagine he was a match for the two warlords; that all he needed to do was offer them land that was not Britain's to offer. It was like the Hoare–Laval Pact over Abyssinia all over again, but on a larger scale.

Changing the Rules

Eden was appalled at the patent dishonesty of this turn of events. He was a man of strict ethical standards and considered that any advance in that direction would tarnish Britain's honour. He insisted on taking a firmer attitude with the dictators. His disagreement with the Prime Minister became clearly evident at a Foreign Affairs Committee meeting on 17 February. Churchill was present and supported Eden. But Chamberlain was now intent on negotiating with Mussolini over possible Italian colonies, including Abyssinia.

At that time, an anti-Nazi German diplomat named Wolfgang zu Putlitz, worked in the German embassy in London. He told MI5 that Ribbentrop 'regarded Mr Chamberlain as pro-German and said he would be his own Foreign Minister. While he would not dismiss Mr Eden, he would deprive him of his influence at the Foreign Office. Mr Eden was regarded as an enemy of Germany.'

Putlitz insisted the only way to deal with Nazi Germany was to stand firm. The Government's policy of appeasement was 'letting the trump cards fall out of her hands. If she had adopted, or even now adopted a firm attitude and threatened war, Hitler would not succeed in this kind of bluff.'[3]

Eden realised that he could not last long in foreign affairs by continually opposing the Prime Minister, and felt he had no choice but to resign. Explaining his reasons to the House, Eden maintained that it was time for England to stand firm and not give in to the Nazis. It was the end of attempting to maintain the rule of law in Europe by placing deterrents in the way of aggressive nations. Britain and its former allies must not allow Hitler's well-planned programme of aggression to unfold.

As soon as Eden resigned, Halifax was appointed Foreign Secretary in his place. He had been Eden's deputy, but had undertaken important diplomatic manoeuvres with Germany because of his former vice-regal status as 'the man behind the throne'.

Churchill finally admitted to despair when he heard the news. The rules had changed and he felt helpless in the face of Government actions. What was happening demonstrated very clearly that Chamberlain and Halifax were set on appeasing Hitler and the Nazis instead of standing up to them. He was unable to sleep that night because it was the exact opposite of what he had been attempting to achieve for years, and precisely what he wished to avoid. To give in to Hitler's demands by offering him more and more territory could only result in him taking even more. It was a truism of English history that every schoolboy learned.[4]

He considered whether appeasement was a rational realpolitik hypothesis, and concluded it was not. He knew how easy it was for anyone to be flattered and manipulated, like Halifax and Chamberlain, because they had already made up their mind what they wanted to believe beforehand. Both were vain. He also knew from history that there was only one way to stop the tyranny of blackmail and threats – it was by crushing the tyrant. It meant war.

The attitude of the leading appeasers was like an attempt to muddle through by thinking wishfully that everything would come out right in the end. It was the same slippery attitude that Sam Hoare had taken with Laval over Mussolini's intentions to invade Abyssinia – buy him off with a bit of land. But what can you do when you know your government is taking the wrong path?

Churchill knew they were afraid of another war, but it was his best option. 'War is terrible,' he would repeat, as the situation grew more and more explosive, 'but slavery is worse.'[5]

Former Foreign Secretary Anthony Eden shared the French worry that if Germany was not stopped now, war would erupt in three years when it was ready.

French Foreign Minister Pierre Flandin was agitated: 'If you do not stop Germany now, all is over.' But Chamberlain was convinced that Britain's finances could not support a war.

Churchill had also been Chancellor of the Exchequer, and knew the state of Britain's Treasury. He also knew that judgement was a matter of priorities. To his mind, it was better to arm for war than have to grovel at Hitler's feet. He was aware that any agreement with Hitler would involve losing the British Fleet and all its safe harbours all over the world. As a former Lord of the Admiralty, he knew that Britain would be powerless without the Royal Navy, since Britain was a small island surrounded by an ocean that was protected by its Fleet. It would be starved into submission without it.

The problem was how to convince the Prime Minister that he was wrong. Winston had often worked with Chamberlain before, and thought he had built up considerable goodwill. But privately he considered Chamberlain to be extraordinarily ignorant. He was also exceedingly stubborn. Once he had an idea in his head, he would become deaf to any other ideas from anyone else.

28

The Munich Dilemma

1937–38

Churchill was now sixty-two. Stress had caused a stomach problem that made it difficult for him to stand up. He was put on a special diet by his doctor, but the indigestion continued.

Sarah visited him in January with her new husband, Vic Oliver. Churchill hoped she would be happy. Light entertainers, like dance band leaders, were considered frivolous at that time of international crisis when there were heavier responsibilities to be borne. But light entertainment was needed by young people who wanted to dance the time away at night clubs. They were not yet aware of the imminence of war.

Oliver earned good money from a radio series. He had become a successful comedian because British audiences found his accent and formal Austro-Hungarian mannerisms funny. Sarah enjoyed touring theatres with him in an erratic and restless life. Nevertheless, Churchill could not take his son-in-law seriously. He was more concerned about defence deficiencies in the British Isles through the early months of the New Year, and people continually asking him for help or advice. He had often to explain that he was not in political office and had no influence on the direction the Government might take. The Government had even approached the BBC to prevent him from broadcasting his views, because they differed from official policy.

'You say it is Government policy,' Churchill wrote to Inskip, 'and yet it may not be right.'

Now that Chamberlain was Prime Minister, the gap had widened between Winston's world view and the government's. There was growing public opinion that Hitler did not want war. Nevertheless, small European nations closer to Germany, like Czechoslovakia, recognised the dangerous situation and feared an invasion by German forces.

When speaking at Oxford, Churchill decided to say nothing of the continual shortages of war material for fear of causing defeatism, but he continued to warn that this and the following year were ones of Britain's maximum weaknesses.

Meanwhile, he carried on dictating his latest chapters at Chartwell, and audiences streamed into the House of Commons to hear what he had to say about the impending war. His oratory and political reputation had been maintained for over thirty-five years. Despite that, he was still not offered a Cabinet position.

According to Lloyd George, no Cabinet Minister would want Churchill 'because of his dominating intellectual force and experience'.[1]

One result was that – although always busy with family and friends, painting and books, working happily on his estate, and entertaining flocks of visitors to Chartwell – Winston felt isolated from the political mainstream. So he was unaware of further alarming news of RAF discrepancies between what was being manufactured and what would be required for war. The Cabinet was told that it was impossible for necessary supplies to be completed before November 1939. It was a year away.

He told the Anti-Nazi Council that, in the absence of emergency regulations, the supply situation could only encourage the Nazi gangsters to acts of aggression and violence. He wrote his views in an article, for the Foreign Office to reply. They thought his article was too violent during the present sensitive state of diplomatic relations with Germany, and might do some harm. Nevertheless, his opinions were published on 17 September in the *Evening Standard.*

What he did not realise at the time was the pointlessness in being conciliatory to Hitler, since he was following a double agenda – to create a harmless picture of his military intentions while preparing relentlessly to carry out his real massive and ruthless programme for war. The result of his propaganda tactics was to put at rest the minds of British politicians and the public by telling them more of what they wanted to hear. He had been hugely successful in deceiving the German public to obtain absolute power. Now he used more temperate words to deceive and disarm the British Government, Britain's media, and the British public.

Power and Resolution

Among the subjects that Halifax had discussed with the Nazis was a partial understanding about colonies. Very likely it was the reason why Chamberlain imagined that Hitler would accept an offer of territory in Africa in exchange for peace. Evidently he had not read *Mein Kampf,* which clearly expressed Hitler's intention to expropriate far bigger territories in Central Europe and Russia, and the Middle East, as huge German colonies, instead.

One of the few who had read it was Britain's Ambassador to Berlin, Nevile Henderson. He had been impressed that someone so little educated as Hitler had written it. He was unaware that Hitler had been helped by his friend Rudolf Hess, now Deputy Fuhrer of the Nazi Party, or that the Führer had borrowed a multitude of ideas from others. Henderson thought it too long and rambling and could have been cut by a third. Since he anyway supported appeasement of Germany, and cared little about who owned Slav lands, he viewed Hitler's memoir differently from most other readers.

Hitler had also raised the matter of European disarmament with Halifax, even suggesting a possibility of beginning by abolishing bomber aircraft. Evidently it was his biggest concern. The British Government thought that 'although it entailed the risk of enabling the German army to dominate Europe', it also removed 'the risk of a knock-out blow at the outset of a war'.[2]

Both Hitler and Chamberlain despised the League of Nations as a sham, since it could not impose its views by force. In the debate on 21 December about Halifax's visit to Hitler, Churchill took the opportunity to express the importance of supporting the League, both as a necessary centre of any coordinated military effort against aggression, and as a foundation of morality in international affairs.[3]

Churchill warned Parliament that the Prime Minister hoped 'that by great and far-reaching acts of submission, not merely in sentiment and pride, but in material matters, peace may be preserved'. But, he asked, what price will we have to pay for it? 'No one can compute it.'

He warned also that smaller nations would move to the side of 'power and resolution'. He added ominously, 'I predict that the day will come when, at some point or other, you will have to make a stand, and I pray to God, when that day comes, that we may not find, through an unwise policy, that we have to make that stand alone.'[4]

However, whenever Churchill spoke in the House or published his articles in the press, there were always dissenting opinions. Whereas *The Yorkshire Press* commended him for expressing the sentiments of the nation, the *Evening Standard* opposed his call for collective action and even cancelled his contract for further articles. But Churchill was a bestseller, and the *Daily Telegraph*, which opposed Chamberlain's policy of appeasement, agreed to publish Churchill's fortnightly articles instead.

Victors and Vanquished

Hitler had also been putting more and more pressure on Austria to become part of Greater Nazi Germany. Its Prime Minister, Kurt von Schuschnigg, had managed so far to keep Austria neutral and independent, despite pressures from Austria's Nazi Party, by believing he had the support of Mussolini. Now, in response to Hitler's threats and persistent warnings, he decided to call a referendum in which Austrians could vote for or against independence from Germany. Hitler told him bluntly that he would not accept it. Then Halifax telegraphed Schuschnigg on 11 March to state that Britain could not be responsible for advising him on any action that might endanger his country, since the British Government could offer no guarantee of protection.

When Mussolini, too, announced that he would do nothing to guarantee Austria's independence, Schuschnigg resigned. German troops marched into Austria the same evening, and the Nazis arrested all opponents. A steady stream of those who had opposed the Nazi regime was very quickly and forcibly escorted to concentration camps. Hundreds of others were shot. Tens of thousands attempted to flee.[5]

George Weidenfeld, an Austrian Jew who would become a successful publisher in England, recorded how on 12 March 1938, 'while Austria began to burn, its youth danced'. Despite the annexation of their country, the carnival season with its masked balls continued as usual. It was the popular *Wiener Fasching*, where everyone wore fancy dress and pretended to be someone else at a whole series of balls. There was the Architects' Ball, the Lawyers' Ball, the ball in the Konzerthaus, the Academicians' Ball, and the ball of the *Konsularakademie* for the diplomatic corps. Since Chancellor Schuschnigg had been summoned to Germany by Hitler, a senior minister, Guido Zernatto, turned up dressed as an Austrian fascist storm trooper, apparently to reassure everyone.

Hitler ordered Schuschnigg to comply with his wishes *at once*. 'I demand obedience,' he told him. 'And I shall enforce it if necessary with my armies.'

He told General Walter von Reischer, who commanded the Munich defence district, 'Before Herr Schuschnigg studies my ultimatum, I want you to take him into the next room and show him the whole of your strategic plan for the occupation and garrisoning of Austria.'

> Suicides were a frequent occurrence among Jews who did not know how to face a future made suddenly so bleak and dangerous. Among those who killed themselves were several well-known writers and lawyers. A British dental student who studied in Vienna wrote in a private letter five days after the *Anschluss*: 'A family of six Jews have just shot themselves, a few houses down the street. They are well out of it.'[6]

The Austrian Nazis were as vicious as those in Germany, brought up in a cesspool of antisemitism from the days of Karl Lueger in the Austro-Hungarian Empire, a racist forerunner of Hitler. There were 200,000 Jewish people in Austria. Some 30,000 were arrested and sent to concentration camps. As threats of torture multiplied, as many as 10,000 Jews were believed to have killed themselves. The Austrian Nazis' tendency to sadism was little different from the German Nazis. Some of the Jews who had managed to avoid arrest and escaped, looked lost. Suddenly, they had no country, no family, no employment, and no one to help them.

III

THE ROAD TO WAR

29

The Approaching War

1937–38

Hitler's well-calculated and well-timed annexation of Austria was debated in the House of Commons on 14 March, when Chamberlain agreed to a fresh review of Britain's defence programmes. Churchill warned against any delay, and again pointed out Britain's grim choices – either to take speedy measures to ward off the dangers, or submit to German rule over the British Isles. He identified Czechoslovakia as the next country likely to be threatened by Hitler. It was a heavily industrialised nation that manufactured and supplied armaments that protected Romania and Yugoslavia. It was now almost surrounded on three sides by a Greater Nazi Germany. Hitler was well aware that without weaponry from Czechoslovakia, all of them would be powerless to resist invasion by German forces.

Churchill was sceptical of Chamberlain's promise to rearm to preserve peace. It was too late for that. He continued to believe that the small states of Europe had to be united in a system of collective defence. But it was not enough, since they also had to believe that they could rely on Britain, when Britain could not rely on itself. Once again, Churchill affirmed his staunch belief in the usefulness of the League of Nations for collective security against an aggressive enemy. He wanted to see a treaty organised by Britain and France. Even at this late stage, he felt, it might 'arrest this approaching war'.

But, even after Germany had marched on Austria in 1938, the Chamberlain Government continued to abandon Baldwin's pledge for air parity, which he had made in March 1937. Inskip told the House of Commons that the promise of 1,500 front-line aircraft had not been made with any assurance that they would not be out of date. He insisted that everyone knew their designs would be obsolete.[1]

Britain faced a dismal state of affairs with no guarantee of protection from air attack and an inevitability of further claims for more territory by Hitler. Only France's Premier Blum declared that the French would come to the aid of Czechoslovakia if it were attacked.

The British Cabinet's Foreign Policy Committee cautiously took a different stance. Its attitude was revealed when Inskip described Czechoslovakia as 'an unstable unit in Central Europe'. It was in fact a jumble of fragments left over from the vanished Austro-Hungarian Empire. He told colleagues that he saw no reason why Britain should take any steps to maintain its existence, since Chamberlain's priority was anyway to please Germany. He believed that Czechoslovakia should be requested to make a territorial concession of the German-speaking border areas known as the Sudetenland. But that mountainous area was Czechoslovakia's only natural defence against aggression. Equally important, it was the source of most of its industrial production and wealth, including its arms industry.

Faced by this new paradox, there was some popular feeling that Churchill ought to be offered an important ministerial role, like Air Minister. As for policy, 'he would have to be kept in chains', said Thomas Jones. But Chamberlain had no intention of appointing Churchill as a minister in his Government, since their world views and intentions were diametrically opposed. He and Halifax rejected Churchill's call for a Grand Alliance, convinced that the majority in the House would agree with them.

Hitler was now not only in complete control of Austria, but intent on bombarding Czechoslovakia with aggressive propaganda to convince its German-speaking citizens and influence the world in favour of his demands. Churchill continued to insist that security for Britain lay in an Anglo-French treaty of mutual defence. In his most recent article in the *Evening Standard* he urged the Government to join in the French declaration to aid Czechoslovakia if she were attacked by German troops. Chamberlain had no intention of doing any such thing.

World Mastery

Churchill pointed out to the House that the victors of the last war were now the vanquished and those who had once begged for an armistice were now aiming at world mastery. But Halifax disagreed that Hitler was after conquests on the scale of Napoleon. He was particularly indignant at Churchill's approach to leading French politicians in Paris for a binding alliance, as if Winston were the Foreign Secretary and not him.

In the first of Churchill's articles commissioned for the *Daily Telegraph*, Churchill pointed out that if France broke, everything would break. And Nazi domination of Europe would look inevitable.

Suddenly, on 19 August, Major Ewald von Kleist visited Churchill at Chartwell. He belonged to an anti-Nazi group of German officers who opposed German troops invading Czechoslovakia for fear it would start a second world war. Churchill agreed with him that, once begun, such a war would be fought to the last man and be destructive for all parties. He felt encouraged at evidence of an anti-Nazi group in Germany.

Churchill's nature was built to challenge conflicts, and also to focus on several tasks simultaneously. He wrote throughout the summer months to complete the fourth *Marlborough* volume and the opening chapter of his *History of the English-Speaking Peoples.* The work was a much-needed distraction from despair and an antidote to the boredom of waiting impotently for the Government to acknowledge what he viewed as an imminent war, unless they acted against it.

Clementine was the one who frequently became mentally and physically exhausted by his enormous energy that produced 'the tensions and exhilaration of life at Chartwell'. She needed long vacations in order to recuperate, while he galvanised himself and others into action. Now he could only wait, while she left for Austria to recover from fatigue and the constant challenge of the costs of him entertaining political colleagues and cronies.

Sarah was now in America with her husband. Mary and Diana were in Austria with Clementine, when he returned to Blenheim for Christmas, after doing his best to calm and reassure Clemmie by writing her a great number of long and tender letters. He told her how much he missed her. He felt lonely without her understanding. Only Randolph was left to keep him company.

Chamberlain kept in personal touch with Churchill, and made occasional optimistic claims that Churchill rejected as wishful thinking. Halifax kept in personal contact with him, too. Inskip had no good news, but repeated the same bleak story that Britain was unprepared for war, and added that it *never* would be: at least not for a year or more. Nor, if it came, could it put an army in the field for many months after the outbreak. It was all very depressing, because it was likely.

Churchill's fourth volume entitled *Marlborough, His Life and Times* was published on 2 September 1938: the same day that Germany mobilised and Hitler announced that Sudeten Germans needed to be protected from their Czech rulers.

Churchill felt that the imminent invasion of Czechoslovakia could be stopped if there was enough protest from sovereign nations. According to his meeting with Soviet Ambassador Maisky, Russia was keen to examine, with Britain and France, ways and means to defend Czechoslovakia against a German invasion. He also wanted to invoke Article II of the League of Nations Covenant under which they had to consult if war was imminent. Churchill passed on the course of their discussion to Halifax. But the British Government did not want to become involved with Russia.

Churchill sympathised with Chamberlain's dilemma while disagreeing with his course of action. He was still concerned about the unpreparedness of the RAF to keep enemies away from bombarding Britain. But evidently the Prime Minister had accepted the numbers that the Air Ministry had circulated to reassure the public, and genuinely did not know the real ones. At least, 'It ought to make Neville think. He does not know the truth: perhaps he does not want to.'[2]

Chamberlain seemed to be single-mindedly launched on his own new policy of replacing parity in the air with conciliation with Hitler, and most of the Cabinet supported him.

Surrendering the Future

Churchill was the first to understand Hitler's strategy to establish Vienna as the centre of distribution of wartime resources: 'Romania with its oil, Yugoslavia with its minerals and Czechoslovakia with its munitions.' Consequently, he referred to the abandonment of those nations as 'surrendering the future'.[3]

'When everyone else has been thrown to the wolves,' he remarked, 'we are left to face our fate alone.'

As for France, which was seen as weak and indecisive, it was continually changing its leaders and governments, as if playing a game of musical chairs. Evidently they were unable to take the imminent war seriously in such confusing circumstances. It was felt better for Britain not to make any commitments with her, and to keep Germany guessing.

Halifax's recommendation about Churchill's idea of a Grand Alliance was that the difficult negotiations it would entail would give time for Germany to view it as a provocation. And Germany could 'dispose of Czechoslovakia' before a Grand Alliance could be finalised. It was 'a disagreeable business', but the Cabinet agreed with Halifax to put pressure on the Czech government to accept Hitler's demands for the Sudetenland. It should be undertaken 'as pleasantly as possible'.

Without knowing about the Cabinet's defeatist decision about Czechoslovakia's fate, Churchill viewed their inaction as leading to a broad and inviting stairway that led down into a dark gulf. Historians, he said, would never understand the Government's choice. He was unaware that they had already spent two and a half months discussing the choice between the need to economise and the need to increase Britain's defence programme. They had simply been muddling through again. Nothing had been concluded because of 'the burdensome cost of defending Britain', as Inskip would explain on 8 February 1938.

And yet, Chancellor of the Exchequer Sir John Simon would announce a budget surplus of £28 million on 1 April. Their prudence with their budgets was evidently misguided – it was more a question of judgement than cash in hand.

Churchill took a holiday, chasing the sun in the south of France. He failed to find it, and withdrew to his room to continue writing, while Deakin remained at Chartwell to correct footnotes and references and check Churchill's added sentences and paragraphs. Churchill dined with the now former Prime Minister of France, Flandin, who was pessimistic about French morale.

On 10 May the *News Chronicle* published a survey which showed that 56 per cent of people who were questioned said they wanted Churchill in the Cabinet. It was at that point when the news media discovered that Churchill, who was strapped for funds to maintain Chartwell, had put his country home up for sale: 80 acres with a floodlit swimming pool, and a fine house with five reception rooms, nineteen bed and dressing rooms, eight bathrooms, and three cottages.

He had been spending too much time making speeches and fulfilling public duties that did not bring in any money. The cost of producing books with all his researchers and secretaries had been too great to pay. Overhead costs to maintain his lifestyle had eaten into his shrinking royalties from writing.

Brendan Bracken examined Churchill's finances and explained to him that, if he could complete his *History of the English-Speaking Peoples* in eighteen months, he would receive £15,000 towards the £18,000 owed to his stockbroker. The industrialist Sir Henry Strakosch agreed to be responsible for Churchill's share portfolio for three years, if Churchill undertook to 'incur no further liability'. Churchill was able to withdraw Chartwell from the real estate market as a result.

30

Overture to Genocide

Most people rarely, if ever, encounter intolerance on such a massive and grotesque scale as Hitler's character revealed by his obsession with serial and mass murders. His attitude towards deliberately killing millions of people was so casual that his Nazi clique of propagandists and police officers, generals and bureaucrats, nimbly accepted his plans in the same matter-of-fact way. Cabinet meetings sought to find the easiest or most cost-effective means to get rid of people. It was made easier by the fact that the main focus of those egotists was their own status and ambitions. There was no time, nor room under the spotlight of ambition and status, to consider other people. Others were merely tools to satisfy their own wishes. It was those others that they talked about as targets for extinction.[1]

A clue to the origin of Hitler's facility to destroy any number of people without hesitation or much thought, emerges from his letters from the front as a Private in the First World War who was still uncertain of himself and forced to mature on the Western Front. One of the few people who had befriended him was his landlord, to whom he described his battlefront experiences 'clearing out the trenches' after an advance, by machinegunning British and French soldiers he found cowering in their trenches when under attack, defenceless and afraid, instead of taking them as prisoners of war. That experience of slaughtering victims would be repeated again and again when he had the power and opportunity to murder others.

> We marched in columns through a forest to our right and emerged with our ranks intact in an elevated field. Four marksmen were dug in ahead of us. We took up positions behind them in large trenches and waited… Finally came the command 'Forwards.' We climbed out of our holes and sprinted across the field… towards a small farmstead. Left and right shells were exploding, and in the middle English bullets were humming, but we paid them no mind. For ten minutes we took cover and then again came the command 'Forwards'… Now the first of our numbers were falling. The English had trained their machine guns on us. We threw ourselves on the ground and slowly crawled forward in a furrow. 'We fought like this for three days until the English were finally taken care of.'[2]

Although most people in the West now take human rights for granted as an entitlement of democracy, they appear to have no idea what had to be achieved over thousands of years to fight for individual rights and establish them in the constitutions of democratic countries. They were finally bequeathed to us as a consequence of philosopher and revolutionary Thomas Paine, who proclaimed that leaders who viewed their people as property rather than citizens were illegitimate tyrants. His book, which had a profound influence on society, was called *The Rights of Man.* It was published nearly two centuries before the Nazis took control of Germany.[3]

Rulers of Germany and Russia had been enemies of an open society for centuries, and still were. Had their populations been treated as free citizens, there would have been plenty of opportunities for open debate without the threat of imprisonment, but both societies were closed and ruled by threats that imposed fear. Thomas Paine maintained that the only legitimate form of government was one framed on a social contract based on a constitution that clearly outlined everyone's rights, responsibilities and limitations. All legislation should be undertaken through parliament, and be aimed at increasing the quality of life of all people.

In the competitive hierarchy of the Nazis, they got rid of others to promote themselves. It involved 'reputation savaging and manipulation by antisocial and psychopathic types.' Totalitarian police states provided plenty of opportunities for destructive and subversive people who wished 'to advance themselves in the reputational hierarchy' by denigrating others. Such individuals 'are so dangerous that they can demolish the structure of an entire society'.

One of the foremost crowd experts with experience of that intolerant personality type was the late Elias Canetti, who had experienced at first hand the magnetism and destructive power of intolerant crowds. He had watched hysterical mobs rioting in the streets and setting buildings on fire in the July Revolt in Vienna in 1927, when he was a student. He had managed to escape from Austria before it was annexed by the Nazis, and moved to England in 1938.

Canetti would become a Nobel prizewinner in literature as the author of *Auto-da-Fé* published in 1935. He won the French *Prix International* in 1949, the Grand Austrian State Prize for literature in 1967, the Literary Award of the Bavarian Academy of the Fine Arts in 1969, and nine other literary awards. In his *Crowds and Power* (1960), Canetti would describe the self-centered cruelties of Muhammad bin Tughluq, the Sultan of Delhi, a tyrant whose overwhelming power and sadism made all his subjects live in fear. The all-powerful Sultan remains as a record for comparison with the almost inconceivable and grotesque behaviour of Hitler.

Fortunately for our understanding of his character, a famous Arab traveller named Ibn Battuta spent seven years at the Sultan's court and 'learnt what it was like to live in deadly fear of him'. His account tallies with a history of those times written by Ziauddin Barani, who described his own impressions of the Sultan's government and his subjects.

The Sultan of Delhi was highly cultured and possessed an elegant literary style and considerable imagination. He was equally fascinated by Persian literature, mathematics, physics, logic, and Greek philosophy. It was the dogmas of philosophers that had the most powerful influence over him, because they were 'productions of indifference and hardness of heart'.

'To reach the interior of the palace,' Canetti wrote, 'one had to pass through three doors. Outside the first door were a number of guards, and also trumpeters and flute players. When an Amir, or any other person of note, arrived, these sounded their instruments and said "So-and-so has come. So-and-so has come."

'Outside this door there were also platforms where the executioners sat; so that, when the Sultan ordered a man to be executed, the sentence was carried out here and the body left lying for three days and nights. Thus anyone approaching the palace would come first on corpses. Heaps and mounds of them were always lying there; the sweepers and executioners who had to drag out the condemned and put them to death were worn out with the heavy and endless labour.'

The Sultan's aim was to murder so many of them, and banish the entire remaining population from Delhi, so that he could enjoy the capital city on his own.

Not satisfied with only one example of an intolerant and self-centred homicidal type, Canetti described a westerner who suffered from schizophrenia and shared the same fixation of self-aggrandisement and entitlement, and had no time for other people. He was a German judge at the Court of Appeal in Dresden named Daniel Paul Schreber, who died in 1911. He would become famous for his own description of the world, viewed through his disorderly mind which was overwhelmed by conspiracy theories and a sense of catastrophe.

Hitler's attitude was not unlike Schreber's. He could not tolerate anyone competing with him for attention, they had to be cancelled or destroyed if they dared. A significant element in the drawings that young Hitler had submitted to the Academy of Fine Arts in Vienna was that they were streetscapes with classical buildings. He did not paint portraits or scenes featuring people, except as minor decoration in the streets he painted, and sold in cafés and beer gardens when he was a student in Schwabing. In Hitler's imaginary world people were far less important than things.

Contemplating those two situations of a need to get rid of people may help to understand Hitler better when, on 29 April 1937, he explained to the regional director of the Nazi educational camp how he intended to get rid of the Jewish people.

> With me the main thing is never to take a step that I may have to withdraw or that will damage us. You know, I always go to the extreme of what I feel I can risk, but no further. You have to have a nose for what you can and cannot do. In a struggle against an enemy as well.[4]

In a secret speech to a private audience Hitler went on to say, 'I do not intend to immediately challenge my enemy to a physical fight. I do not say "Fight!" because I believe in fighting for fighting's sake. I say "I want to destroy you. And now, I'll ask my wits to help me to manoeuvre you into such a corner that you cannot lash out at me because you would suffer a fatal blow to the heart." That's how it is done.'[5]

The recording of his voice reveals how he spoke relatively calmly to begin with, before lashing out at the end with 'That's how it is done' coming out as a triumphant shout, like a violent whiplash. What he said was typical of the way he had so far achieved power, by always going to the limit of what he could get away with, which was the essence of his foreign and domestic policies.

Hitler never set aside his final solution before making war on the Eastern Front; although he spent the first half of 1937 persecuting the Church, by the latter part of the year he had begun denigrating German-Jews with his taunts and raising the spectre once again of 'Jewish Bolshevism'. Goebbels found his claims contradictory, since Stalin was particularly intent on persecuting Jewish communists in the Soviet Union. So how could all commies be Jews? It made no sense. But Hitler was unconcerned about contradictions in his speeches or his policies. 'Who were the leaders of the Bavarian Soviet republic?' he would reply to Goebbels.' Who led the Spartacus revolution in Schwabing in 1918?'[6]

In reality, 'It was a Schwabing revolution, with Schwabing personalities taking control of the whole city of Munich, of the whole state of Bavaria. Men of ideas drove out men of business, men of speculation drove out men of practical experience, men from the world of the arts drove out men from the world of politics, men of cafés drove out men of offices.'[7]

Not only did he confuse German-Jews with Russian Bolsheviks, but also with intellectuals, with the cultured middle-classes, with communists, and Jews with Christians. He despised them all: so he rolled them all into one category he called 'the enemy', to make them easier to destroy. Lenin had used similar justifications to get rid of all the people he disliked when he had taken control of Russia and made his own little list of enemies to be eliminated, including priests and schoolteachers and other leadership figures who might rival him.

Despite his sentimental attraction to Wagner's operas – largely because of the heroic Siegfried and *Götterdämmerung* – the Nazis hated culture. Their attitude would be immortalised in the ominous remark attributed to Goering, but actually misquoted from a play by popular playwright Hanns Johst; 'Whenever I hear the word *culture,* I reach for my pistol.'

Hitler's opportunity came in October, when the anti-Semitic violence seemed to be getting out of hand in Berlin. A new stream of anti-Semitic boycotts began to be put in place by local leaders of the Nazi Party in other parts of Germany, preventing Jewish shopkeepers from conducting any business.[8] It pressed more Jewish families to sell their businesses and leave Germany; and the plundering of Jewish homes and Jewish companies increased, while most Jews were deprived of a livelihood.[9]

There had been approximately 50,000 Jewish businesses in Germany before the Nazis took power. Only 9,000 would still exist by September 1939.[10] Inevitably in such dire circumstances, they were exploited unscrupulously by the Nazis, so that sellers received only a fraction of what their business was worth. German authorities became even greedier by imposing a series of fees on any Jews leaving Germany. There was even a tax for 'fleeing the Reich'. When it was still possible for Jews to leave, the Nazis discouraged many by allowing them to take too little with them to start a new life abroad. Now they were trapped.

On November 8, Julius Streicher and Goebbels opened an anti-Semitic exhibition in Munich's German Museum aimed at depicting Jews as subhuman. Its intention was to justify persecuting them in the most horrible ways, as a prelude to inventing excuses for exterminating them.

Removing Hjalmar Schacht as economics minister in late November disposed of the final obstacle that had so far prevented the Nazis stealing from Jewish families and Jewish companies on an even larger scale.[11] Nazi policy now was 'depriving Jews of every basis of existence'.[12]

Coupled with the Nazi campaign of disposing of all German-Jews was Hitler's foreign policy of 'aggressive expansionism.' The annexation of Austria by Germany in March 1938 increased the persecution of Jews, since another 190,000 Austrian Jews were added to the number of German Jews.

Hitler's plan to absorb Austria into a Greater Germany met with little resistance. All it needed was for Hitler to invite the Austrian Chancellor Schuschnigg to Berlin and show him the military plans already prepared to destroy his government for Schuschnigg to realise he was defeated. After an ultimatum from Hitler, he resigned on March 11 in favour of Hitler's puppet.

The date generally considered to be the beginning of persecution of German-Jews is 30 January 1933, when Hitler became Chancellor of Germany. Although he had already planned to dispose of them even before he wrote of his ambition in *Mein Kampf* in 1925, it had taken him about four years of stirring up hatred against Jews in Germany to reach the point of fake legitimising his endeavours. The anti-Jewish Nuremberg Laws were established by decree for anyone who had three or four Jewish grandparents. German citizenship was denied to anyone who did not have so-called 'pure' German blood – which was, of course, a ridiculous fantasy.

In 1937, Hitler and the Nazis defined all Jews as 'enemies.' Austrian Jews would suffer the same fate as German-Jews who had not viewed themselves as a different race from gentile Germans with their Prussian culture, but were having an unscientific racist theory forced on them and others by the Nazis. Even as early as 1849, the German-Jewish Gabriel Riesser had proclaimed to applause, 'We are not immigrants – we were born here – and so we cannot claim any other home: either we are German or we have no homeland.'[13]

It was a cry which had rung down the centuries from all sorts of nations in the East and West and the Middle East, where Jews had contributed to society and the economy, and the stability of the nation, but been viewed by the envious rabble with jealousy and hatred. Despite support from monarchies and other forms of government, it had always ended the same way – with sullen resentment by the rabble and apprehension by leaders who were anxious about possible civil wars or revolutions by the illiterate masses.

Unscientific race theories had been raised before by several second-rate thinkers who had not understood Darwin's theory of evolution. One of them had been Arthur de Gabineau at the end of the nineteenth century. The greatly esteemed philosopher and statesman Alexis de Tocqueville responded in a letter to him that, 'I remain, as before, opposed in the extreme to your doctrines. I believe they are probably quite false. I know that they are certainly very pernicious… The consequences of both theories is that of a vast limitation, if not a complete abolition of human liberty.'[14]

It was precisely what happened when those theories were projected into the real world and humanity and liberty were abolished.

31

The Nazis of the Middle East

'On June 17, 1939 – less than three months before the beginning of the Second World War – a Saudi Arab claiming to be an emissary of King Ibn Saud presented himself at the Berghof, Hitler's residence in the Bavarian mountains. The man was described as the royal counsellor Khalid al Hud al Gargani, special envoy of King Abdul Aziz Ibn Saud. According to the US political agent in Jeddah, Gargani was the principal advisor to the King.'[1]

A German spy named von Hentig noted that Gargani met afterwards with head of naval intelligence Admiral Canaris, and General Wilhelm Keitel the Chief of the German Supreme Command. He further recorded that Ibn Saud wanted to prevent any press coverage of his negotiations with Germany. Canaris and Keitel agreed that the king should be given 6 million Reichsmarks for him to purchase 4,000 rifles and 8 million rounds of ammunition. Light anti-aircraft guns and armoured cars would also be supplied. They expected there would be enough money to set up a small munitions factory in Saudi Arabia.

Weapons and ammunition would be delivered as quickly as possible. Similar negotiations had already begun between Saudi Arabia and Mussolini, who was Germany's partner in the war against the Allies. Ibn Saud had opened negotiations to obtain friendship with Italy and Germany in case Britain lost the war, as seemed most likely. He was in desperate need of money, since a deep fall in the numbers of pilgrims visiting Mecca in 1939 had diminished the head tax and drained the Saudi treasury:

> Also he was seriously in debt. He owed some $200,000 to Philby's trading company in Jeddah for Ford cars and Singer sewing machines delivered but not paid for, some $100,000 to Britain for arms purchases, $100,000 to Russia for a shipment of petroleum products in 1932, and about $120,000 to a Polish company from which he bought machine guns in 1930. He could not pay wages to his administration or army.
>
> But obtaining help from Hitler would have costs as well as benefits. There were signs that $750,000 held in his name by the bank Misr at Cairo would be frozen, should he enter into a pact with Hitler through Fritz Grobba, who was at this time resident in Tehran, the main centre for German secret works in the Middle East.[2]

Part of Grobba's work included supporting a mysterious figure who would cause considerable trouble for Britain throughout the coming war and afterwards by stirring up Arab hatred against the West and the Jews at every opportunity. Known by the English as the grand mufti of Jerusalem, al-Haj Amin al-Husseini was Hitler's man in Palestine, constantly working for German support for Arab independence.[3]

Grobba would take the mufti to one of Germany's slave labour camps near Berlin, to show him how the Nazis were already destroying Jews in Europe, as an example to follow in the Middle East. The Nazi Master Plan for the extermination of populations in the East to make way for German colonisers would involve millions of murders by lethal gas, starvation and disease; many in specially designed murder camps throughout Germany and occupied Poland and other Nazi-occupied territories first, they were described as 'innocent' concentration or re-education camps. Part of the plan was to transfer their victims to where slave labour was needed to keep Germany's wartime armaments industry increasing its production capacities – by 'extermination through labour' – or to brothels for German troops, or to Nazi murder camps to destroy older victims and younger children.[4*]

The Glorification of Terror

T.E. Lawrence had been convinced, with Churchill and most of the Arab Bureau, that the Jewish farmers and Zionists would initiate enormous improvements in the Middle East, which had remained inert and unchanged for centuries. Obviously, the Arab peasants and farmers and Bedouin did not have the skills or technologies to improve the country, whereas the Jewish immigrants did – as they had done in most of the countries where they had settled. They also had ambition and purpose for the future, which the Arabs did not: *they* were immersed in the past. Moreover, they did not appear to want to change. They were accustomed to the hardships of surviving from day to day in the desert by raiding other Arab encampments for slaves, women, cattle and plunder, with the strong exploiting the weak. Even when offered help they resisted the incursion of others on to what they considered to be holy land intended only for Muslims.

---

* Photographic evidence would appear in 2017 of the mufti with Fritz Grobba studying the Nazis' Trebbin slave labour camp in 1943, where Hungarian Jews were used as cheap labour before murdering them. While Hitler expressed contempt for Arabs and North Africans as racially inferior to Germans, his priority was to be assured of the much-needed oil for Germany's military machine.

Harry St John Philby – who lived among the Arabs for many years and became a Muslim and a Haji – described them as sullen and disputatious, and given to hysterical outbursts, instead of reasoning that they might benefit. It was because they knew only one book, which was the Quran, and they had learnt it by heart from the age of five, or sooner, so that they were totally absorbed in it. Their days and hours between sowing and harvesting their corn were spent in prayer. When not praying, and not raiding each other's tribal territory, they discussed the words attributed to the prophet by his messengers, as if seeking hidden clues. That, as far as they were concerned, was a normal way of life. Any changes were forbidden to them by the pronouncement in the Quran against innovation.[5]

That state of mind had come about since the Prophet Muhammad had united the Arab tribes into a single Islamic state in 630 CE. His holy book, the Quran, was based partly on Judaism and partly on Christianity. Its intention was largely to prevent Arab tribes from killing each other and stealing from each other, as they had done ever since anyone could remember. It had left a residue of suspicion against non-believers, so that they would not cooperate even in their own interest, because they failed to view Western culture as an improvement on theirs. Their priorities differed from those of the West.

Philby had written to his first wife in London that he thought the Puritanical Wahabis were mad with their thought police, their authoritarian rule over women, their slaves and their Ikhwan swordsmen.

A Hearty Welcome Home

It is not easy to follow all the threads that run even further back than the First World War against Germany and their Turkish allies in 1918; after which Churchill was handed the responsibility to solve the Middle East crisis. Those threads that would lead inexorably to the Gaza War in 2023, go back more than fourteen centuries, because Islamist extremists have long and resentful memories. That was when an intense hatred existed among illiterate and superstitious Arab masses against more progressive leaders dedicated to change, and against the more modern West. Wahabis and other extremists refused to escape from their self-imposed prison of past history. All that can be done in this brief account is point out some of the most significant milestones along the way.

In 1918 T.E. Lawrence took the Zionist leader Chaim Weizmann to see the Emir Faisal in the desert. When he viewed the Jews as likely importers of western modernity to the stagnant Middle East, Feisal sympathised with the Zionist movement and 'accepted the possibility of future Jewish claims to territory in Palestine.[6]

'We will do our best, in so far as we are concerned, to help them through: we will wish the Jews a most hearty welcome home.' Faisal felt that 'there exists room in Syria for us both and that neither can be a success without the other.'

Nevertheless, in 1920 at the Nebi Musa Festival in Jerusalem, the Arab masses began a hysterical pogrom against Jews. Amidst a crowd of nearly 70,000, their leaders incited the Arabs to use force. Arabs began attacking Jews in the Old City, shouting slogans like 'Palestine is our land, the Jews are our dogs!'[7]

It was the mufti who 'provoked the April pogrom' as the religious leader of the Palestinian Arabs.[8]

Sir Herbert Samuel was the new High Commissioner of Palestine. Ironically, he had appointed a 25-year-old former and future enemy of the West to be the most powerful Arab in Palestine, 'with consequences more profound than anyone at the time could conceive. That man was Amin al-Husseini.'[9] Samuel failed to be aware of the mufti's sinister character and his obsession with brutal violence and mass murders. Al-Husseini 'turned out to be an implacable enemy not only of Zionism but also of Britain', culminating in his sinister alliance with Hitler's Germany in the Second World War:

> The illusion of calm was broken in April 1920 at the annual pilgrimage festival of Nebi Musa. The crowd that year was far larger than in previous years – some 70,000 Muslims poured into Jerusalem, some of them armed, chanting nationalist and militant slogans. Prominent Arabs addressed them from the balcony of the Arab Club. The mayor – an older, more hardline relative of the mufti named Musa Kazem al-Husseini – urged the crowd to 'spill their blood' for Palestine. Over the next three days, mobs attacked Jews in the Old City, looting shops and homes. Five Jews were killed and over 200 injured, including 18 critically. Two sisters, aged 25 and 15, were raped.[10]

It was eerily reminiscent of what would occur a century later in a repetition of history on 6 October 2023 in an incident that triggered a war in Gaza between the Israeli Defence Force and Hamas terrorists in Palestine who gloried in perpetrating atrocities against Jews. They raided private homes of Jewish families to murder, rape, kidnap hostages, and behead Jewish babies.

The riots created considerable visibility for al-Husseini and increased his influence in the Arab community. 'After being appointed Grand Mufti, al-Husseini, an Islamist hater of Jews, emerged as the most influential and effective leader of the Arab community in Palestine. Thus al-Husseini instigated a bitter century of conflict between Palestinian Jews and Palestinian Arabs. This later widened into a series of larger Arab-Israeli wars, initially incited by the Grand Mufti, but later continued by Islamic militant terrorist organisations like the PLO.'[11]

Agreements between Israel and Egypt signed on 17 September 1978 led in the following year to a peace treaty between those two countries, the first such between Israel and any of its Arab neighbours. Brokered by US President Jimmy Carter – between Israeli Prime Minister Menachem Begin and Egyptian President Anwar

Sadat and officially titled the 'Framework for Peace in the Middle East' – the agreements became known as the Camp David Accords, because the negotiations took place at the US presidential retreat at Camp David, Maryland. Sadat and Begin were awarded the Nobel Prize for Peace in 1978 for their contributions to the agreements.

The Camp David Summit with Palestine in 2000 with President Clinton and the leader of the terrorist group Hamas ended in failure, because Yasser Arafat claimed he would be killed by his supporters if he signed. Terrorist attacks on Israel by the PLO, Al-Fatah, and other terrorist groups working from Jordan, Lebanon and Egypt, turned Palestinians into pariahs to those and other Arab states who refused to help them. Other terrorists included Hamas, Hezbollah, Black September, and other groups funded largely by Iran to weaken Israel, because it was the only democratic nation in the Middle East and America's only dependable partner. The relationship between Saudi Arabia and Palestine was one of distrust. The result of being shunned by everyone outside and controlled by terrorists inside turned the Gaza strip into a keg of dynamite awaiting a spark to ignite it.

It would be a simplification to say that the Gaza War in 2023 was part of Hitler's so-called "Plan Orient"- because the struggle by Islamist extremists to restore the defunct Caliphate had been lingering from centuries earlier – but it could be described as another link in the chain of events from the seventh century to the collapse of the corrupt Caliphate in 1918, and what followed after, that led us to our most recent stupidity.

32

An Ultimatum

1938–39

Churchill searched for a way to protect Czechoslovakia's integrity by forming an alliance with France, and any other state under threat from Germany, but feared that Chamberlain's conciliatory approach to Germany would 'blunt the edge' of preparations for the Czechs' defence. It would leave them vulnerable as a sacrifice to keep the Nazis at bay for a little longer.

At least the House of Commons had woken up to the reality of the delays in air expansion, even if it meant that Lord Swinton resigned when he was made the scapegoat for all the bungling. Churchill began to correspond with Sir Kingsley Wood, who replaced him. At the same time, those who thought Churchill should be in the Cabinet asked for his advice; in particular the new Secretary of State for War, Leslie Hore-Belisha, and First Lord of the Admiralty Duff-Cooper, who opposed appeasement.

Since the Austin factory in Birmingham would be among the first to manufacture war material in the event of war, Churchill made a visit to see it for himself. His experience as Minister of Munitions in the First World War had made him more than familiar with mass production systems, assembly lines, and union problems. He also visited the Fleet at Duff-Cooper's invitation, to see the new submarine interception system named Asdic.

One of the results was his concern at the lack of anti-aircraft defences for the cities and other vulnerable centres. Some were on order, but hopelessly below the number required. Both he and Morton believed that it might also be too little to strengthen their hand in order to make diplomacy work over Czechoslovakia.

Czechoslovakia

Everything that Churchill had predicted was being confirmed by Hitler's subsequent actions. Nazi propaganda continued its lies in order to justify invading and annexing Czechoslovakia. Nazi terror was imposed on Austria. And the Nazis continued to terrorise Jewish families within the German and Austrian borders. Churchill did his best to make threats in his newspaper articles that if Germany attempted to crush Czechoslovakia, all the major nations would be brought into the war. He repeated what he had previously told General von Kleist, that it would be fought 'to the bitter end'.*

Churchill was convinced Britain would fight if Germany invaded Czechoslovakia, but Herman Goering told the French Ambassador that it was not so. On the contrary, he'd had assurances from London that 'Britain would not lift a finger'.[1]

Duff-Cooper wanted to send the British Fleet to Scapa Flow as a warning for Germany to desist, but the Cabinet turned his suggestion down as a possible provocation. It led to a pause for re-evaluation – during which Hitler took the initiative again. Evidently he had already made his plans and was not about to back down now. He firmly demanded that the Sudetenland be transferred instantly to Germany.

The British Cabinet did not warn him off, as would have happened immediately in those far-off times when the British Empire had been virile and powerful and respected. Instead, Chamberlain and Sir John Simon decided at a special Committee meeting on Czechoslovakia to negotiate directly with Hitler. No Czech leaders would be invited to participate in the negotiations to sell them out.

At a second meeting of the Committee on 10 September at 10 Downing Street, a telegram was read out from the British Minister in Berlin cautioning them not to threaten Hitler.

They found Churchill waiting for them in the hall at the end of the meeting. He assured them that the French and the Russians were ready for an offensive against Germany, and insisted it was the last chance to stop the landslide by sending an ultimatum to Hitler.

Hoare assured Churchill that his information about French and Russian intentions was not the same as their own. Churchill was undeterred: he visited the Foreign Office next day, to advise Halifax to warn Hitler that a violation of Czech territory 'meant immediate war'.

But Halifax had already decided that the only way to avert war was to separate Czechoslovakia from the Sudetenland and give it to Germany. The Nazis would have read his intentions in *The Times* four days earlier.

On 11 September, the British Government agreed to a four-power conference with France, Germany and Italy: not that they wished to discuss the issue any longer, but to iron out the details of transferring the Sudetenland to Hitler. The Czechoslovak government was not included in the negotiations; nor was Russia.

Churchill viewed their decision as a betrayal. He wrote to Lord Moyne that owing to the mishandling of the German problem and the neglect of Britain's defences over the past five years, Britain was now faced with the bleak choice between war and shame. He was sure that the British Government would choose shame, and then have to fight a war afterwards on worse terms than Britain would get by fighting right now.

---

* Von Kleist would be hanged by the Nazis after a failed bomb plot against Hitler nearly six years later.

Leo Amery noted in his diary that some of the young MPs, Harold Macmillan in particular, were clamouring for a rebellion to get rid of Neville and replace him with Winston.

Several days later, on 14 September, Chamberlain announced to the Cabinet that he was going to persuade the Czechs to surrender the Sudetenland to Germany, since Britain and France were not ready to fight a war over it. He flew to meet Hitler in Berchtesgaden next day to discuss a referendum with him. It was Chamberlain's first ever flight in an aeroplane, and he knew almost nothing about Nazi Germany. He seemed unaware that he was at a considerable disadvantage; certainly not in a favourable position to negotiate with Hitler. But vanity caused him to see himself in the heroic mould as a saviour.

Chamberlain stated at his meeting with Hitler that he would not oppose the separation of the Sudetenland from Czechoslovakia; so all that was required was to iron out the details of a transfer to Germany and obtain Cabinet approval.

The Prime Minister took care to avoid a debate in Parliament on his return to London, in case his decision was overruled by an opposition group. Parliament would be informed only after the Government had committed itself. What the ministers decided was that 'it should be stated pretty bluntly to the Czech President, Edouard Beneš, that if he did not leave himself in our hands then we would wash our hands of him'.[2]

The Czechs were warned not to mobilise their army. They were to wait to be sacrificed.

The World Waited Breathlessly

Churchill flew to Paris on 20 September 1938 to persuade the French to support Czechoslovakia if German troops invaded. But Reynaud and Mandel told him they were in a minority. Returning to London, he told the press that Czechoslovakia was being forced to hand over the Sudetenland to the Nazis by threats. It would not bring peace to anyone. On the contrary, it would release twenty-five German divisions for the Western Front and also give the Nazis access to the Black Sea.

It was a chilly, damp grey day when the whole world waited breathlessly for an answer to Hitler's demands. The first German war had ended only twenty years previously, and the killing fields had been so unexpectedly brutal that the slaughter had left horrifying memories that still lingered with the sadness of huge losses of Britain's and France's heroic youth. Despite life continuing from day to day in the British Isles since then, there was no appetite for another world war. But Britain was apparently doomed to mindless brutality all over again, since the Government had been given an ultimatum by Nazi Germany. The two most influential politicians in England now trudged wearily and closely together down one of Westminster's famous streets near the Prime Minister's residence at 10 Downing Street, deep in conversation about the possible consequences, while several waiting press photographers took the opportunity to snap their photo in the street.

The two men ignored them. The short, stockier one in his autumn overcoat and dark Homburg hat was Winston Churchill. He held a cigar loosely in one hand as he listened anxiously to what the 6ft-tall Foreign Secretary told him, as he loomed over him with solemn features beneath his modest black bowler hat. It made him look like any other civil servant and reflected his mild and formal personality. Halifax was an honourable man and a firm patriot, like Churchill, who had devoted his life to his country and its people, although some now considered he had betrayed them by appeasing the Nazi dictator. But Great Britain had been placed in an impossible situation under threat from powerful enemies when unprepared for war. Despite the fact that it maintained the biggest empire the world had ever known, which comprised about a quarter of the global population, its treasury was meagre compared with the enormous costs of the British Empire and the Indian Raj. Providing infrastructures, law and order, education and justice to protect a quarter of the world's people cost a fortune and kept the government parsimonious and frugal, even stingy. Consequently, Britain had not joined the arms race, and now bitterly regretted making itself vulnerable to attack by leaving rearming too late.

It is likely that Churchill knew the strengths and weaknesses of both Halifax and Prime Minister Neville Chamberlain better than anyone. Chamberlain had been his helpful mentor when he had entered politics as a young man. And Lord Irwin – as Halifax had previously been known – had been an impressive figurehead as a previous Viceroy of India. Halifax was still perceived by some as 'the power behind the throne', since he was a personal friend of the king.

The famous chimes of Big Ben marked the hour from the summit of its tower beside the Parliament buildings nearby as the two men huddled closer to communicate their thoughts.

Churchill had been out of office for years after his party had been voted out of office. But he had continued to search for information about the strength of Britain's enemies in order to warn the Government, the media, and the public, about the looming threat from the other side of the English Channel. He had continually urged the nation to rearm in readiness for war. And Halifax was privy to much of what went on in Chamberlain's mind, but not all of it.

The world still waited while Halifax and Chamberlain had continued to appease the Nazi dictator, while worrying what to do about the troublesome upstart now he had become Germany's Chancellor and main rabble-rouser. No doubt Halifax informed Winston Churchill that Prime Minister Chamberlain had decided to sign a treaty with the German dictator in Munich that would give Germany and Italy free rein to carve up Europe and the Americas between them.

Hitler had already annexed Austria, and intended to crush Czechoslovakia next year as an overture to further victories without firing a shot. And Chamberlain had been seen as helping him to grow even more powerful militarily, since the Prime Minister and his Foreign Secretary believed that Germany was now far too powerful to resist, and it would be wiser to befriend Herr Hitler.

From the perspective of the twenty-first century, history is seen as an admonitory figure accusing both Lord Halifax and Chamberlain of appeasing a brutal warlord who cared for nothing and no one but his own self-indulgent ambition for total dictatorial power. The very word 'appeasement' has become toxic as a consequence of what we know with hindsight of his brutal atrocities to unarmed populations of old men, women and infants, of Nazi ethnic cleansing, and the Holocaust – all as a consequence of misunderstanding Chamberlain's and Halifax's motives. Halifax had always believed it was better to compromise to avoid bloodshed and economic ruin, until he would shortly become convinced that Hitler had a secret agenda and continually lied to give himself time to prepare and act to his own advantage – that he could never be trusted to keep his word. He and Chamberlain wrongly believed that Hitler was a reasonable man. Their judgements were unrealistic because they had both been brought up as gentlemen whose words could always be trusted. And they had expected the same of others. Now they were lost in a labyrinth of criminal deceit while the world returned to feudalism.

And yet, they were not two of a kind. While Halifax was loyal to the Prime Minister, his motives were genuine, and he gave sound and reasonable advice. Despite his special relationship with the royal family, and the pomp and splendour he had enjoyed when Viceroy of India, Halifax was a modest man, whereas Chamberlain was vain. Pride in being a gentleman had corrupted him into feeling superior to the coarse and peasant-like Hitler, whom he had patronised. The German aristocracy had patronised Hitler too, and he had been well aware of what they thought of him. Now he had turned the tables on them. While Chamberlain and his Foreign Minister had believed that normal people would be prepared to compromise, and that no one wanted another war, they had been wrong. War was exactly what Hitler and Mussolini wanted. It would give them their own way to carve up Europe, North Africa, and the Americas. And they saw no reason to compromise with anyone.

Chamberlain flew back to see Hitler at Bad Godesberg two days later on 22 September, taking Sir Horace Wilson with him. This meeting with the Führer should have been a revelation to Britain's Prime Minister, when Hitler immediately dismissed Chamberlain's plans because they would take too long to finalise and he was in a hurry to take Czechoslovakia. He wanted immediate occupation of the Sudetenland by German troops. Chamberlain agreed that all Czech fortifications and war material would be handed to Germany intact.

When Hitler asked Wilson in a private meeting what would happen if the Czechs refused, Wilson said, 'I will make those Czechos sensible.'

Chamberlain returned to London on 24 September and described the conclusions of the meeting with the inner Cabinet. He was convinced that Hitler did not intend to take over the rest of Czechoslovakia. He emphasised that the population of the Sudetenland were mostly German-speaking and this German takeover was racially motivated: they were their own kind. He appeared to think he had established a personal friendship with Hitler, and was convinced that Hitler would not go back on his word.

When the full Cabinet met next day, the Prime Minister urged them to agree to the immediate transfer of the Sudetenland to Germany. Halifax, Hailsham, Duff-Cooper and Hore-Belisha were uneasy and expressed their doubts at the wisdom of forcing Czechoslovakia to give in to Germany. But Inskip, Kingsley Wood, Malcom MacDonald and Lord Stanhope advised them to agree.

Churchill arrived at 10 Downing Street at the conclusion of the meeting, and urged the Prime Minister to issue a joint declaration with Russia, warning Germany off. He was told that Sir Horace Wilson was about to take a message to Hitler, and that it was not a retreat. But Chamberlain was annoyed when Lord Halifax issued a communiqué from the Foreign Office without first showing it to him. It stated that if Germany invaded Czechoslovakia, France would be bound to come to her assistance, and Britain would stand by France.

Chamberlain sent Lord Runciman as a so-called 'conciliator and mediator' to Prague to tie up the loose ends. Runciman made his visits scrupulously to Czech and German leaders. The American correspondent William Shirer was present at Runciman's first press conference on 4 August. Shirer wrote of it in his diary:

> Lord Runciman arrived today to gum up the works and sell the Czechs short if he can … Later Runciman, a taciturn, thin-lipped little man with a bald head so round it looks like a misshapen egg, received us – about three hundred Czech and foreign reporters – in the reception hall … Runciman's whole mission smells …[3]

The Czechs were finally convinced by Britain's plan for Czech withdrawal from the Sudetenland within four days. They understood it was all over for them. The situation made it clear that, as far as Chamberlain was concerned, he dismissed the Czechs as foreigners. As he referred to them in his broadcast to the nation, they were people 'in a faraway country … of whom we know nothing'.

He telegraphed Hitler on 28 September, requesting a further meeting to settle the final details.

Chamberlain was giving an account to the House of Commons when Hitler replied by inviting him to Munich. He jubilantly told his cheering supporters in the House that he would fly to a meeting called by Hitler with French and Italian representatives. Halifax telegraphed the British Minister in Prague that the Czechs should immediately accept the British plan. President Beneš had no choice – he agreed. The Sudetenland was now part of Germany.

A Return to Medievalism

At the Savoy Hotel in London that night, a young guest named Colin Coote recorded that Churchill was in 'a towering rage and deepening gloom' at the Government's sacrifice of their honour. When Coote heard newsboys in the Strand shouting out that the agreement had been signed, he dashed out into the street to buy a paper.

Churchill was in his country home at Chartwell when Chamberlain returned from Munich. Churchill had only one visitor that morning. He was a young BBC producer named Guy Burgess. Churchill showed him a message from President Beneš and asked Burgess what he should do.

'Here I am,' he told Burgess, 'an old man without power and without party. What advice can I give?'

Burgess had already taken the only option he could see that might work, in company with four other former students who had been with him at Cambridge University – he and they had become secret agents for Soviet Russia. Churchill was unaware of it. The Soviet spies would become infamous much later on when found out, as 'the Cambridge Five'. Like Churchill, they believed in an alliance against Nazi Germany because they were convinced that the Nazis could not be beaten without Soviet Russian help. But it was not something they could mention openly at the time or they would have been viewed as traitors and might even have been shot to death by a firing squad.[4]

Churchill gave Burgess a copy of his new book, which was a collection of his speeches in Parliament. Burgess said: 'You alone have the force and authority to galvanise the potential allies into action.'

On 14 December, the American Ambassador had served four years in Berlin. He wrote in his diary, 'Today the Czechoslovak Minister called, tremendously concerned about the fate of his country because democratic countries do nothing and thus give Mussolini, Hitler and Japan increasing sway over the world. He said Russia, although an ally of his country, and France, is helpless.'

He remarked on how our modern civilisation was drifting back to medievalism.

War correspondent William Shirer would note later on that, 'The primary cause of the Continent's upheaval was one country, Germany, and one man, Adolf Hitler … I saw the European democracies falter and crack and their confidence and judgement and will paralysed, retreat from one bastion to another until they could no longer, with the exception of Britain, make a stand.'[5]

33

The New Deal

1938–39

President Roosevelt's 'New Deal' economy brought greater social justice and welfare for Americans in the neutral United States, particularly for the immense number of marginalised families. It had already begun to provide a million more jobs by the end of 1938. Congress agreed to allocate $3.75 billion to infrastructure development and industrial expansion. Textile and steel industries increased production, followed by the boot and shoe industry and the building industry. Residential home building broke recent records by the end of the year. Some 23 million received some type of government welfare.

America avoided demagoguery and dictatorship because Roosevelt understood Keynesian economics and applied it consistently in relief, public works and labour legislation. He'd spent an extra year studying economics at college as a young man and said later on, 'and everything I was taught was wrong'.[1]

Both Roosevelt and Churchill were always conscious of the need to stimulate employment, and both followed what Keynes had declared; that 'it is worse, in an impoverished world, to provoke unemployment than to disappoint the *rentiers*'. The primary aim should be to manage domestic expectations. Despite the economic double-talk, like Churchill, FDR understood how quickly distressed, unemployed people could lose their identity, become discontented, and disturb society.

It was an honest as well as a compassionate way to use public funds. Four million jobless Americans, instead of remaining unemployed, would go to work for the United States government in a programme of public works. 'They built swimming pools, parks and gardens, schools and roads, among other projects, working through the winter … The flood control and hydroelectricity provided by the Tennessee Valley Authority, created in May of 1933, set the backward South on the road to an industrial economy …'

The economy grew by about 9 per cent a year on average during Roosevelt's first term in office as President of the United States, which was the strongest peacetime economic growth in US history.[2]

Roosevelt possessed considerable courage and skill in defying countervailing trends, not only with his economic programme but with his political opponents. Part of his skill was finding the right kind of specialists who could dance rings around the cruder Republicans. But there were those who believed that the fascists and Nazis protected America against the scourge of communism. They were sufficiently anti-Semitic to turn a blind eye to Hitler's racist policies in Europe.

Homegrown Fascists

There were all sorts of fascists in the United States, too. There were those who openly wore brown shirts to show their 'America for the Americans' virtues, and were jealous of the man most responsible for carrying out the President's successful economic policies, Henry Morgenthau, because he was Jewish. Talented Jewish people were also abundantly successful in the film industry, in finance, in the women's garment and men's tailoring industries, in the legal profession, and in government agencies. But their success did not cause as much resentment in such a multicultural melting pot, compared with the more primitive and spiteful envies and resentments and jealousies in Berlin, Vienna, and Budapest, where there appeared to be more discontented and bitter people than anywhere else, who harboured envy and hatred against other segments of society who were doing better than them.

Those who wore brown shirts in America supported Nazi Germany, whereas America's Black Shirts opposed communists, atheists, and civil rights for African Americans. White Shirts claimed to stand for economic liberty. There were also Khaki, Blue, and Gray Shirt groups in the United States, and a national fascist organisation known as the Silver Shirts, which included anti-Roosevelt, anti-communist, and anti-Catholic attitudes.[3]

All believed in American neutrality and isolation from Europe. But, when Japanese troops continued advancing into China, and the German Air Force attacked and bombed Republican towns in Spain, and the German Condor Legion fought alongside Franco's Spanish troops, American Secretary of State, Cordell Hull, warned in Nashville, Tennessee, on 3 June, that it was an illusion to imagine that the US could remain isolated during a period of victory by dictators of totalitarian regimes. 'We cannot withdraw from the world,' he said.

He emphasised that there was never a time when America's influence was more needed to support international law.

A week later in England, Churchill was shocked when talking to the American columnist Walter Lippmann over dinner to hear that the United States Ambassador to Britain, Joseph Kennedy, was telling his friends that Britain would surrender to the Nazis when war came.

As German, Austrian and Czech refugees fled from the Nazis in Europe, many sought safety in the United States. Roosevelt made sure that those already there as visitors would not be forced to return. But dedicated American isolationists prevented further residence permits from being issued.

The Netherlands, Denmark and the Dominican Republic agreed not to place restrictions on refugees, while Britain continued to allow up to 20,000 Jewish people a year to enter Palestine, but no more. Ships carrying Jewish refugees escaping from the Nazis were intercepted and sent to the island of Mauritius, where they languished in internment camps. Some who fled Nazi persecution managed to make their way to Britain.

British rule in Palestine was endangered by Arab riots in Jaffa and Hebron, where the British Army was outnumbered by hysterical mobs. British General Ord Wingate created small guerilla forces of armed Jewish Zionists and trained them to defend Jewish populations and property, while terrorists from both sides fought each other in savage cycles of violence.

Egypt, Iraq and Saudi Arabia pressed the British Government to halt Jewish immigration, while Poland and the United States urged Britain to allow refugees from Europe to enter Palestine. Britain's Colonial Office gave in to Arab pressure and imposed barriers to Jewish immigration, with an upper limit in cases of emergency.

A Palestine White paper ruled that there could not be a Jewish majority. Its population stood at 445,437 and could rise to a level of only 545,475, whereas the Arab population now stood at 1,501,698. Churchill had been right in saying the Arabs would flock to the Jewish parts of the country that were being developed.

Alfred Duff-Cooper had just resigned from the Cabinet in disgust at the Government's cowardice towards Germany. He spoke up in the House of Commons against the restrictions imposed on future Jewish immigration, to explain that it was the strong arm of the British Empire that had opened the door for them when all other doors were shut. 'Shall we now replace that hope – that we have revived – by despair, and shall we slam the door in the face of the long-wandering Jew?'[4]

Worse than the Reds

World attention was focused on Hitler's victories, and the way he had managed to occupy two countries without having to fire a shot. Grisly news continued to emerge, not only from the Nazi-occupied nations, but also about Stalin's purges of Red Army officers in the Soviet Union. It still left room for headlines about the bloody losses by Spain's Republican Government in the civil war. As the Republican town of Teruel fell, it left about 20,000 dead as well as 14,000 Nationalists killed.

After the bombing of Guernica with its loss of civilian lives, came air raids over Barcelona, Tarragona and a few coastal towns by German and Italian bombers. On 16 March 1938, 815 people were killed in another air raid on Barcelona, which refused to surrender to General Franco's fascist troops. The slaughter continued on both sides as power in the Spanish Civil War swung from communist to fascist forces. Ruthless brutality from both sides bled their enemies to death without mercy. Whatever cruelties the Japanese committed against civilians in China was matched by atrocities committed by both sides on each other in Spain's civil war.

'I can scarcely describe the horror that I have conceived since my interview with Franco three days ago,' wrote British Field Marshal Sir Philip Chetwode to

Lord Halifax. 'He is worse than the Reds and I could not stop him executing his unfortunate prisoners.'[5]

Italians fought beside Spanish Nationalist troops against Catalonia on 23 December. After nearly three years of civil war, by 31 March 1939, the whole of Spain was under the rule of General Franco as its sole dictator.

America was not involved. President Roosevelt continued to show that it was possible to organise a sound economy and get things done without imposing dictatorial laws and using secret police against opponents. He spent $400 million on constructing 'super-highways' for the increased traffic, as Hitler had done with the German *autobahns* and Mussolini with his *autostrada* to facilitate the swift movement of military forces to trouble spots. Roosevelt increased taxes and expenditures to create employment.

At the same time, as a result of a $25 million loan, American aircraft and pilots and machine guns began to be sent to the Chinese forces still attempting to fight off Japanese invaders.[6]

The Nazi Menace

Britain's Prime Minister Chamberlain was not only completely taken in by Nazi pageantry and propaganda, and Hitler's displays of power, and the empty promises he made that he intended to break, but was also strangely ignorant of the economic, industrial, and political importance of the United States and its Constitution. Evidently he considered friendship with Germany more important than forming an alliance with America.

'Roosevelt moved to counteract the poor impression made by Ambassador Kennedy, and developed a gradual campaign to raise American awareness of the importance of Europe, by moving another ratchet up from his "we will not stand idly by" and the "Quarantine" speeches.'[7] He broadcast to the nation against the 'dangers from sheer force', from which there can be no peace; against threats of war; against the refugee problem of 'floods of millions of helpless and persecuted wanderers with no place to lay their heads'; against religious persecution; and against the threat of German arms.

His mastery of tactics and oratory, his use of key words and emotional phrases, equalled Churchill's. His speech was also recognised as a reproach to Ambassador Kennedy, who remarked that he felt he had been stabbed in the back. For, although Kennedy and the celebrated aviator Charles Lindbergh admired fascism because they enjoyed power, most American isolationists preferred democracy.

When Martha Dodd's memoir was published in the United States in April 1939, it opened the eyes of Americans who knew nothing about Europe and readers who still failed to understand the danger of the Nazi menace. She was the daughter of Roosevelt's Ambassador to Germany. She wrote about the sadistic reality of torture in Hitler's so-called concentration camps where murders of innocent people took place daily. She had spoken to some of the people who had managed to escape after being made to watch friends tortured to death. The trauma of those who had been able to flee never left them: their lives too were ruined.

Gallup Polls in November 1938 showed that 94 per cent of Americans disapproved of the Nazis' treatment of Jews and 97 per cent disapproved of their treatment of Roman Catholics. In addition, 57 per cent approved of President Roosevelt's withdrawal of the US Ambassador to Germany. Perhaps most significantly, 92 per cent of Americans did not believe that Hitler had no more territorial ambitions, as he claimed. And 60 per cent thought the Munich agreement was more likely to lead to war than peace. Roosevelt was one of them.

34

The Alarm Bell

1939

Returning to England from Munich on 30 September 1938, Neville Chamberlain waved his worthless piece of paper triumphantly in the air for the press reporters at the airport to see what he regarded as a signed agreement with Hitler. He repeated the empty gesture again for the cameras outside 10 Downing Street in Westminster.

At first there was a popular feeling of relief in Britain at being brought back from the edge of war. Then dismay gradually set in as they began to realise that the Czechs had been sacrificed to Hitler for his signature on a flimsy piece of paper. Many felt it was a betrayal and a humiliation. But Chamberlain was jaunty in his delusion that he had achieved 'peace in our time' for his country.

Clement Attlee, the leader of the Labour Party, took a different view when he claimed it was not a victory for reason or humanity; instead it was a victory for brute force. Sir Archibald Sinclair, the leader of the Liberal Party, agreed with him. Yet, even at that stage, they were unaware of Hitler's intention to invade Europe, or that he already planned to conquer the world. It was too bizarre to contemplate, just as most people failed to grasp what was happening in Nazi-occupied countries or behind the fences and machine gun emplacements of Nazi concentration camps, because it was too grotesque to imagine. Normal people did not behave that way.

It was questionable whether Britain's secret intelligence service needed to spread rumours that Hitler intended to annex the whole of South America through ardent local fascist parties and sympathisers in Argentina, without a battle; from where they would be only a short step to creating bridgeheads from which to attack the United States. The intention of the SIS was to persuade the United States to join in the war as Allies against Nazi Germany. It provided plenty of material for President Roosevelt to warn Americans of their own peril.

Churchill spoke in the House of Commons on 5 October. He had already claimed that the Munich Agreement would not lead to peace. Now he warned that it would not lead to a reduction in tensions in Europe, as Chamberlain claimed. It simply meant that small and vulnerable nations would have to make the best terms they could with Nazi Germany.

Germany was the only nation to gain from the fraudulent Munich Agreement. Hitler had already annexed Austria and the Sudetenland without having to use his armed forces. That alone had increased the size of German territory from 186,000 square miles to 225,000, and its population from 68 million to 79 million, with gains also in industrial power and raw materials.

The former Czech President Beneš had resigned and saved his life by seeking exile in England, while Austria's former leader was securely locked up in a German concentration camp.

Hitler's next step was to expel all Polish Jews from Germany. Twenty thousand were ordered out of their homes and sent by train and truck to the Polish border. They were the lucky ones. No one else would be able to escape from the Nazis as soon as Germany trapped them by sealing its borders.

The dramatic incident of *Kristallnacht*, the 'night of broken glass' took place on 9–10 November 1938 in Munich and Berlin, when 7,500 Jewish shopkeepers were intimidated, threatened, and attacked during a period of fifteen hours, while they watched the destruction of their stores, and their homes being looted by brown and black-shirted thugs. About a hundred Jewish people were murdered right away, and 20,000 were taken to concentration camps at Dachau, Sachsenhausen, and Buchenwald.

The shock of photos of the spectacular smashing of Jewish shop windows finally alerted the world to the grotesque criminal nature and brutality of the Nazi regime. Churchill called it 'the alarm bell'.

The Red Terror

At the same time, Stalin's reign of terror in Soviet Russia destroyed more and more Red Army officers, who were tried and executed, or imprisoned without rational reasons. At one point on Russia's borders with Japanese-held frontiers, the Japanese assumed that the USSR would be far too weakened and demoralised to defend its more remote territories by the loss of about 700 Red Army officers whom Stalin had murdered. But the Red Army fought to hold its borders even while Stalin's purges of officers continued.

But for the moment at least, the Red Terror in Soviet Russia served only as a backdrop to the perils that directly involved Great Britain.

The Munich debate began in England on 3 October 1938 in an increasing atmosphere of doubt and discontent by the nation, and lasted for three days. Anthony Eden, Clement Attlee, Sir Archibald Sinclair and Winston Churchill spoke out against Neville Chamberlain's policy. Churchill called the Munich Agreement a 'total and unmitigated defeat'. He warned of the propaganda lies that would soon come again from Goebbels before the Nazis struck somewhere else and the rest of Czechoslovakia would soon be swallowed by the Nazi regime.

Churchill repeated that what had happened had been made possible by five years of neglect of Britain's air defences. Consequently, the nation was unprepared for war. He attacked the Government for not preventing Germany from rearming, for not arming Britain, and for abandoning the League of Nations without making any alliances. He warned that the independence of Britain and France was at risk. What he found particularly menacing and depressing was that Britain was falling under the power and influence of Nazi Germany, so that Britain's very existence now depended on Germany's goodwill.

Churchill's delivery of his message was slow and sombre, and filled with a sense of doom, which made his pronouncements impressive and convincing – even to members who had supported the Munich Agreement. His sober presentation made them realise the truth of the awful things they had done, and what they should have done, and raised fears for Britain's security.

'Do not suppose this is the end,' he warned them. It was only the beginning of the reckoning, the first bitter taste of what was about to come. There was now no future in Europe except war at Hitler's choosing.

The House of Commons voted that night. Thirty Conservatives refused to vote for Prime Minister Chamberlain, even though he was the leader of their Party.

The Munich Sellout

Back home again at Chartwell, Churchill was in despair. All he felt he could hope for was that the United States would play a role in Europe. Meanwhile, the Prime Minister had adjourned Parliament so that there would be no more criticism of his Munich sellout. Chamberlain was still filled with a personal sense of achievement and elation about his importance to the world, and pride in his claimed friendship with Hitler. He stubbornly wrote to his sister that he was undeterred by Churchill.

New pressures inside the Cabinet by Kingsley Wood to increase the size of the Royal Air Force, and Hore-Belisha to increase the army, were met by Sir John Simon with the same appeasement arguments that Chamberlain did not want to upset Hitler. There were plenty of people in Britain who supported Chamberlain's pro-Nazi stand. Some of them had been disturbed by Churchill's attacks on the Government, and wanted to have him replaced by a Government supporter. There were three attempts to unseat him. But isolating him from influence did not reflect the country's wishes. More individuals wanted him offered a post in the Cabinet. Some wanted him to lead a 'National Opposition', which the Liberals agreed to support.

Churchill had secretly attempted to persuade the popular Irish Taoiseach, Éamon de Valera, to join the Allies, but he would not. He and Ireland's President had decided to remain neutral. In September 1939 de Valera demanded the Irish ports back that had been passed to Britain as Irish Treaty ports to protect the British Isles from German U-boat attacks. Churchill urged Parliament for the return of at least the port of Berehaven.

The House felt it would be unwise to occupy it by force. But Churchill believed that three quarters of the Irish population would support the Allies. Foreign Secretary Anthony Eden was more realistic in assuring him that neutrality prevented Ireland from cooperating. Small neutral nations were terrified of reprisals by Germany.

Britain was not yet ready for war. The logistics were not yet in place; nor were Britain's armed forces trained for landing and invading from the sea. And Prime Minister Chamberlain did not possess the knowledge or ability to conduct a war: he was a committee man.

As Churchill wrote to Admiral Pound, 'Our army is puny as far as the fighting front is concerned; our air force is hopelessly inferior to the Germans; we are not allowed to stop them receiving their vital supplies of iron ore; we maintain an attitude of complete passivity dispersing our forces ever more widely … Do you realise that perhaps we are heading for *defeat*?'[1]

One humiliation came after another when Churchill became convinced that Britain could cripple the German Navy by blockading much-needed supplies of Scandinavian iron ore from reaching Germany. Shipments were sent to Germany from Narvik in Norway and Lulea in Sweden. Churchill had received the suggestion on 23 December from Fritz Thyssen, who was from one of Germany's leading industrial families. He had thought it wise to flee from Germany to Switzerland and then France. He claimed that victory would go to the side that controlled iron ore supplies. The idea would ultimately lead to the disastrous Allied invasion of Norway the following year.

Churchill was more optimistic about the Royal Navy in a broadcast to the nation on 20 January, after he had heard they had forced the German battleship *Graf Spee* to scuttle itself in Montevideo harbour. It had been the pride of the German Navy. He told his audience triumphantly that 'half the U-boats with which Germany began the war have been sunk'.

He did his best to create confidence in the public's attitude and at the same time encourage neutral countries to join the Allies by his show of strength. He praised the neutral Finns who were standing up defiantly against the far bigger Soviet Russian forces that were invading their tiny country. Everyone saw the Finns' victories as a sure sign that the Red Army was by no means as powerful as had been thought.

Halifax were not impressed with Winston's broadcast and urged him to toe the party line – which meant his and Chamberlain's. Churchill humbly apologised by claiming he had thought he was. Then he made another inspiring broadcast, saying: 'Everyone is wondering what is happening about the war.' He seemed to be prompting a decisive reply from the hesitant PM and his Foreign Secretary. 'He had become the orator of the government.'[2]

Chamberlain was strangely silent about the broadcasts. Then, when the fifth meeting of the Supreme War Council was planned to take place in Paris, Churchill was invited to attend it for the first time.

Step By Step

During the entire period when Churchill was out-of-office, apart from using his platform as an MP in the House of Commons, he had used newspapers and broadcasting to keep the public and the Cabinet informed of the menace of foreign adversaries, which he knew about better than anyone else. He had continually implored an indifferent government and public to wake up to the reality of an expanding Fascist Italy and Nazi Germany. To do so, he had to think for an unthinking readership. His newspaper reports on foreign affairs and the defenselessness of Great Britain increased in 1936-1939.[3]

In May 1936 he described how Nazi Germany was rearming and how Great Britain was unprepared for war. Its navy must be stronger. Britain's superior fleet of battleships and cruisers was still the senior service, before it became apparent from the bombing of civilians in Guernica in the Spanish Civil War in August, that air supremacy had now become far more important than ruling the seaways.

In 1937, working class discontent boiled over in France to the brink of civil war between hostile partisan forces of the political left and right – a sure sign of instability and undependability – leaving the possibility of one less partner for Great Britain in the event of war, particularly as France possessed the biggest army in Europe. But 'War is not imminent,' he noted in October. Nevertheless, he prudently put out feelers for help to the United States in December. Just as Hitler had planned his rise to power stage by-stage in Germany, so Churchill anticipated every one of his moves step-by-step.

The bellicose secret societies in the Japanese army, who murdered more moderate politicians who disagreed with their warlike aims, mirrored what had been happening in Germany during the rise of the Nazi Party. Nothing seemed to escape Churchill's attention and his sophisticated analysis and assessment of each situation. 'What did Japan think of us?' In July he was writing about 'The Rape of Austria,' as Hitler drove through Vienna in his motorcade to be greeted with wild enthusiasm by Austria's Nazi Party at his annexation.

Not only did Churchill ferret out facts and circumstances in Europe for the Cabinet to think about, he did exactly what he had done when he had been an ambitious second-lieutenant of 23 in the cavalry in 1898. He had written a book about his skirmishes on the border of the North-West Frontier of India with Afghanistan, and made sure that the Prime Minister had read and praised it. He had sought visibility as a future leader then, and did so now, to show he had the experience and knowledge and attributes to defy Nazi Germany.

In 1938 he reviewed world security, praising the fleets of both Great Britain and France, and criticising Britain's army which was far too small for an intercontinental war; still more like a colonial police force to protect its colonial subjects from invasion. He had already begun to focus on air power, where he compared Britain's RAF unfavorably with other European powers: 'Germany 3000, Italy 1200, Great Britain 1500, and France 1000.'[4]

By 1939 he wrote about 'Mussolini's Choice.' Next came 'The Russian Counterpoise.' Then 'President Roosevelt's Message,' and 'The Anglo-Turkish Alliance.' The Epilogue to his series of newspaper articles may have sounded optimistic, although he cannot have felt that way at the time. Nevertheless, he had to strike a reasonable balance between warning of the imminence of war and comforting readers with the thought that Britain would overcome all setbacks as it had always done in the past, if he hoped to convince them. Churchill was no complainer – he was an enthusiastic soldier filled with optimism about defeating the enemies of a democratic and open society, whether it was to maintain peace or prepare for war.

He had known for years what Hitler was up to; what all nationalists aspire to, and what all dictators attempt to do when given an opportunity to seize power. But after years of warning an indifferent government and public who had done their best to ignore him, he was relentless, while they were unwilling to see the bleak truth of appeasement, which was that it showed weakness to an enemy eager for war. Even so, they found it easier in their languid way to refuse to believe him. 'People would simply not believe that Germany would attack France and Belgium.'[5]

'Here then, in an hour when all is uncertain, but not uncheered by hope and resolve, the tale stops. Great Britain stands in the midst, and even at the head of a great and growing company of states and nations, ready to confront and to ensure what may befall. The shock may be sudden, or the strain may be long-drawn: but who can doubt that all will come right if we persevere to the end.'[6]

He emphasised the outbreak of the previous war as an example of how apathy can be changed in an instant. 'If a score of people are sitting around a conference table in strenuous argument, and one of them draws a pistol and shoots two or three of his opponents, the whole temper of the conference is altered, and it becomes very difficult to recall its members to the other points upon the agenda. Three days before Britain entered the Great War, four members out of five in the Cabinet and nine out of ten in the House of Commons would have been found inveterately opposed to our intervention upon the Continent. Four days later these proportions were reversed.'

He went on to point out that 'An episode like the trampling down of Czechoslovakia by an overwhelming force would change the whole current of human ideas and would eventually draw upon the aggressor a wrath which would in the end involve all the greatest nations of the world.'[7]

The Phoney War

German troops were barely involved with British forces in this period when both sides appeared to be weighing each other up, and Britain was pathetically short of war material. Churchill attempted to drum up support for a plan to scatter floating mines in the Rhine. A French plan was to support the feisty Finns by bombing Russia's oilfields in Baku. Both schemes seemed to get no further than talk, because no one had any idea what the German Army was about to unleash in Europe.

It was during the lull before an impending storm that Chamberlain made a fool of himself by remarking to the Conservative National Union that 'Hitler had missed the boat'. It was one more indication of how out of touch he and Halifax were with the harsh real world of foreign affairs.

The meeting of the Supreme War Council in Paris from 12 September 1939 failed to raise a spark of interest by the French. Churchill attempted to persuade them to be decisive after having failed to persuade Chamberlain. Reynaud 'was wobbly'. Deladier was all for waiting to see what might happen.

American diplomat Sumner Welles had been sent by the President as a special envoy to sound out possibilities for a negotiated peace with Germany. When he met Churchill on 12 March, Winston told him straight out why the war must be fought to a finish. Welles was extremely impressed with their conversation. He had expected to be disappointed but listened as if mesmerised for three hours to what Churchill told him.

Minutes of the meeting recorded that: 'Mr Welles expressed the opinion that Mr Churchill was one of the most fascinating personalities he had ever met.'[8]

Seeing Chamberlain's position weakening, Prime Minister de Valera demanded the return of the Irish treaty ports on the south coast of Ireland, which were vital for the safe passage of Britain's food supplies against German U-boats. Chamberlain meekly gave in, hoping for friendship from Ireland. Éamon de Valera stated that there could be no friendship until Britain gave him the six Protestant counties in the North.

Publicity built up for Churchill from his articles in *Picture Post* and the *New Statesman and Nation*. More of his articles were published in the *Daily Telegraph,* and he was interviewed by the *Daily Herald.* Several other newspapers questioned Chamberlain's decision to exclude Churchill from the Cabinet. It was strange, one of them remarked, that Churchill was left out in the cold while lesser men fumbled with vital matters that Churchill could handle as a master.[9]

Chamberlain confirmed in February 1939 that if either Britain or France was attacked, either would come to the aid of the other. It seemed like a change of heart on the Prime Minister's part, so that Churchill wrote to Halifax that perhaps the Government position was moving closer to his own. But Chamberlain's correspondence with his sister showed that the Prime Minister had been taken in once again by another of Hitler's speeches offering friendship with Britain. Chamberlain felt so optimistic at Hitler's words that on 10 March 1939, he gave it as his opinion to the press at the House of Commons that Europe was now 'settling down to a period of tranquillity'.

Is This the End?

Only five days later, on 15 March, Hitler ordered the German army to invade the rest of Czechoslovakia. It was exactly what Churchill had prophesied would happen after the cowardice of signing the Munich Agreement. German troops now occupied Prague.

Chamberlain was urged to change Britain's policy as a consequence of Hitler's occupation of the whole of the country. He gave an indication that he now realised at last that he had been duped by Hitler, by asking in a speech he gave in Birmingham, 'Is this the end of an old adventure, or the beginning of a new?'

Two days later, Churchill again pressed him on the subject of placing anti-aircraft defences on full alert.

On 28 March, thirty Conservative MPs, led by Eden, Churchill and Duff-Cooper, proposed setting up an 'All-Party Government', as they and the public had lost confidence in this one. Three days after that, Chamberlain surprised them by issuing a guarantee of Poland's independence. He seemed to have established a firm red line at last. Churchill insisted that the Soviet Union should be brought in as a partner, but Chamberlain did not like the idea. Churchill was convinced that Britain needed the cooperation of other nations, even if they were not democratic.

They had hardly absorbed the new dilemmas that Poland raised when Italian troops massed on the borders of Albania and invaded its territory. With Great Britain hesitant and off balance, the opportunity was seen as a free for all. Churchill knew it was another alarm bell. He looked to the British Fleet, on which the security of the British Isles depended, and found it scattered and vulnerable across the Mediterranean. He immediately took control of the situation as if he were the First Lord of the Admiralty.

'When everyone else was dazed and hesitating,' according to Harold Macmillan, Churchill 'found maps to study. He made phone calls to determine the locations of all British warships in the Mediterranean. He advised Chamberlain where he felt they should be, telling him what action should be taken that night. He also called 10 Downing Street for Parliament to be summoned.'

At the debate on Britain's unpreparedness, Churchill expressed the view that expansion of German power was not in Soviet Russia's interest, so that they could be expected to ally themselves with Britain and France. He detested Bolshevism, but insisted it was time for everyone to put prejudices aside in order to cooperate with each other in this emergency.

One of Chamberlain's letters to his sister noted that Churchill had expressed a 'strong desire' afterwards to the Chief Whip to enter the Cabinet. The Prime Minister had not rejected the suggestion, because it caught him 'at a moment when I was certainly feeling the need of help'.

Chamberlain finally announced on 15 April that he would set up a Ministry of Supply, as Churchill and others had been attempting to persuade him to do for some time. But he did not offer the position to Churchill. He chose the Minister of Transport, Leslie Burgin. As soon as the post was announced, there were more calls for Churchill to be included in the Cabinet. The *Evening News* recommended that he should be First Lord of the Admiralty or Secretary of State for Air.

About ten days later, Churchill urged the House to introduce compulsory military service. He was 'warmly cheered' and the Bill was passed. His speech so impressed the House that he became a centre for supporters to gather around.

35

An Age of Extremes

1939

Winston felt he had done all he could, although he was still not a member of the Cabinet. He turned back again to his writing to make some money. There was more work to be done on the *History of the English-Speaking Peoples.* Since his secretary had been taken ill, he now employed Kathleen Hill full-time, and had a team of historians and researchers to help him with details as he worked to complete it in accordance with a scheduled deadline to pay off his debts. She found the house alive and restless when he was home, but still as a mouse when he was away.

In one of his next articles in the *Daily Telegraph*, he predicted another invasion of European territory by Hitler, most probably Poland. Once again, he recommended cooperation with Soviet Russia. But Chamberlain was far too prejudiced against the USSR and stubbornly resisted any interference in what he considered to be his own affair. Horace Wilson continued to take orders from him on Anglo-German economic ties, while their appeasement of Hitler continued.

Sir Nevile Henderson was now at the British Embassy in Warsaw. He was asked to press the Poles to make concessions to Germany. It looked like a repeat situation of the disappearance of Czechoslovakia, which had been thrown to the wolves. Henderson felt a first step should be for the Poles to give the free city of Danzig back to Germany. Chamberlain agreed, and told the owner of the *Daily Telegraph* that: 'It might be possible to arrange things.'

A senior officer at the Foreign Office was heard to remark that Sir Horace Wilson was 'working like a beaver for a Second Munich'.[1]

That Churchill was not in the Cabinet not only surprised the public, it amazed Germany. On 5 July 1939, Hitler's Minister of Finance, Count Schwerin von Krosigk, told two British diplomats in Berlin that Churchill should be in the Cabinet, saying, 'Churchill is the only Englishman Hitler is afraid of.' But Chamberlain feared that Churchill would prevent him from giving Danzig to Hitler once he was in office.[2]

Soon afterwards, on 14 August, Churchill took a trip to Paris. He was shown round the famous Maginot Line. It was a concrete fortress just inside the French border and faced Hitler's Siegfried Line in Germany, with the intention of stopping German troops crossing the French border. French officers who showed him round claimed it was impregnable. He was dismayed to find a 200-mile gap at the end facing the coast at Dunkirk. His spirits dropped when he was told the gap was protected by 'field-work'.

Churchill continued work on his history, and wrote more articles for the *Daily Telegraph* and the *News of the World*, as well as meeting with streams of visitors to Chartwell. He predicted to General Ironside that Hitler was going to make war on Poland. Then Italy would join Germany. Egypt would be captured by Italy. And Hitler would make an alliance with Soviet Russia.

Stalin had enough secret agents established in influential positions to know which nation was the strongest military power. Since England was indecisive and unprepared, he made a pact with Germany instead. Now he would gain control of Estonia, Latvia and Lithuania, and take a piece of eastern Poland in return for supporting Hitler.

A month later, on 1 September, Hitler massed German troops on the Polish border. All the might of the German army and air force was to be thrown in to a *blitzkrieg* invasion of Poland. Polish troops not only faced German forces on one side, but also Russian troops invading their territory on the other. The simultaneous invasion of Poland would involve swift troop advances with tanks and armoured vehicles on three fronts, and overwhelming air dominance to destroy the Polish air force on the ground before it was ready to take off.

Programme of the German Workers' Party

It was the first war in which unarmed civilians, including women and children, were deliberately targeted for mass slaughter and individual murder on such a large scale. What had been rehearsed on a smaller scale in Spain was now unleashed on Poland. It was largely a consequence of the weapons, like heavily armed tanks, and bombing and machine gunning from the air. Hitler had no use for the Poles – he despised the entire race, and would not hesitate to destroy them all. It would be far easier to annex and colonise the country without any Poles left in it, only obedient German colonisers.

SS Death's Head regiments were trained to massacre civilian populations without mercy. They followed in the rear of advancing German troops. Every day in every Polish city, town and village that German forces reached, the SS rounded up and executed local Polish priests, teachers and officials, to deprive those remaining of leadership. Sooner rather than later, the others would be either shot out of hand or herded into concentration camps to be murdered, or used as slave labour until they dropped dead of malnutrition, disease and exhaustion. Polish youths had little chance to resist them. In the event of any Poles assaulting or killing even one German soldier in retaliation, the SS took hostages of ten, twenty, thirty or more Polish civilians and killed them all instantly in public view, as examples to cow the rest.

The German Army made no difference between Catholics, Jews or Protestants; they were all the same to Hitler, and all targeted for extermination. There was panic all round, with people running in every direction, believing they could escape, even when being machine-gunned from the air. Entire families were massacred.

General Halder – who had once planned secretly to have Hitler arrested as a madman – now discussed Hitler's intentions with his fellow officers. After which, one named Colonel Edouard Wagner noted in his diary; 'It is the Führer's and Goering's intention to destroy and exterminate the Polish nation.'[3]

Hitler had elaborated on his intentions in *Mein Kampf*, but it seemed that, although there were plenty of buyers for his book, it was confusing and heavy going to read, and few managed to penetrate it with care or took it seriously. And yet, four years earlier, his 'twenty-five intentions' had been clearly itemised in the Programme of the German Workers' Party, which had merged with the Nazi Party. His priority would be the unity of all Germans everywhere in a Greater Germany. After that came equality with other nations. Third was to obtain more territory as colonies for Germany's growing population.

The other twenty-two points concerned the ambiguous and unscientific race theories that he had invented, that Germans were supermen and other races should be exterminated. Poles would be wiped out first. Then it would be the turn of Czechs, Slavs, Jews and Gypsies. Now he proceeded to turn his fantasies into reality.[4]

Churchill broadcast urgently to the United States. 'Listen,' he said. 'No, listen carefully … Don't you hear it? It is the tramp of armies crunching the gravel of the parade grounds … the tramp of two million German soldiers and more than a million Italians …'

When the Alarm Bell Rang

Churchill was woken up on 1 September by a phone call from the Polish Ambassador, Count Raczynski, to tell him that German bombers were flying over Warsaw and dropping bombs. German troops were advancing simultaneously on the capital city. Churchill passed on the news to General Ironside, who telephoned the War Office. Then Churchill attended an emergency meeting at the House of Commons.

The British Government sent a message to Berlin, warning the Germans to stop all action against Poland without hesitation. But Ambassador Sir Nevile Henderson was told to soft pedal the message by making it clear that it was not an ultimatum.

There was no response by midnight, when Britain had still not declared war on Germany. Churchill wrote to Chamberlain in the morning, hoping that a joint declaration of war would be announced by that afternoon at the latest. He waited for an answer in his London flat in Morpeth Mansions, but Chamberlain did not reply.

Morpeth Mansions was a red brick block within walking distance of Westminster Cathedral and Downing Street. The small London flat occupied the two upper levels, which provided the advantage of a roof terrace with views over the centre of London.

Churchill was still waiting for a summons when the Cabinet met at 4.15 p.m. at 10 Downing Street. Halifax announced that negotiations were still in progress as German troops advanced further into Poland. Now it was Sir Samuel Hoare who was concerned at the delay and fearful of public opinion if something wasn't done about it. Leslie Hore-Belisha backed him up by remarking that: 'Public opinion was strongly against our yielding an inch.' As far as they were concerned, an ultimatum should be sent at once, to expire at midnight. Inskip supported them both.

Chamberlain read out an appeal for Britain to fulfil its obligations to Poland. Then he agreed to a midnight ultimatum.

As one historian would write: 'Perhaps Hitler's biggest single misjudgement was his failure to appreciate the depth of the hostility he had aroused in Britain. The main object of his *blitzkrieg* in France was not to destroy the French army, which he felt he could do any time he wished, but to shock Britain into making terms.'[5]

According to one of Germany's leading generals, Hitler wanted to sound out England on dividing the world between Britain and Nazi Germany.[6] Even if true, Britain would be bargaining from a position of weakness.

Reality at His Heels

Doubts about the fairness of the terms of the Treaty of Versailles in 1919 had lingered long afterwards, and were exploited by German propaganda that continued to insist that Germany was a victim of a conspiracy. That conspiracy theory created a lingering doubt and uneasiness that would be demonstrated two decades later. Now, when the Second World War was imminent, the modern poet W.H. Auden fled from Europe to neutral America on 1 September 1939, 'with reality snapping at his heels'. The pact between Stalin and Hitler allowed Nazi Germany to invade Poland without having to worry about any danger from Soviet Russian forces.[7]

Not only had the 1918 Armistice and the 1919 Treaty provided an opportunity for Germany to build up new supplies of arms, ammunition and armour, but it had also enabled a new generation of German youths to grow up to military age and be trained for sacrifice on new battlefields in order to continue the German War.

Auden was one of many political left-wingers who chose to romanticise communism and Soviet Russia. But now, after a panicked flight from the imminent onslaught in Europe, he sat in a bar on 52nd Street in New York City to collect his thoughts over several much-needed drinks. In an attempt to sort out his conflicting emotions, he jotted down several ambiguous lines of poetry that expressed his thoroughly shattered and confused feelings. Like most people, he had been aware of only small fragments of information about the situation leading up to the war, and based his faulty conclusions on his limited knowledge; which was what most people in England had been doing for years and denying the unimaginable.

Throughout all those years when Churchill had uttered his warnings about the rise of Nazi Germany and the probability of war, millions of ordinary people had gone about their daily affairs without listening to him, or had thoughtlessly dismissed his warnings. They had made wrong-headed assumptions about Hitler and Nazi Germany. Those false assumptions mirrored the paradoxes that had emerged and hovered over the delegates to the Peace Conference in Paris in 1919. There was now no doubt in most people's minds that both the earlier war and this one were German wars that had cost millions of lives and would cost millions more. But the German public had been deliberately brainwashed by German propaganda to believe that they were in the right. Many people in England were as uninformed and wrong-headed as Auden, who had also been deceived by the naivety of his German friends and lovers.

After his first visit to Germany, Auden had exclaimed, 'Berlin is a bugger's daydream. There are 170 male brothels under police control.'[8]

Those in Tor district offered boys in lederhosen. 'Berlin boasted an erotic demimonde consisting of an estimated one hundred thousand women and thirty-five thousand men who regularly prostituted themselves … It also became the world's premier tourist destination for sexual predilections of all kinds.'[9]

Like many others who haunted the artificial Berlin of witty cabarets and the sex trade for tourists, he had been contaminated, by the 'gaily coloured froth on top' of a completely artificial German world, 'that many people mistook for the true, the happy Germany before the eruption of the new barbarism', as the popular artist George Grosz wrote of that inter-war period:[10]

> Foreigners who visited us at that time were easily fooled by the apparent light-hearted, whirring fun on the surface, by the nightlife and the so-called freedom and flowering of the arts. But that was really nothing more than froth. Right under the short-lived, lively surface of the shimmering swamp was fratricide and general discord, and regiments were formed for the final reckoning … And we knew all that; or at least we had forebodings.[11]

Resolution in the House

Neville Chamberlain rose in the House at 7.30 a.m. on Saturday, knowing that there had been considerable unease at the delays. Now the House expected firm resolve. But that was not Chamberlain's way. To their astonishment, he spoke again of further negotiations with Hitler. Most of the Members in the House were shocked and horrified. A delegation of Cabinet ministers went to Chamberlain's room afterwards to put a powerful case against any more delays. Chamberlain promised to consider their request and left hurriedly for 10 Downing Street.

Duff-Cooper went to Churchill's flat at Morpeth Mansions and found Churchill, Eden, Boothby and Bracken already there. Boothby was convinced that Winston should go to the House of Commons to break the Prime Minister and take his place. He should not accept office under Chamberlain. They also insisted that Eden should be in the War Cabinet to avoid Churchill being outnumbered.

In the meantime, Chamberlain phoned Halifax to tell him he wanted him immediately at 10 Downing Street. Halifax warned him over the phone that his statement in the House had gone badly, and that they thought he was half-hearted and hesitant; that the result had been an unpleasant scene. Having warned the Prime Minister, Halifax hastened to Downing Street, where he and Chamberlain dined together. Chamberlain told him he was aware that the House were infuriated at his statement, and he did not believe the Government could stand, 'unless we could clear the position'.

A thunderstorm had broken out while Churchill wrote a letter to Chamberlain with fresh ideas contributed intermittently by the others in his flat, as late as 10.30 p.m.. He requested clarity of the situation and of the part he should play in it. Heavy rain whipped the rooftops and poured down on nearby St James's Park as he wrote. Clementine poured drinks for his anxious friends, who included Eden, Boothby, Duncan Sandys, Duff-Cooper and Brendan Bracken. All were angry at Chamberlain's apparent complacency and inability to act, and his backtracking on his promises to take a stand against Hitler. They and Clementine begged Winston to take a lead.

The rebel group of seven or eight members of the Cabinet had been determined to corner the Prime Minister. As soon as Winston signed his letter, they pressed through the rain to deliver it to Chamberlain by hand, arriving soaking wet at 10 Downing Street, to find him still dining with Halifax. They refused to leave until the Prime Minister had withdrawn all ideas of further negotiations with the Nazis and agreed to an ultimatum being delivered to Germany in the morning.

Winston and Clementine heard the announcement on their wireless set at Morpeth Mansions at 9 a.m. on 3 September 1939; 'If Germany did not halt its attack on Poland within three hours', Britain would be at war.[12]

Several air raid sirens began to howl outside. Winston and Clementine climbed up to the roof to see what was going on. Thirty or forty barrage balloons tugged anxiously on their cables over anti-aircraft gun emplacements. They went down into the air raid shelter with a bottle of brandy, although the basement had not yet been fortified with sandbags to provide effective protection.

The air-raid warning turned out to be a test or a false alarm. As soon as the sirens wailed the 'all clear' over Westminster, Churchill drove to the House of Commons with Clementine, to hear Chamberlain's account. Most pedestrians they passed on the way carried gas masks in cardboard boxes slung over their shoulder by a piece of string. Sixty-eight million gas masks had already been made and distributed to the public in readiness for war.

Now that the Government had finally sent an ultimatum to Germany, Churchill suddenly felt calm after all the arguments and striving of the past years to get something done. He was detached from all the trivialities of human affairs, in order to face something far more important and urgent. He felt thrilled and fearless about the future, as he had done when he had been an army officer under bombardment on the Western Front in the last war. The same exhilaration came to him as he had felt in battle, when he had confessed how happy he was at the battlefront.

For the whole of the past decade he had been out of office as a back-bencher, and out of favour by the Government. But when he spoke in the House of Commons, his listeners had recognised 'the voice of a man of stature, and of integrity'.[13]

Churchill was plunged in deep thought about the future as they drove in silence to the Prime Minister's residence. It was his second world war against Germany. It was fortunate that he had experienced the first one with its grim and grinding and relentless death tolls, because it helped him to prepare for what was to come. On one hand, he reflected, Chamberlain's dithering had provided another eleven months for Britain to rearm. On the other, the Prime Minister had made a cardinal error in not involving Soviet Russia in his meetings. He had been motivated by his own narrow self-righteousness and pride. Now Great Britain was confronted not only by Nazi Germany, but also by Soviet Russia.

Churchill had been remarkably patient and sympathetic towards Chamberlain. He could not forget how the Prime Minister had launched him on his own political career in Oldham in 1929, when he had been only twenty-six:

> Mr Chamberlain himself came to speak for me. There was more enthusiasm over him at this moment than after the Great War for Mr Lloyd George and Sir Douglas Haig combined. There was at the same time a tremendous opposition; but antagonism had not wholly excluded admiration from their breasts. We drove to our great meeting together in an open carriage. Our friends had filled the theatre; our opponents thronged its approaches. At the door of the theatre our carriage was jammed tight for some minutes in an immense hostile crowd, all groaning and booing at the tops of their voices, and grinning with the excitement of seeing a famous fellow citizen whom it was their right and duty to oppose. I watched my honoured guest with close attention. He loved the roar of the multitude, and with my father could always say 'I have never feared the English democracy.'[14]

Clementine snapped him out of his reverie to point out that their vehicle had arrived at its destination. She waited in the car while Winston hurried in through the front door of No. 10 to see the Prime Minister. When her husband came out only a few minutes later and hastened back to the car, he called out to Clementine: 'It's the Admiralty. That's a lot better than I thought.' Back again in the car, he told her he had also been given a seat in the War Cabinet.

Churchill had served as First Lord of the Admiralty with distinction in the First World War, when General Lord Kitchener, the Commander in Chief of the British Army, had complimented him on the fact that the British Fleet had always been ready for battle.

As soon as his new appointment was announced officially, the Board of Admiralty signalled it to all ships. It was said that, as word spread of his appointment as First Lord of the Admiralty, faces began to smile with relief and confidence, and pride-full eagerness. Officers and men quickly passed on the message to each other – Winston was back![15]

36

Unworldly Innocence
1939

In January 1939, Winston wrote to Clementine from Paris:

> They all confirm the fact that the Germans had hardly any soldiers at all on the French Frontier during the crisis. And [Prime Minister] Blum told me, (secret) that he had it from Daladier himself that both Generals Gamelin and Georges were confident that they could have broken through the weak unfinished German line, almost unguarded as it was, by the fifteenth day at the latest, and that if the Czechs could have held out only for that short fortnight, the German armies would have had to go back to face invasion.
>
> On the other side there is great preponderance in the air, and it depends what you put on that how you judge the matter.

He added:

> I have no doubt that a firm attitude by England and France would have prevented war, and I believe that history will incline to the view that if the worst had come to the worst, we should have been far better off than we may be at some future date.

Some people in the West who give serious thought to their fate, continue to wonder, if that were the case, what had the British Cabinet been so afraid of that had placed them and other European nations in danger? Why had the Government so abjectly continued to give in to Hitler's demands? And what was the root cause of the Second World War?

> Roosevelt had recognised from the earliest moment of the Third Reich that Western democracy probably could not coexist with it. He came to believe, by early 1939 at the latest, that the United States would be required as the indispensable force to rid the world of Nazism and that it would then emerge not only as a post-isolationist country but as the pre-eminent nation on earth. Supreme political artist as he was, he cannot

> have failed, by the beginning of 1939, to have glimpsed this destiny that would carry his country to heights no nation had ever occupied and himself to a position in American history rivalled, if at all, only by Washington and Lincoln.[1]

Hitler and his diplomats, his propagandists, and his generals, had successfully managed to bluff Britain and its allies about Germany's real goal. It was particularly surprising since he had laid it out for his followers in *Mein Kampf.* Goebbels would refer to Hitler's book when he claimed that the French premier should have remarked after its publication, 'This man cannot be tolerated in our vicinity. Either he disappears or we march!' But they didn't do it. 'They left us alone and let us slip through the risky zone, and we were able to sail around all dangerous reefs. And when we were done, and well-armed, better than they, then they started the war!'[2]

His remark emphasised that it was not so much the aggression of the post-First World War years that caused the Second World War, but Britain and France's spinelessness in failing to react to it when it was still possible to resist it between 1925 and 1933. Instead, no government possessed the will to stand up to bullying, or even form a proper understanding of the situation.

Historian Paul Johnson claimed that: 'Britain and France, even without America, might conceivably have contained Hitler in 1933–34, had both been resolute and willing to act in concert.'[3]

By doing nothing, the Allies returned Europe to that point in 1918 when Germany had been winning the war. Hitler now established Germany as the dominant power in Europe. His next step would be to destroy Soviet Russia, as he had said he intended to do in *Mein Kampf.*

The Minds of Leaders

When social psychologist Gustave Le Bon investigated the causes of the French Revolution, he pointed out that writers and historians had been perplexed because they had not analysed the minds of its leaders. There are still plenty of mysteries that have not been resolved about the causes of the Second World War. One is the state of mind and attitude of Britain's leaders and the appeasers of the Nazis in the Cabinet and the Foreign Office and elsewhere in the 1930s, which led up to the outbreak of war in 1939. They appeared not to have recognised that since the old Europe had gone, so had polite and old-fashioned diplomacy, when gentlemen negotiated with gentlemen. The new situation required a more modern, realistic and resolute hand.

Of the many different mindsets between each of the members of the Cabinet and Winston Churchill, perhaps the most important one was that Churchill was a 'modern man' and a lifetime learner, who would never stop learning until he stopped breathing; whereas the attitude of most of the others seems to have been imprisoned in complacent illusions of their status from the Victorian past. The young Winston had managed to shake off the romantic tradition of Christians grovelling piteously on their knees to the deity for help, instead of rolling up their sleeves and helping themselves, when he faced the brutal truth of warfare as a soldier in his early twenties. It confirmed him in his belief that God was not much interested in human affairs. It was up to us to be vigilant and always prepared to defend ourselves.

The British public school sentiment of the times is not easy to describe, because it was unlikely to have been fully understood by the naive schoolboys themselves, who had to learn it obliquely from schoolmasters who did not understand it either. Certainly, they could not express those sentiments clearly enough for the concept to be effective in the real world outside of a school chapel, where small boys were obliged to sit and listen to whatever mindless nonsense their teachers might utter about fair play for all. There was no such thing.

There was a romantic stirring in their hearts to do good for society, out of feelings of guilt for the inequalities and injustices they saw around them, and a tendency for socialists to blame it on themselves instead of recognising it as a reality of life.

Prime Minister Neville Chamberlain had been educated at Rugby, which had been the original source of that noble but unrealistic sentiment that, today, would be considered puzzling, patronising, or laughable. Instead of being prepared for the unforgiving evolutionary process that had existed since the beginning of human life, they were taught cricket and learnt how to lose gracefully. Chamberlain had been no match for Hitler in negotiations, because he was honest to a fault when dealing with a schemer who used lies and threats, and promises that he had no intention of fulfilling. Chamberlain, on the other hand, had been careful to maintain his punctilious good manners, as if dealing with another gentleman of the old school.

Churchill remarked in his memoir at the age of thirty-six how dignified Chamberlain had been in his message of support to the electorate when he had spoken on young Winston's behalf:

> He spoke for over an hour; but what pleased the audience most was that, having made a mistake in some fact or figure to the prejudice of his opponent, he went back and corrected it, observing that he must not be unfair.[4]

Chamberlain did not wish to be unfair to Hitler, either. He always gave him the benefit of the doubt, until he finally realised he had been hoodwinked. Churchill, on the other hand, was a former professional soldier who had fought in several different types of wars, and knew that meekness was a losing tactic and hesitation a short-cut to the grave. Monsters had to be crushed immediately, before they grew too strong to defeat.

On 22 August 1939, Churchill's old bodyguard – who had since retired from Scotland Yard to manage a small group of grocery stores – received a telegram from his old boss. It said simply, 'Meet me Croydon Aerodrome 4.30 P.M. Wednesday'. Churchill took him to Chartwell and offered him his old job. Since Thompson's respect for him had never wavered, he agreed with alacrity.

'Large numbers of organised Nazis are already in England,' Churchill told Thompson. 'I can look after myself in the daytime, but I need you to take care of me at night.'[5]

Thompson borrowed Churchill's Colt, and immediately began to patrol the grounds at Chartwell. When a state of national emergency was declared soon afterwards, Churchill informed him that his position was now official and he would work from Marlborough Street police station. Thompson collected a Webley from Scotland Yard and returned Churchill's Colt.

37

A Man of Stature

1940

Great Britain was still the moral leader globally, and much admired and envied for possessing the largest empire in history to back its moral leadership with force, if necessary. Major and minor European nations had turned to Britain to save them from the possible onslaught by Nazi Germany; which they would have been unlikely to have done without the backing of the Empire. Even so, Britain looked weak now, as a consequence of its previous show of weak and unsure leadership, and was no match against Germany's military might.

On returning to London from Paris, Churchill was thrust into the poorly executed disaster of the Norwegian Campaign of April 1940, to cut off Germany's supplies of essential resources, including steel and oil. Minutes of the meetings of the War Cabinet after its failure revealed a 'lack of advance planning, infirmity of purpose, ill-coordination between the services, and clutching now at one objective and then at another'.

German command of the air outweighed Britain's historic command of the seas. It confirmed what Churchill had been protesting to the Government about for seven years. The Norwegian fiasco was the result of complacency and smugness between the wars, when generals and admirals had refused to modernise and were dismissive and fearful of enemy air superiority at the same time, because they had no idea what to do about it.

'Even his gift for spirit-lifting oratory seemed to desert him during that dismal April.'[1]

He looked tired and worn in his attempts to achieve combined operations between army and navy. Despite the failure of the Allied invasion of Norway, the German Navy lost three cruisers and ten destroyers. But the Allies lost Norway to the Germans, because Hitler believed that the best way to obtain essential resources from a country was to invade and devastate it.

With Britain's failure and retreat came a lack of confidence in its ability to hold Germany back. Confidence dwindled in Whitehall too, as they faced the fact that they were unprepared for modern warfare.

In the debate in the House on the failure in Norway in early May 1940, Chamberlain attempted to defend himself, but he failed to impress anyone. The normally mild Attlee, who responded as leader of the opposition party, was unusually feisty in the way he deflated the PM. Other speakers who might have been critical of Churchill chose to blame Chamberlain for his misdirection of the war, instead. Attlee placed the responsibility for the disaster also on Simon and Hoare, but not on Churchill. He admired him as a genuine individual who knew what others did not and had not been properly supported. Admiral of the Fleet Sir Roger Keyes said, 'I have great admiration and appreciation for my right honourable friend the First Lord of the Admiralty. I am longing to see proper use made of his great abilities.'

He added, 'One hundred and forty years ago Nelson said, "I am of the opinion that the boldest measures are the safest, and that still holds good today."'[2]

Perhaps the unkindest cut of all to Chamberlain's pride came from L.S. Amery, although his speech was far too long. But he ended it forcefully with the famous quotation from Oliver Cromwell that culminated with the words; 'You have sat too long here for any good you have been doing. Depart I say, and let us have done with you. In the name of God, go.'

It might have marked the end of Chamberlain on its own, but it was reinforced by a speech from one of the most admired wartime prime ministers in history, Lloyd George, who was still persuasive, and had the affection of the House.

'He has appealed for sacrifice,' Lloyd George said of Chamberlain. 'I say solemnly that the Prime Minister should give an example of sacrifice because there is nothing which can contribute more to victory in this war than that he should sacrifice the seals of office.'[3]

Churchill made his reply about the failed Norwegian Campaign at the end of two days of debate. It was 10.11 p.m. when he rose from his seat in the House and spoke for forty-nine minutes. He had to manoeuvre with the problem of loyalty to the Prime Minister, and also to defend the armed services. Despite those handicaps, he spoke vigorously with a slashing speech, because he knew how crucial the deciding vote would be for the future of Great Britain.

'When the motion [to support the Prime Minister] was put to the vote, the nominal Conservative majority of 213 fell to only 81. It was a devastating blow for Neville Chamberlain.'[4]

The Prime Minister had already gone white in the face. Now he looked grim and ill as he strode out of the House. He invited Churchill to his room, where they spoke until midnight, when Chamberlain finally admitted he could not continue as Prime Minister.

The Phoney War was over thirty hours after the vote, when the German Army launched its invasion of France through Belgium, using its well-practised *blitzkrieg* techniques.

Crucial Days

The days from 24 to 28 May were the most crucial in changing the course of history, as members of the British War Cabinet debated 'whether to negotiate with or to continue the war against Hitler'.[5]

It was 'Then and there,' wrote historian John Lukacs, that 'Adolf Hitler came closest to winning the Second World War ...' Churchill had finally to overcome the Cabinet's sense of defeatism and resignation towards Hitler, and replace their frightened delusions with his own more realistic world view, his vision of history and his fierce attitude towards the Nazis. It was not so much a matter of morality but realism – about what they could expect to happen if they continued to submit to Hitler's wishes.

Up until as late as 30 September, the date of the Munich Agreement, even Churchill had no idea of the extent of Hitler's grotesque ambitions, and thought he might have to be bought off with a few small territories like Malta or Gibraltar, or a minor African colony.[6] What Hitler really planned was so audacious, criminally vicious, and grimly inhuman, that no one outside of the Nazi hierarchy could have conceived of its possibilities.

'The summer of 1940 brought an end of old Europe, sweeping off the stage of history the notion of a world managed by a concert of civilised European powers, within a frame of agreed international conventions and some system of moral absolutes.'[7]

According to Professor Lukacs, 'Churchill's situation within the War Cabinet was much more difficult than most people, including historians at that time, thought.' And, 'the danger, not only to Britain but to the world, was greater and deeper than most people still think'.[8]

That was the critical state of affairs that Churchill had to contend with to win over his political colleagues. Although he shared their ideals to improve society, in the end, it was the fact that he was a soldier and a realist who understood what Britain was facing that convinced them of his suitability to lead the nation. He was not about to allow Britain to be destroyed by the German military machine.

None of them possessed his wartime experience or his military attributes. And, by now, they had begun to feel ashamed of the previous Government's desire to appease the German warlord by sacrificing the entire population of Czechoslovakia to his ambitions. It had not worked. Now Hitler demanded even more territory. And he would go on doing so. He would never be satisfied.

According to Churchill's account six years later, in the first volume of his history of the Second World War, he met Chamberlain and Halifax at 11 a.m. on Friday morning, 10 May, when the German offensive began. The Prime Minister artfully suggested that he was about to resign and be replaced by Halifax.

Churchill would famously write of the event, 'As I remained silent a very long pause ensued.'

But Churchill's memory was faulty concerning what happened and when. Halifax did not possess the nature to take on such a responsibility. He preferred to be a figurehead. Why should he wish to take over the reins of a war that surely Britain could not possibly win? He was far more suited to dressing up in his impressive diplomatic uniforms to represent Queen Victoria as Viceroy of India at the Durbar and other colourful functions that lent status to Great Britain. He had acted effortlessly as a diplomatic functionary when he had been known as Lord Irwin from 1925 to 1934.

It appeared that Chamberlain had hoped to give his friend a second opportunity by placing him in a position in which he might feel obliged to accept. But Halifax was content to have a justification for refusing the PM's offer by reminding Chamberlain that he was disqualified as a peer in the House of Lords, not the House of Commons. It left the prime responsibility to Churchill.

Churchill's biographer Roy Jenkins would dispute that recollection by insisting that the critical meeting actually occurred on Thursday afternoon, when the Chief Whip, Captain Margesson, had been present. According to Margesson, Halifax had already excluded himself from becoming Prime Minister at 10.15 a.m. that morning because he had thought he would become merely a cipher if he had accepted, as someone else would have to conduct the day to day affairs of war. Despite his many diplomatic skills, Halifax was not a warlord.

'I thought Winston was a better choice,' Halifax was alleged to have remarked: 'Winston did not demur. Was very kind and polite but showed that he thought this the right solution. Chief Whip and others thought feeling in the House has been veering towards him.'

Or, so said a cryptic note scribbled by the Foreign Office permanent under-secretary, Cadogan, who had met Halifax immediately he had returned from 10 Downing Street, and learned the gist of what had occurred. That was the best explanation of how the destiny of great Britain and Europe, and the United States, and everywhere else, fell onto the willing and capable shoulders of a man who had always believed that an incredible destiny awaited him, and had prepared for the event all his life.

The Starting Pistol

Once he was Prime Minister, Churchill put it bluntly to his closest colleagues by telling them on 4 June, 'We shall go on and we shall fight it out, here and elsewhere, and if at last the long story is to end, it were better it should end, not through surrender, but only when each of us lies choking in his own blood.'[9]

His bewildered, meek and mild colleagues seemed to understand self-sacrifice. It was an essential part of the code of English patriots then. It gave them continuity with their Anglo-Saxon ancestors who had settled the country in the distant past. All knew there was no way that Churchill was going to turn the other cheek to Hitler. The days and weeks and months of appeasing the little tyrant were over.

But the damage had already been done. Hitler had an instinct for sniffing out weakness and seizing opportunities to exploit it.[10]

It must have been an uncanny and dreamlike feeling for Churchill to find himself in the coalition War Cabinet with Neville Chamberlain and Lord Halifax, Clement Attlee and Arthur Greenwood. Time had overtaken Chamberlain and left him stranded somewhere behind. Churchill described him almost affectionately as the 'Old Umbrella'. He belonged to the Victorian era of prim rectitude, and failed to understand the twentieth century to the end of his days. As for the more spiritual Halifax, he lived even further away from the harsh reality of the times – almost in the Byzantine era, since his main desire was to bring back the Church of England to its former days as a 'High Church', barely dissimilar in its religious rites and rituals from the Roman Church. He appeared to be halfway to heaven, and avoided being contaminated by the material world.

Attlee was an idealistic socialist and Leader of the Labour Party. He was good natured, mild mannered, and often as unrealistic as Halifax. He had spent much of his youth working for the poor and needy in the East End slums of London. Greenwood was the Deputy Leader of the Labour Party. They were both well-intentioned men. Greenwood had spoken out strongly against Chamberlain's policy of appeasing Hitler. Despite their having been chosen for the War Cabinet, none but Churchill understood war, or the dire position in which Great Britain had now been placed.

Churchill knew that now the war had started, it must go on to the end. The Nazis had to be destroyed before they destroyed the world. But even now, Halifax and Chamberlain still appeared to imagine they could parley with Hitler and bring him round to their way of thinking.

Neither the politicians nor civil servants liked to be stirred up into activity by Churchill. And that was precisely what he had to do, and did, from then until the end of the war.

What Churchill did when he became Prime Minister was what he had always done; he galvanised people around him by forcing them to think, perhaps for the very first time, about the seriousness of Britain's situation. The former world leadership of Great Britain had made them self-satisfied and complacent. He forced them to act, not simply continue to administer the affairs of the nation in their habitually languid and cautious ways, with little thought or awareness of what was happening outside their narrow departments, their private clubs, and weekend leisure pursuits.

His oratory was at its peak when he assured the War Cabinet, the news media and the public, as Britain's new Prime Minister, that there was no way he would continue selling out to Hitler, as the previous Government had done, with its meek and mild ideals that invited defeat.

All the while, his critics aimed their barbs at him without mercy. 'Half-cocked as usual,' they said. They were entirely oblivious to the real perilous situation, and ignorant of Churchill's strategic and tactical skills. As he remarked ruefully long afterwards, 'It was a marvel that I survived.'

Years later, in the comfort and seclusion of his study at Chartwell, he would write in his memoirs of the Second World War of what happened soon after he was appointed Prime Minister: 'Thus, then, we all started on our common task.'[11]

Churchill wrote that confident remark with self-satisfaction after reflecting on the event with composure. But, by then, he had the advantage of knowing with hindsight that he and Great Britain and its Allies had achieved victory over Nazi Germany.

He appeared to have forgotten – or wished to forget – other more dire moments, like Clementine writing hopefully to encourage her sister on 20 September 1939 that Britain had only just begun fighting against Nazi Germany, whereas Germany's war machine was at its peak. Or what he had said to his Scotland Yard bodyguard, Walter Thompson, on 10 May 1940, when the Inspector had remarked to his boss on the enormous task that lay ahead.

Tears had come into Churchill's eyes as he'd replied: 'God alone knows how great it is. I hope it is not too late. I am very much afraid it is. We can only do our best.'

Epilogue

The Führer of the Arab World

When Winston Churchill had been appointed as Britain's new Colonial Secretary in 1920, he had organised a formal Cairo Conference to decide how best to fill the critical leadership vacuum left in the Middle East at the end of the First World War. Two years had already elapsed since the League of Nations had approved of Britain's administration of the huge territory of Mesopotamia, which had been ruled largely by Turkey before its defeat by the Allies in 1918. Already there were signs of chaos with the emergence of a multitude of Arab warlords and tribal strife in attempts to grab territories and plunder them. Now there was the added fear that either the Turkish army would return, or the new Soviet Red Army would sweep down from the Bolshevik civil war in the north and annex parts of Arabia.

The two main priorities of the Paris Peace Conference in 1918–19 had been obtaining war reparations from Germany and applying self-determination to most of the fragments of territory left orphaned by the sudden collapse of the four major empires – Germany, Austria, Turkey, and Russia. Stability was required in accordance with the Balfour Declaration of 1917 and the official mandates by the League of Nations, in which the Middle East was to be administered largely by Great Britain and – in Syria and Lebanon – by the French. The League was committed to allowing Jewish people to immigrate to Palestine as their right, and not on sufferance.

Winston had found his new portfolio unwelcome and unattractive. He had wanted to be Chancellor of the Exchequer, like his father had been. Situated at 11 Downing Street, the Chancellor's residence was closest to the Prime Minister's seat of power in No. 10. But Prime Minister Lloyd George had been adamant, and Winston had no choice.

Nor was it in his nature to do anything half-heartedly; so he had accepted the position as a challenge to his planning and management abilities. Part of that challenge would be a number of confrontations with the fanatical enemies of Great Britain.

Churchill already possessed a reputation as a smooth conciliator who nearly always received respect from both sides. But, as he would discover in the Middle East, fierce conflicts that required solutions, like compromises, were far too emotional for trade-offs among people with rigid ideas they imagined were voiced directly to them by God.

As a modern man, he had not been aware of the complete absence of reasonableness in the territory, when he had chosen somewhere between a dozen and twenty outstanding specialists to plan and establish new frontiers for the conglomeration of different tribes who inhabited the area, or passed through it in nomadic style with the seasons. They had included T.E. Lawrence – still known as the heroic Lawrence of Arabia – who only a few years previously had famously organised Arab irregulars for the Arab Rising that had helped to defeat the Turkish Empire and end the Great War in 1918.

Another specialist had been the famous explorer and author, now known as Major Miss Bell – formerly celebrated by the general public as the accomplished Gertrude Bell, who had published a number of books about her travels in Arabia. She spoke several Arabic, Persian, and other Oriental languages. Her particular first-hand knowledge was derived from her expeditions, when younger, to Petra, Daraa, Palmyra, Beirut, Damascus, and Hayil – which had been the stronghold of the Raschid dynasty, who were pretenders to the throne of Arabia and the Caliphate. That trip had caught the attention of Lawrence when he had worked for the Arab Bureau in Cairo. He had recommended Bell to British Intelligence, and she had been trained as a spymaster.

It was Bell's job to make sure that 'nobody suffered as a member of an oppressed minority in a country split by racial, religious, and economic differences'.[1] It included the Druze and Kurdish minorities.

Churchill had been given the thankless job of acting as a peacekeeper between a collection of different tribes whose culture was based on a seventh-century desert ideology of cruelty and hatred towards others.

It had been the second time in thirteen years that he had observed Jewish efforts to develop a thriving agricultural economy in Palestine out of the formerly useless desert terrain, which was largely a barren wasteland of sand dunes and rocky outcrops, with a blazing sun beating down from a cloudless sky. And, once again, he encountered one obstacle after another placed in his way by Arabs who were prepared to destroy whatever it was that they could not have for themselves. Always in the background was the mufti initiating violent riots and encouraging bloodshed to clear the British and Jews out of the vast territory, in which nothing new was supposed to happen, according to a statement in the Quran forbidding any sort of innovation since the Prophet's time in the seventh century.

According to the nomadic Arab way of desert life, each day should be filled with prayers and discussions about the Quran and other holy books. As for work, or surplus, or profit, although they planted corn in sown areas, there was no surplus, and therefore no income. Profits were derived from invading caravans with knives and swords. Stronger tribes raided weaker ones for slaves, women, cattle and goats. It was a wild and desperate frontier life where any weakness was exploited to the full, and had been almost from the beginning of time.

Reasons why discontent among Arab tribes often reached boiling point was thought by the British and French to be sullen envy that broke out into hysterical rages, or chanting and threats, by a peasant population at the arrival of educated Europeans, who were more successful than they were. It was the traditional Arab hatred of strangers who did not share their beliefs, daring to set foot on the land that they believed was holy. The result was that it had been sterile for centuries when life in the Turkish Caliphate had stood still without clocks to mark the time. Only the agricultural seasons changed from sowing to threshing and harvesting, with intervals to exploit an opportunity to attack a weaker tribe for plunder.

It had been infuriating for the *fellahin* to see strangers arriving from Europe, and succeeding by growing crops in the desert where they had failed. Al-Husseini encouraged them to take out their frustration and anger on successful Jewish farmers:

> After the 1920 Nebi Musa riots, Amin fled to Transjordan and hid among the Bedouin tribes. By 1921 – after clashes for supremacy with other Arab nationalists who continued to squabble with each other for dominance – Amin became the Mufti of Jerusalem and President of the newly created religious organisation, the Supreme Muslim Council. He was a Sunni Muslim. He and his Arab rivals for power had one thing in common; they continued to demand a stop to Jewish immigration, and to prevent Jewish families and Zionist organisations from buying back land in what had been Jewish territory in Biblical times.[2]

One of the grim ironies of the situation was that it had been the distinguished Liberal politician and former Home Secretary – now High Commissioner of Palestine – Sir Herbert Samuel who had made the grave error of appointing Haj Amin al-Husseini as Grand Mufti of Jerusalem. The Jewish Samuel had thought he was making a goodwill gesture in appointing an Arab to high office to show 'fair play'. He had failed to understand that fair play was not a concept that existed in desert regions or frontier towns. Nor had he yet recognised the extreme hatred felt by Arabs towards the British administrators. It overrode all other considerations. Amin returned his favour by raising the April riots, and the High Commissioner was forced to realise he had turned the mufti into a sinister and untrustworthy leader of the Palestinians. Husseini was a born rebel, not only a dedicated enemy of all Jews, but also a sworn enemy of the British.

Churchill's Welcome

Churchill had taken a train to Jerusalem from Cairo, all those years ago, on 24 March 1921. He had stopped off at Gaza early the following morning, to be welcomed by a large crowd of shouting Arabs. His spirits were raised by the unexpected welcome from cheering crowds shouting 'Cheers for the Minister!' 'Cheers for Great Britain!'

Even bigger mobs of hysterical Arabs called out 'Down with the Jews!' and 'Cut their throats!' Winston had no idea what they were shouting when the train moved off, but felt optimistic about the possibilities of his negotiations in Jerusalem. Arabs rioted in Haifa the day after he arrived, demanding a stop to further Jewish immigration. Police opened fire to disperse frenzied mobs.

But, as a minister of the Crown, Churchill's diplomatic discussions were undertaken between educated leaders of nations. Although Emir Abdullah accepted Churchill's assurances that the rights of the existing Arab population would be preserved, the hostile local Arabs refused to listen. Their political and religious leaders warned Churchill that if Britain ignored their demands for an end to Jewish immigration, 'then perhaps Russia will take up their call some day; or perhaps even Germany'.

It was not just the British or the Jews that the Arab peasants rioted against. They were in conflict with their own leaders. When Abdullah visited the Mosque of Omar, he was assailed by a hostile crowd with shouts of 'Palestine for the Arabs' and 'Down with the Zionists'. They had to be dispersed by British police. The illiterate and superstitious mobs did not trust their leaders, and the leaders despised the rioting mobs. It would take years for the British or French to understand the religious clashes between tribes or the hatreds between rural peasants and villagers, villagers and city dwellers ... Even when some westerners began to recognise that endless clashes of opinions persisted and no two people would agree about anything, the desert way of life of nomadic tribes, and the imaginative religious superstitions carried forward through the centuries were inconceivable to the European mind.

Threats came, not only from Muslims in Palestine, but also from Muslims in India and Iraq, who had decided that the whole of Palestine belonged to the Arabs. Religious leaders presented Churchill with a five-point memorandum, the essence of which was that Jewish immigration should be halted. No matter what benefits he offered in terms of financial investments by Britain, or construction of cities that would provide employment and raise their impoverished style of living, the Arab masses were stubbornly against any improvements. Innovation was a Western concept against the wishes of the Prophet Muhammad. The very idea of modernisation was anathema to religious zealots who wanted to remain exactly as they had been at the time of the prophet in the seventh century.

The Arabian Monarchs' Approval

'Churchill favoured a scheme whereby Faisal would accept the throne of Iraq, and his brother Abdullah the throne of Transjordan, in return for Western Palestine – from the Mediterranean Sea to the River Jordan – becoming the location of the Jewish National Home under British control.'[3]

After drawing the most suitable frontiers between the major Arab tribes, and considering the cyclical movements of nomadic Bedouin to fresh seasonal pasturelands and back, other factors had to be considered within each geographical boundary, such as densities of populations, and the possibility of oilfields, water too. Churchill's team of specialists also considered the separation of Sunni and Shia Muslims. One of their final steps had been to approve rulers for each territory. A great deal of thought was shared about bloodlines of descent from the Prophet Muhammad. The Emirs Faisal and Abdullah fulfilled the necessary qualifications.

When it came to sorting the strong from the weaker leaders, Lawrence of Arabia's personal relationship with the Hashemites proved to be invaluable. He had already recognised the bravery in battle and the princely poise in the Emir Faisal, who would ultimately be enthroned as King of Iraq. He was a leader whom others followed without question. His brother, Prince Abdullah, was installed as King of Jordan. The Hashemite dynasty now came under the protection of the British Empire in terms of financial support, arms, and the aid of a British intelligence officer provided to advise each monarch.

King Ibn Saud was different. He would carve out his own territory of Saudi Arabia by pacifying the disputatious Arab tribes with the swords of his Ikhwan warriors who – as militant Islamic fundamentalists – showed no compassion. And such was the leadership of Ibn Saud that he had most of his wild and fanatical swordsmen under control – at least most of the time. There would always be clashes of opinions between the monarchy and its zealous fundamentalists. But each knew they needed the other.

King Ibn Saud's greatly enlarged territory would become the foundation of the Kingdom of Saudi Arabia. As for the establishment of the Jewish homeland in Palestine, Churchill took good care to obtain approval from all the Arabian monarchs. Faisal welcomed them back home.

Neither King Ibn Saud, nor King Faisal, or King Abdullah, would be the cause of future conflicts. It was the superstitious and illiterate peasantry, the *fellahin*, whose hatred was palpable towards all non-Muslims. They preferred to follow the instructions of the mufti of Jerusalem. And, on 29 August, anti-Jewish riots broke out again in Palestine. A royal commission established to investigate the situation found that the mufti had been involved.

Lawrence had warned Churchill's bodyguard from Scotland Yard, at the beginning of the trip, that Churchill's life would be at risk 'from the instant we were on Arab soil'. When they reached the hotel, Lawrence took Thompson aside and told him, 'Churchill is in great danger. Never, on any account, let him out of your sight. Trust nobody, black or white. Guard him as you would your own life – even in the sanctuary of his own bedchamber.' According to Lawrence, 'The Arab masses were dangerous and inflammable.'[4]

On 19 April 1936, two Jews were killed in Jaffa. Two days later a general strike was proclaimed in Nablus. On 12 January 1937, the Royal Commission established that the mufti had been responsible for increasing the violence. On 17 July the British attempted to arrest him. Al-Husseini hid in the Al-Aqsa Mosque area. He fled from Palestine to Beirut, then to Damascus, and on to Iraq, where he attempted to organise a pro-German coup between 1939 and 1941. British administrators sent in an army to prevent it from happening. He fled from Iraq and arrived in Tehran on 1 June 1941. He fled from Iran for Turkey, where he spent a month in the Italian embassy for protection. Then he arrived in Italy on 11 October and communicated with Mussolini.

Whatever he had discussed with Mussolini, *Il Duce* sent him to Berlin to meet Hitler. He arrived in Berlin on 6 November. On 28 November he met Germany's Foreign Minister Joachim von Ribbentrop, and Hitler later on the same day,

The mufti remained in Germany throughout the Second World War, where he was involved in and led anti-Jewish meetings. He broadcast anti-Semitic propaganda over the radio, encouraged anti-Jewish activities, and organised the Arab Legion to fight alongside German troops.[5]

Hitler set al-Husseini up in a luxurious mansion in Berlin's elegant Klopstock Street, from where he was driven along the Wilhelmstrasse, where most of the government ministries were located. The chauffeur-driven Mercedes drove him to the corner of Voss-Strasse, where he stepped out and entered the Reich Chancellery. He would have felt completely at ease in the grandeur of the long red marble walls of the corridors that led him to Hitler's private office and study, since he had been hailed on arrival in Berlin by cheering crowds as 'The Führer of the Arab World'.

What he discussed with Hitler was Hitler's 'Plan Orient'. In order to introduce it into the Middle East, the mufti was given a tour of one of the biggest Nazi concentration camps, where he was shown how to murder and dispose of all non-Muslims across Arabia. The Arabs wanted them out, in the same way as Hitler had wanted all foreigners out of Germany and Austria. It was felt to be a fair exchange of Germany's death-dealing technologies and methodology, for Middle East oil.

Oil would be desperately needed for General Rommel's light panzer tank divisions fighting the Allies in the Desert War in North Africa. Hitler and al-Husseini were convinced that Rommel's Afrika Korps would win the battle at El Alamein against the Allies.

As it would turn out, they were wrong. Rommel's tanks came to a halt, one after another, between minefields planted by the British Army in the campaign for a desert victory against Nazi Germany. They had run out of oil because British Intelligence had intercepted shipments to North Africa by torpedoing the oil tankers intended to service the Afrika Korps in the desert.

When it became clear that Germany would lose the war, the mufti fled once again. He arrived in Paris in May 1945. He planned to escape to Cairo as soon as he could, where he intended to continue warring against Great Britain. He had many leisure hours to consider his future and dwell on the past when in Paris:

> What if the German military had been victorious at the decisive Battle of El Alamein in Egypt and had gone on to conquer Palestine and the rest of the Middle East? What if Germany had won the Battle of Britain and conquered the British Isles? What if Churchill's government had then collapsed, to be replaced by a pro-Nazi puppet regime in London? What if Hitler had won the war?[6]

The hate-filled 'Führer of the Middle East' was the link between all the trouble spots in the Arab world, where he moved with deliberate intent from Jerusalem to Gaza, from Beirut to Iraq and Iran, creating riots wherever he went. If any one individual could be blamed for the chaos and destruction in the Arab world, which has seeped into the West, Amin was the link between then and now.*

* Amin Al-Husseini would be replaced as leader in 1964 by the Palestine Liberation Organization (PLO).

Acknowledgements

In addition to over 500 sources listed in the end notes of both volumes, the author wishes to acknowledge, in particular, the following four books by Sir Winston Churchill's official biographer, Sir Martin Gilbert, who had access to all of Churchill's official documents and private and official correspondence. There is also a perceptive analysis of the situation at the critical moment when Winston Churchill and his War Cabinet had to decide whether to hold to the agreement that Chamberlain had signed with Hitler to stay out of the German war, or make war on Nazi Germany.

Sir Martin Gilbert, *Winston Churchill: The Wilderness Years* (Macmillan, London, 1981).

Sir Martin Gilbert, *Churchill: A Life* (Holt, NY, 1991).

Sir Martin Gilbert, *A History of the Twentieth Century* Vol. 2 & 3 (Morrow, NY, 2001).

Sir Martin Gilbert, *Churchill and the Jews* (Simon & Shuster, UK, 2007).

John Lukacs, *Five Days in London, May 1940* (Yale University Press, New Haven, 1999).

About the Author

John Harte has written twenty-two books of modern social history about what caused us to be where we are today; several are still scheduled for future publication. Eight titles are about Winston Churchill, with references attributing over 3,000 sources, including other historians or historical documents. Only one other historian has written as many books about Churchill. That was his official biographer, the greatly esteemed Sir Martin Gilbert, who had access to all of Churchill's correspondence and official documents. Since John studied all of Gilbert's books, his narratives also benefit from the products of Sir Martin Gilbert's scholarship.

The author was born in London, England, and educated at St Paul's School and Carleton University in Ottawa, where he studied psychology. His home is now in Canada, where he writes books about the movers and shapers of history who gave meaning and purpose to our lives. Most are about injustice and the struggle for societies to achieve common decency. In the course of his travels and studies he has observed the decline or collapse of several different countries and, as described in these pages, all for the same reasons.

Author's website: www.johnhartebooks.com

Notes

Preface

1. Dr. Mark Hyman, *Young Forever* (Little, Brown NY, 2023), p.xix.
2. John Simpson, BBC News. Youtube, 2016.
3. Christopher C. Harmon, *Terrorism Today,* Introduction (Routledge NY, 2013).
4. Harmon, ibid., p.115.
5. Karl Polanyi, *The Great Transformation: The Political And Economic origins of Our Time* (Farrar NY, 1044) Beacon Boston: p.299.
6. Amanda Turnbull, reference: Balkan 825, 'The Psychology of Grotesque in Modern American Literature (2018).' An MB thesis from Rollins College.
7. Karl Polanyi, ibid., p.25.
8. Ibid., p.5.
9. Ibid., p.30.
10. Karl Popper, *The Open Society and its Enemies* (Princeton University, 1945), p.420.
11. Karl Popper, Ibid.
12. Winwood Reade, *The Martyrdom of Man* (1872).
13. Karl Popper, Ibid.
14. Heraclitus.
15. In an online interview by the Hoover Institution in 2014.
16. Winston S. Churchill, *Great Contemporaries* (Butterworth London, 1937), pp.17–25.
17. Ibid., p.33.

1. Nazi Ideology

1. German Chancellor Otto von Bismarck.
2. Sir Martin Gilbert, *A History of the Twentieth Century* Vol. 2 & 3 (Morrow, NY, 2001), p.705.
3. *Nazism – 1919–1945. A Documentary Reader, Vol. 2. State Economy and Society, 1933–39*, Ed. J. Noakes & G. Pridham (University of Exeter, 2000), pp.361–362.
4. Kagan, Ozment, Turner, *Western Heritage* (Prentice Hall, 2007), pp.922–923.
5. Gilbert, *A History of the Twentieth Century*, p.706.

6. Ibid., p.707.
7. Arthur Koestler, *Arrow in the Blue* (Collins, London, 1952), pp.85–89.
8. Gilbert, *A History of the Twentieth Century*, p.730.
9. Ibid., p.731.
10. Tony Judt & Timothy Snyder, *Thinking the Twentieth Century* (Penguin, London, 2012), p.164.
11. Dane Kennedy, *The Highly Civilized Man* (Harvard University Press, Cambridge, 2005), p.46.
12. Gilbert, *A History of the Twentieth Century*, p.733.

2. A Real Man of Genius

1. Lloyd George fell from power in 1922 when the Liberal Party declined and splintered into fighting factions. He became mistrusted by the electorate during an economic downturn and a series of strikes, after which he lost his credibility.
2. According to former Prime Minister Lord Balfour who wrote him a letter of congratulations.
3. Sir Martin Gilbert, *Winston Churchill: The Wilderness Years* (Macmillan, London, 1981), p.14.
4. W. S. Churchill, 2, 243, 247, 451, 1964, 83.
5. Norman Rose, *Churchill: An Unruly Life* (S&S NY, 1994), pp.58–59.
6. Ibid., p.63.
7. W.S. Churchill, *The World Crisis* Pt 1, Chapter 3 (Butterworth, London, 1931).

3. German Blood

1. Gilbert, *Wilderness Years*, p.16.
2. Gilbert, *A History of the Twentieth Century*, p. 443.
3. Ibid., p.448.
4. Benito Mussolini, *Force and Consent* (1923).
5. Ibid.
6. Gilbert, *A History of the Twentieth Century*, p.752.

4. Hard Times

1. Gilbert, *Wilderness Years*, p.15.
2. J.M. Keynes, *The New Republic* magazine.
3. 'Ideas alone are not [sic] flesh and blood', Barbara Tuchman, *Practicing History*, p.40.
4. To use a phrase coined by historian Barbara W. Tuchman in her *Practicing History*.
5. Gilbert, *Wilderness Years*, p.19.
6. Sonia Purnell, *Clementine* (Viking, NY, 2015), p.187.
7. Ibid., p.189.

5. The Unchanging Middle East

1. Martin Gilbert, *Churchill and the Jews* (Macmillan, London, 2007), p.90.
2. Gertrude Bell, *Complete Letters Vol. 2* (Amazon Fulfilment, Poland), First ed. Ernest Benn London, 1927).
3. Roger Scruton, *Gentle Regrets* (Continuum, London, 2005), p.146.
4. Churchill, *The World Crisis*, pp.726–727.
5. *The Lake Regions of Central Africa* (1860). Final chapter: 'The Character and Religions of the East Africans; their Government, and Slavery.'
6. Kennedy, *The Highly Civilized Man*, p.4.
7. Ibid.
8. Ibid., p.7.
9. Ibid., pp.26–27.
10. Isabel Burton, *Life*, Vol. 1, pp.108–109.
11. Ibid., pp.109, 135.

6. Reason or Hysteria

1. Sir Martin Gilbert, *Churchill: A Life* (Holt, NY, 1991), p.493.
2. Gilbert, *Wilderness Years*, p.22.
3. Ibid., p.23.
4. Gilbert, *Churchill: A Life*, p.494.
5. Tom Hickman, *Churchill's Bodyguard* (Hodder, London, 2005), p.67.
6. Gilbert, *Wilderness Years*, p.24.
7. Gilbert, *Churchill and the Jews*, p.91.
8. *San Francisco Chronicle,* 12 September 1929. 'Arab atrocities in Holy Land Ended for All Time, Asserts Statesman in Interview Here.'
9. *New York Times,* 13 September 1929. 'Churchill says Arabs owe much to Jews.'
10. Arthur Koestler who admired Faisal.
11. *Sunday Times,* 22 September 1929. 'The Palestine Crisis', Winston S. Churchill.

7. No Time for Self-Pity

1. Hickman, *Churchill's Bodyguard*, p.73.
2. Gilbert, *Churchill: A Life*, pp.506–7.
3. Gilbert, *A History of the Twentieth Century*, p.498.
4. Ryszard Kapuscinski, *Travels with Herodotus* (Znak, Poland, 2004), p.43.
5. Ibid., p.71.

8. A Flight of Capital

1. *Sunday Chronicle,* 2 November 1930.
2. *Barnett Janner: A Personal Portrait.* Elsie Janner. p.41.
3. Gilbert, *Churchill: A Life*, p.507.
4. Gilbert, *A History of the Twentieth Century*, pp.758–9.

9. The Little People

1. Brigitte Hamann, *Hitler's Vienna: A Dictator's Apprenticeship* (Oxford University Press, NY, 1999).
2. Not translated into English until 1974.
3. Wilhelm Reich, *The Impulsive Character* (Meridian, NY, 1974).
4. Sigmund Freud, *The Ego and the Id* (1923).
5. *The Diagnostic and Statistical Manual of Mental Disorders.* 5th edition.
6. 'In any case,' Freud added, 'most remain *hidden* motives, unless psycho-analysis can uncover them.'
7. Elias Canetti, *Masse und Macht* (Seabury, NY, 1905).
8. Winston S. Churchill, *Great Contemporaries* (Thornton Butterworth, London, 1937), p.166.

10. The Split-Minded Weimar Republic

1. Walter Rathenau, *Ein Preussischer Europiter* (Berlin, 1955), p.329.
2. Eric D. Weitz, *Weimar Germany: Promise and Tragedy* (Princeton University Press, 2018), p.2.
3. Amos Elon, *The Pity of it All* (Henry Holt NY, 2002), p.370.
4. Arthur Koestler, ibid.
5. Amos Elon, ibid., p.372.
6. Richard Rhodes, *The Making of the Atom Bomb* (S&S NY, 1986), p.105.
7. Ibid., pp.105-106.
8. Ibid., p.107.
9. Ibid.
10. Ibid., p.106.
11. Ibid., p.151.

11. The Jewish Dilemma

1. P. Gay, *Freud, Jews and Other Germans* (Oxford, 1978), p.169.
2. Gertrude Himmelfarb, *Past and Present*, ibid., p.200. From an essay by Beatrice Webb.
3. Ibid., p.206.
4. Ibid., p.207.
5. Moritz de John.
6. P. Gay, ibid., p.197.
7. Ibid.
8. Daniel Jonah Goldhagen, *Hitler's Willing Executioners: Ordinary Germans and the Holocaust* (Random, NY 1996), p.28.
9. Ibid., p.170.

12. Hitler's Racism

1. Eberhard Jäckel, *Hitler's Weltanschauung: Entwurf einer Herrschaft* (Stuttgart, 1981).
2. Volker Ullrich, ibid., p.177.
3. Hitler, *Mein Kampf*, ibid., pp. 312, 314, 316.
4. Strasser, *Hitler und ich*, p.79f.

13. My Darling Clementine

1. Mary Soames, *Clementine Churchill* (Houghton Mifflin, Boston, 1979), p.267.
2. Winston Churchill was awarded a Nobel Prize for Literature in 1953.
3. Purnell, *Clementine*, p.52.
4. Ibid., pp.168–9.
5. Gertrude Bell, *A Woman in Arabia* (Macmillan, NY, 2008), p.22.
6. Churchill Archives in Cambridge (CSCT), 14 July 1912.
7. John Grigg, *Churchill and Lloyd George* (Oxford-U, Feb 1996), pp.97–112.
8. Purnell, p.182.
9. Gilbert, *Wilderness Years*, p.22.
10. Ibid., p.23.
11. Sonia Purnell, *Clementine: The Life of Mrs Winston Churchill* (Viking, NY, 2015).
12. Secretary of State for India, Sir Samuel Hoare.
13. Purnell, p.193.
14. Winston S. Churchill, *His Father's Son: A Life of Randolph Churchill* (Orion, London, 1997), p.65.
15. Purnell, pp.196–7.
16. Ibid., p.169.

14. Inside Germany

1. Peter Gay. Ref. to Gottfried Benn, poet. *Freud: A Life for Our Time* (Norton, NY, 2006), p.171.
2. P. Gray, *Freud* etc. Ibid., p.176.
3. Ibid.
4. Ibid., p.172.
5. Peter Gay, Ibid.
6. Ibid., pp.173–4.
7. Amos Alon, Ibid, p.265.
8. Ibid., p.268.
9. Gay, p.41.
10. Adolf Rapp, *Grossdeutsch-Kleindeutsch* (1922), p.178.

11. Milton Himmelfarb, *Jews and Gentiles.* Ed. Gertrude Himmelfarb (Encounter, NY, 2007). p.101
12. A.L. Rowse, *The Poet Auden: A Personal Memoir* (Methuen, London, 1987).

15. The Future of Civilisation

1. Gay, p.526.
2. Ibid., p.528.
3. Ibid., p.529.
4. Freud, *The Future of an Illusion* (1930).
5. Gay, p.550.
6. Martin Green, *The von Richthofen Sisters: The Triumphant and the Tragic Modes of Love* (Basic, NY, 1974), pp.199–200.
7. Hitler, *Reden. Schriften, Anordnungen*, doc 94, 121, pp.252, 371 (16 Dec. 1925 & 11 April 1926).

16. Hitler Unhinged

1. Paul Schmidt, *Hitler's Interpreter: The Memoirs of Paul Schmidt*, Bonn, 1950 (Macmillan, London, 1951), p.394f.
2. Ibid. pp.395–8.
3. Ernst von Weizsäcker, *Erinnerungen* (Munich, 1950), p.244.
4. Stephen Kotkin online interview by Peter Robinson about his book, *Joseph Stalin: Waiting for Hitler* (The Hoover Institution, 2019).
5. William L. Shirer, p.133 (Diary Entry for 22 September 1938).
6. Joseph Goebbels, p.109 (Diary Entry for 24 September 1938).
7. Shirer, p.127 (Diary Entry for 26 September).
8. Henderson, *Fehlschlag einer Mission*, p.187.
9. Goebbels, p.127 (Diary Entry for 3 October 1939).
10. Bernd-Jürgen Wendt, *Grossdeutschland* (Verlagsgesellschaft mbH, Berlin, 1987), p.166f.
11. An expression used by Thomas Paine in *The Rights of Man* (1791).
12. Michiko Kakutani, *New York Times*, September 2016.

17. The Nazi Power Grab

1. Paul Johnson, *Modern Times* (Weidenfeld, London, 1983), p.285.
2. Hitler's claim.
3. Gilbert, *Churchill: A Life*, p.512.
4. Heinrich Himmler, *Holocaust Encyclopedia* (Yale University Press, 2001).
5. Gilbert, *Churchill: A Life*, p.514.
6. Hansard transcript.
7. Gilbert, *Churchill: A Life*, p.515.

8. Gilbert, *Wilderness Years*, p.77.
9. Judt & Snyder, *Thinking the Twentieth Century*, pp.159–160.

18. A Sense of Resignation

1. They would become gently merged and adapted into a two-part television series in 2001.
2. The TV adaptations available on YouTube.
3. Soames, p.266.
4. Richard Toye, *Churchill's Empire* (Macmillan, London 2010), p.182.
5. Rhodes James, *Victor Cazalet: A Portrait*, 19 April 1933 (Hamish Hamilton, UK, 1943), p.154.
6. Rhodes James, *Memoirs of a Conservative* (Weidenfeld, London, 1969), p.385.
7. Gilbert, *Wilderness Years*, p.77.
8. Michael Carritt, *A Mole in the Crown: Memoires of a British Official in India* (Rupa, 1985), pp.63–64.
9. Eric Hobsbawm, *The Age of Extremes* (Vintage, NY, 1994), p.200.
10. D.K. Fieldhouse, *The Colonial Empires* (Delacorte, NY, 1966), p.393.
11. Kagan, Ozment, Turner, *Western Heritage* (Prentice Hall NY, 2007), p.829.
12. The savagery of the 'Amritsar Massacre' by General Dyer and his Indian troops is continually brought up as evidence of either British Imperial bullying or the stupidity of British Colonial Army culture. More thorough recent research clears his reputation. Nigel Collett, *The Butcher of Amritsar* (Bloomsbury, London, 2005).
13. J.F.C. Welldon, *Recollection and Reflections* (Cassell, London, 1915).
14. *The Times,* 4 October 1897. On India's frontier policy.

19. Politics of Hatred

1. Gilbert, *Churchill and the Jews*, p.95.
2. 'Moses', Winston S. Churchill. *Sunday Chronicle*, 8 November 1930.
3. Gilbert, *Churchill and the Jews*, p.99.
4. Source: Albert Einstein papers.
5. Letter of 19 December 1934. Churchill papers, 2/231.
6. Sir Arthur Wauchope.
7. Gilbert, *Churchill: A Life*, p.523.
8. Hansard transcript.
9. Gilbert, *Churchill: A Life*, p.524.

20. Germany's Iron Cage

1. Green, p.7.
2. Gilbert, *Churchill: A Life*, p.530.

3. Koestler, Ibid.
4. Gilbert, *Wilderness Years*, pp.116–7.

21. The Old Grim Choices

1. Gilbert, *A History of the Twentieth Century*, p.845.
2. Ibid., p.846.

22. Implacable Enemies

1. Gilbert, *Churchill: A Life*, p.543.
2. Gilbert, *Winston Churchill: The Wilderness Years*, p.118.
3. At a Conservative Party Conference in Bournemouth.
4. Gilbert, *Churchill: A Life*, p.547.

23. The Endless Repetitions of History

1. Hansard.
2. General Volkogonov.
3. Gilbert, *A History of the Twentieth Century*, Vol. 2, p.64.
4. *Life* magazine, 20 April 1953.
5. John and Carol Garrard, historians of the Soviet Writers Union.
6. Gilbert, *A History of the Twentieth Century*, Vol. 2, p.64.
7. Ibid., Vol. 2, p.65.
8. *Bezhin Lug (Bezhin Meadow).*
9. H.G. Wells, *The New Machiavelli* (Lane, London, 1911).
10. Judt & Snyder, *Thinking the Twentieth Century*, p.70.

24. Dead Past and Unknown Future

1. Geoffrey Best, *Churchill: A Study in Greatness* (Penguin, London, 2001), pp.142–143.
2. Rose, *Churchill: An Unruly Life*, p.222.
3. Gilbert, *Churchill: A Life*, p.550.
4. H.A.L. Fisher, *History of Europe* (Eyre & Spottiswoode, London, 1935).
5. Gilbert, *Churchill: A Life*, p.553.

25. Hitler's Territorial Ambitions

1. Gilbert, *A History of the Twentieth Century*, Vol. 2, p.99.
2. According to the minutes of its meeting in March.
3. Gilbert, *Wilderness Years*, p.155.
4. Alan Campbell Johnson.
5. Gilbert, *A History of the Twentieth Century*, Vol. 2, p.101.
6. Gilbert, *Churchill: A Life*, p.561.

26. The Hitler Menace

1. Gilbert, *A History of the Twentieth Century*, Vol. 2, p.100.
2. Gilbert, *Churchill: A Life*, p.576.
3. Johnson, p.76.
4. Gilbert, *Churchill: A Life*, p.579.
5. CSCT, December 1938.

27. Pro-German Feelings

1. Gilbert, *Wilderness Years*, p.211.
2. Johnson, p.360.
3. Spartacus Educational online.
4. Dating back to continual invasions by the Danes who had already been bought off, but always returned to demand more gold.
5. 7 January 1939.

28. The Munich Dilemma

1. Gilbert, *Wilderness Years*, p.180.
2. Ibid., p.211.
3. Ibid., p.211.
4. Gilbert, *Churchill: A Life*, p.588.
5. Ibid., p.589.
6. Gilbert, *A History of the Twentieth Century*, Vol. 2, p.179.

29. The Approaching War

1. Gilbert, *Churchill: A Life*, p.590.
2. Gilbert, *Wilderness Years*, p.213.
3. Ibid., p.218.

30. Overture to Genocide

1. From a study by *Personality and Individual Differences* magazine.
2. Thomas Paine, *The Rights of Man,* February 1791.
3. Jordan Peterson, ibid.
4. Adolf Hitler, *Die Verfolgung und Ermordung der europäischen Juden durch das national-sozialistische Deutschland 1933-1945,* Vol. 1. (Ed.) Wolf Gruner (Munich 2008), doc.276, p.658.
5. Saul Friedländer, *Das Dritte Reich und die Juden: Die Jahre der Verfolgung 1933-1939* (Munich 1998), Vol.1, p.206.
6. Volker Ullrich, ibid., p.658.
7. Martin Green, ibid., p.98.
8. Saul Friedländer, p.257.

9. *Die Verfolgung und Ermordung der europäischen Juden durch das nationalsozialitische Deutschland 1933-1945,* Vol. 1. (Ed.) Susanne Heim (Munich 2009), doc. 6, pp.91, 92.
10. Avraham Barkai, *Vom Boykott zur "Entjudung": Der wirtschaftliche Existenzkampf der Juden im Dritten Reich 1933-1945* (Frankfurt am main, 1988), pp.78-80.
11. Saul Friedländer, ibid., p.257.
12. *Die Verforlung*, ibid., pp.91-3.
13. Amos Elon, ibid., p.177.
14. *The Western Heritage*, ibid., p.816.

31. The Nazis of the Middle East

1. Judge Bert Fish documents. 'Some Notes on the Present Government of Saudi Arabia (11 March 1940)', in *Saudi Arabia Enters the Modern World.* Edited by Ibrahim al Raschid. (Salisbury, N.C. Documentary Productions, 1980), Vol. 1, p.39.
2. Anthony Cave Brown, *Oil, God, and Gold: The Story of Aramco and the Saudi Kings* (Houghton Mifflin, Boston, 1999), p.85.
3. James Barr, *A Line in the Sand: Britain, France and the Struggle for Mastery of the Middle East* (Simon & Schuster, London, 2011), p.360.
4. Adam Tooze, *The Wages of Destruction* (Penguin, UK, 2006), p.472.
5. St John Philby, *Sa'udi Arabia* (Benn, London, 1955), p.265.
6. David Semple. 'Winston Churchill in Jerusalem, 1921', A summary of the visit, online. Manchester Conservatives.
7. Ibid.
8. Ibid.
9. The National Archives.
10. Oren Kessler, *The Times of Israel*, 19 August 2023.
11. Ibid.

32. An Ultimatum

1. Gilbert, *Wilderness Years*, p.226.
2. Ibid., p.229.
3. Gilbert, *A History of the Twentieth Century*, Vol. 2, p.191.
4. Gilbert, *Wilderness Years*, p.235.
5. Gilbert, *A History of the Twentieth Century*, Vol. 2, p.264.

33. The New Deal

1. Eric Rauchway, *The Money Makers* (Basic, NY, 2015), p.xxii.
2. Ibid., p.97.

3. Ibid., p.114; George Wolfskill, *The Revolt of the Conservatives* (Houghton Mifflin, Boston, 1962), p.84.
4. Gilbert, *A History of the Twentieth Century*, Vol. 2, p.217.
5. Ibid., p.242.
6. Ibid., p.215. Chetwode was negotiating an exchange of prisoners of war.
7. Conrad Black, *Franklin Delano Roosevelt: Champion of Freedom* (Public Affairs, NY, 2003), p.483.

34. The Alarm Bell

1. Churchill, *War Papers* 1, p.358.
2. Roy Jenkins, *Churchill: A Biography* (Farrar Straus, NY, 2001), p.568.
3. Winston S. Churchill, *Step By Step: Political Writings 1936-1939* (Bloomsbury London, 1939).
4. W. S. Churchill, ibid., p.142.
5. W. S. Churchill, ibid., p.207.
6. W. S. Churchill. Ibid. p.264.
7. Churchill, ibid., p.207.
8. Minuted by Berkeley Gage of the Foreign Office.
9. Gilbert, *Wilderness Years*, p.247.

35. An Age of Extremes

1. Gilbert, *Wilderness Years*, pp.255–6.
2. Ibid.
3. Gilbert, *A History of the Twentieth Century*, Vol. 2, p.269.
4. Fergus Fleming, Ed., *The Man with the Golden Typewriter* (Bloomsbury, NY, 2015), p.5.
5. Johnson, p.366.
6. Franz Halder, *Kriegstagebuch: Tägliche Aufzeichnungen des Chefs des Generalstabes des Heeres 1939–1942* (Stuttgart, 1962), p.308.
7. The expression was used by the young poet Raymond Aron.
8. David Clay Large, *Berlin* (Basic, NY, 2000), p.227.
9. Philipp Blom, *Fracture: Life and Culture in the West 1918–1938* (Basic, NY, 2008), p.256.
10. *George Grosz, an Autobiography*, Translated by Nora Hodges (Macmillan, NY, 1983), p.149.
11. Ibid.
12. Gilbert, *Wilderness Years*, p.266.
13. Ibid., p.267.
14. Churchill, *My Early Life* (Butterworth, London, 1930), p.359.
15. Gilbert, *Churchill: A Life*, pp.623–4.

36. Unworldly Innocence

1. Black, *Franklin Delano Roosevelt*, p.504.
2. H.A. Jacobsen, *Der Zweite Weltkrieg: Grundzüge der Politik und Strategie in Dokumenten.* (Frankfurt, 1965), 180–1; quoted in Andreas Hillgruber, *Germany and the Two World Wars* (tr., Harvard 1981), pp.56–7.
3. Johnson, p.345.
4. Churchill, *My Early Life*, p.359.
5. Hickman, *Churchill's Bodyguard*, p.80.

37. A Man of Stature

1. Jenkins, p.574.
2. Hansard, Col. 1094–1130.
3. Hansard, 5th series, Vol. 360, Col. 1250–83.
4. Jenkins, p.582.
5. Blurb on the dust cover of John Lukacs's book entitled *Five Days in London; May 1940* (Yale University, New Haven, 1999).
6. According to Neville Chamberlain's diary entry.
7. Johnson, p.369.
8. John Lukacs, p.xii.
9. According to Hugh Dalton's notes.
10. Andrew Roberts, *The Holy Fox* (Head of Zeus, UK, 2015), p.806.
11. W.S. Churchill, *History of the Second World War*. Vol. 2. 'Their Finest Hour,', p.26.

Epilogue: The Führer of the Arab World

1. Bell, *Complete Letters*, p.207.
2. *Encyclopaedia Britannica.*
3. Gilbert, *Churchill and the Jews*, p.47.
4. Tom Hickman, quoting Walter Thompson, *Churchill's Bodyguard* (Hodder, London, 2005), p.11.
5. David G. Dalin & John F. Rothman, *Icon of Evil: Hitler's Mufti and the Rise of Radical Islam* (Random House, NY, 2008), pp.149–151.
6. Ibid., p.67.

Index